Entrepreneurial Ecosystems and the Diffusion of Startups

SCIENCE, INNOVATION, TECHNOLOGY AND ENTREPRENEURSHIP

Series Editors: Elias G. Carayannis, *Professor of Science, Technology, Innovation and Entrepreneurship, School of Business, George Washington University, USA* and Aris Kaloudis, *NIFU STEP Studies in Innovation, Research and Education, Oslo, Norway*

There is ample and growing evidence that intangible resources such as knowledge, know-how and social capital will prove to be the coal, oil, and diamonds of the twenty-first century for developed, developing, and emerging economies alike. Moreover, there are strong indications and emerging trends that there are qualitative and quantitative differences between the drivers of economic growth in the twentieth and twenty-first centuries.

This new era is punctuated by:

- Development of a service-based economy, with activities demanding intellectual content becoming more pervasive and decisive.
- Increased emphasis on higher education and life-long learning to make effective use of the rapidly expanding knowledge base.
- Massive investments in research and development, training, education, software, branding, marketing, logistics, and similar services.
- Intensification of competition between enterprises and nations based on new product design, marketing methods and organizational forms.
- Continual restructuring of economies to cope with constant change.

This valuable new series concentrates on these important areas by focusing on the key pillars of science, technology, innovation, and entrepreneurship.

Titles in the series include:

Entrepreneurial Ecosystems and the Diffusion of Startups

Elias G. Carayannis

Professor of Science, Technology, Innovation and Entrepreneurship, School of Business, George Washington University, USA

Giovanni Battista Dagnino

Professor of Business Economics and Management, University of Catania, Italy

Sharon Alvarez

Thomas W. Olofson Chair in Entrepreneurial Studies, Joseph M. Katz Graduate School of Business, University of Pittsburgh, USA

Rosario Faraci

Professor of Business Economics and Management, University of Catania, Italy

SCIENCE, INNOVATION, TECHNOLOGY AND ENTREPRENEURSHIP

Cheltenham, UK • Northampton, MA, USA

Published by
Edward Elgar Publishing Limited
The Lypiatts
15 Lansdown Road
Cheltenham
Glos GL50 2JA
UK

Edward Elgar Publishing, Inc.
William Pratt House
9 Dewey Court
Northampton
Massachusetts 01060
USA

A catalogue record for this book
is available from the British Library

Library of Congress Control Number: 2018931745

This book is available electronically in the **Elgar**online
Business subject collection
DOI 10.4337/9781784710064

ISBN 978 1 78471 005 7 (cased)
ISBN 978 1 78471 006 4 (eBook)

Typeset by Servis Filmsetting Ltd, Stockport, Cheshire
Printed and bound in Great Britain by TJ International Ltd, Padstow

Contents

Contributors

Sharon Alvarez, Thomas W. Olofson Chair in Entrepreneurial Studies, Joseph M. Katz Graduate School of Business, University of Pittsburgh, USA.

Erkko Autio, Chair in Technology Transfer and Entrepreneurship, Imperial College Business School, UK.

Vincenzo Butticè, Assistant Professor in Entrepreneurship Finance, Polytechnic of Milan, Italy.

Elias G. Carayannis, Professor of Science, Technology, Innovation and Entrepreneurship, School of Business, George Washington University, USA. He is series editor, book co-editor and author.

Massimo G. Colombo, Professor of Economics of Innovation, Entrepreneurship and Entrepreneurial Finance, Polytechnic of Milan, Italy.

Giovanni Battista Dagnino, Professor of Business Economics and Management, University of Catania, Italy.

Rosario Faraci, Professor of Business Economics and Management, University of Catania, Italy.

Nicolai J. Foss, The Rodolfo Debenedetti Chair of Entrepreneurship iCRIOS-Department of Management and Technology, Bocconi University, Italy.

Jonathan Gander, Lecturer and Director of Executive MBA, London College of Fashion, UK.

Adrian Haberberg, Principal Lecturer in International Business Management, University of East London, UK.

Emily Longstaff, Director of Research and Enterprise, University of East London, UK.

Jacob Lyngsie, Associate Professor of Strategic Organization Design, Southern Denmark University, Denmark.

Angelo Miglietta, Professor of Management of International Enterprises and Markets, IULM University of Milan, Italy.

Anna Minà, Assistant Professor in Management, Kore University of Enna, Italy.

Emanuele Parisi, Adjunct Professor in Entrepreneurship and Innovation for Creativity and Start-up, IULM University, and Investment Team Member, Anthemis UniCredit EVO, Milan, Italy.

Dario Peirone, Assistant Professor of Management, University of Turin, Italy.

Paola Pisano, Assistant Professor of Management, University of Turin and Deputy Mayor for Innovation and Smart City of the City of Turin, Italy.

Mike Provance, Managing Partner Growth Kinetics and Adjunct Professor of Strategy and Entrepreneurship, Virginia Commonwealth University, USA.

Alison Rieple, Professor of Strategic Management, University of Westminster, UK.

Dmitry Sharapov, Assistant Professor of Innovation, Entrepreneurship and Strategy, Imperial College Business School, UK.

Llewellyn D.W. Thomas, Associate Professor, LaSalle Universitat Ramon Llull, Spain.

Acknowledgments

We wish to acknowledge the many individuals that, in various ways, have made it possible to compose and publish this book. First, our gratitude goes to the authors of the chapters of this book; they have always responded straight away to our solicitations to send their chapters out to us and to revise them when it was required. With no hesitation we declare that without them and their enduring commitment, this collective editorial effort would never have seen the light. Second, we are indebted to the many participants at the First International Entrepreneurship Research Exemplar meeting "Entrepreneurial Ecosystems and the Diffusion of Startups" held at the University of Catania, Italy, on 23–25 May 2013. Gathering from various parts of Europe and North America, they vigorously contributed their wisdom, judgment and energies to the study of entrepreneurial ecosystems and the diffusion of startups, which was seen as a pretty risky academic endeavor at the time as it was at its very inception. The initial idea to assemble this book emerged out of those discussions and the chapters are an elaboration of works initially presented on that occasion. Third, our universities (University of Denver and Pittsburgh, George Washington University and University of Catania) deserve special recognition for allowing us the time and application required to the turn this volume into reality. Fourth, we recognize the commissioners and Edward Elgar Publishing for their invaluable support in the book's publishing process. Fifth, one of the editors wishes to express his gratitude to Harvard Business School and its faculty for providing the appropriate environment to finalize some parts of the book during his visit to Boston in spring 2017. Last but not least, our respective families merit boundless admiration for patiently tolerating our absences in the preparation of this volume.

Sharon Alvarez
Elias G. Carayannis
Giovanni Battista Dagnino
Rosario Faraci
Boston, Catania, Pittsburgh, Washington,
April 2017

1. Introduction: entrepreneurial ecosystems and the diffusion of startups

Sharon Alvarez, Elias G. Carayannis, Giovanni Battista Dagnino and Rosario Faraci

1.1 PURPOSE

The goal of this book is to contribute to the emerging debate on entrepreneurial ecosystems and the diffusion of startups by providing a set of well-rounded chapters, written by leading scholars from various parts of the world in the field of entrepreneurship and strategy that collectively significantly advance the evolution of the subject in the relevant knowledge domain. We seek to explore new ideas, provoke debate in both academia and practicing business agents, and deliver high-level forward-looking investigation in areas related to these emerging phenomena.

We have gathered nine relevant conceptual and empirical contributions written by 21 authors from the United States and Europe specifically prepared for this endeavor. Taken together, the contributions push forward the porous boundaries of the entrepreneurship field as well as the business conversation and scholarly debate on entrepreneurial ecosystems and startups. In such a way, the book is able to inform academic thinking and offer implications helpful to a range of practitioners such as entrepreneurs, executives, consultants and policy makers.

There are three explicit contributions that the book advances. First, it pulls notable attention and generates substantial awareness on the key issue of entrepreneurial ecosystems design, establishment, organization and evolution. Second, it advances an organized synopsis of the extant literature on entrepreneurial ecosystems to dissect the advances made and the current status of ecosystems research. Third, it portrays a highly valued selection of examples of entrepreneurial ecosystems at work and discusses their implications for entrepreneurial theory and practice. Amongst these examples, the volume illustrates the emergence and impact of AppCampus (a project aimed at leveraging and enhancing the entrepreneurial ecosystem generated by Aalto University and the Windows Phone innovation ecosystem), the main features of UK fashion design micro enterprises, the incubator perimeter mapping methodology, understanding of how social capital affects the funding of products in various industry projects that are crowdfunded by means of Kickstarter online platform and the reasons for knowledge spillover and agglomeration of new ventures in innovation-intensive regions.

1.2 ROOTS

The book is based on a thorough selection of the best works presented on the occasion of a milestone meeting, entitled "Entrepreneurial Ecosystems and the Diffusion of Startups", held at the University of Catania, Italy, on 23–25 May 2013 (see cataniaentrepreneurship2013.wordpress.com/) that was expressly aimed to produce this book. Gathering under the same roof, over 60 interested participants came together from three continents (Europe, America and Asia) and 11 different countries. The meeting was co-sponsored by the Academy of Management's Entrepreneurship Division, and the Department of Economics and Business of the University of Catania. It is worth noting that participants had the opportunity to attend the inaugural session in the premises of JoYà Academy, an idea creation lab in the fashion industry, which is located in a particularly intriguing space with a black tuff volcanic stone atmosphere, imaginative illumination, and artistic installations that, many years ago, hosted the warehouses of the sulphur refinery workshops of Catania. Far from being an intrusive one, the condition of being a collective endeavor has allowed us to strengthen the thematic element of the book, as well as to pursue internal coherence and overall consistency of the volume.

1.3 MOTIVATION

Interest in the key theme "Entrepreneurial Ecosystems and the Diffusion of Startups" is spreading from the rapidly increasing role that entrepreneurial ecosystems and startups are assuming in today's business world. From a remote corner of the study of entrepreneurship and strategy, it has now taken center stage in the field of entrepreneurship. The study of entrepreneurial ecosystems has recently met with unexpected success by attracting a wide-ranging selection of novel contributions:

(a) Research reports and executive summaries by various well-respected institutions, such as the Kaufmann Foundation's report on measuring an entrepreneurial ecosystem (Stangler and Bell-Masterson, 2015), by the Organisation for Economic Co-operation and Development (OECD) (Mason and Brown, 2014) and from Startup Genome and Telefónica Digital (2012) on mapping startup ecosystems.

(b) Case studies for MBA and executive education courses, such as the recent Harvard Business School case, *Rising from the Ashes: The Emergence of Chicago's Entrepreneurial Ecosystem* by Linda Applegate and associates (2017).

(c) Book chapters (Cinici and Baglieri, 2016; Minà et al., 2016) and books, such as *Entrepreneurial Ecosystems* (Boutillier et al., 2016), focused on the role of entrepreneurial ecosystems on economic growth, as well as the well-circulated *Startup Nation* (Singer and Senor, 2011) and the present volume.

(d) Call for papers for special issues of academic journals, such as *Small Business Economics: An International Journal* (Colombo et al., 2015) and *Strategic Entrepreneurship Journal* (Autio et al., 2015).

(e) A few initial articles of premier academic journals dedicated to entrepreneurship and the issue of entrepreneurial evolution (Spigel, 2017).

In a broad sense, an entrepreneurial ecosystem considers the actors and the environment affecting the rise and diffusion of entrepreneurship at the "glocal" level. It encompasses a group of firms, including startups, and one or more coordinating entities, such as firm incubators or accelerators and local policy agencies, which share similar goals and decide to form a network to leverage scale economies, as well as entrepreneurial flexibility and a strong drive to innovate (see Isenberg, 2014; Financial Times Lexicon, 2017). Alongside the recent outburst of entrepreneurship at the glocal level, the rise of new startups and startup ecosystems around the world, as well as new-found developments in existing ones, has picked up. For instance, the *Startup Ecosystem Report 2012* (Startup Genome and Telefónica Digital) argues that countries and cities are shifting from service-based economies to becoming increasingly driven by a new generation of fast-moving software and technology-rooted business organizations. Interestingly, the OECD in November 2013 organized a meeting on entrepreneurial ecosystems (Mason and Brown, 2014), underscoring that the burgeoning issue has far-reaching implications, involving economic development, planning, economic geography and policy perspectives. To be sure, with entrepreneurial ecosystems we do not limit the inquiry to spatially bounded intra-industry or inter-industry contexts, but extend our reach to virtual entrepreneurial ecosystems that are global in nature.

Therefore, while we recognize that the spatial dimension may be relevant to entrepreneurial ecosystems that are located and concentrated in certain regions (Silicon Valley, Israel, Ireland and Taiwan), and in these cases regional conditions are rather important, we concurrently posit that the spatial dimension may today be increasingly superseded by "glocal" and virtual forces given by global drivers of entrepreneurial platforms. We also acknowledge that entrepreneurial ecosystems are inherent drivers of innovation and new business energy and power. Successful startup ecosystems usually foster a long-term view, process-structure recombination across boundaries, and entrepreneurial dynamics to shore up communities of entrepreneurs and investors who share the aspiration to cultivate each other's talent, creativity and network support as shown in the case of Chicago (Applegate et al., 2017).

On the other hand, weak entrepreneurial ecosystems may display a range of key weaknesses that need to be tackled, such as the need for venture capital money to finance growth, the need for enlarged and more intense valuable networking as well as ways to attract skills and talents to speed up growth, and the need for a major coordination role by universities and research centers. In addition, what is also necessary is the presence of change agents and orchestrators that are effectively able to perform as role models and champions of entrepreneurial ecosystems. This is the case in the Scottish entrepreneurial ecosystem as represented by Levie and associates (2014). Finally, entrepreneurial ecosystems are loci or relevant settings where the actual co-existence and operational interplay of the two countervailing centripetal and centrifugal forces of competition and cooperation may actually occur taking the form of actor *coopetition* (Minà et al., 2016). This condition happened in a Canadian hi-tech entrepreneurial ecosystem located in the Quebec region.

1.4   AUDIENCE

As indicated above, this book is aimed at both academics and practitioners. On the one hand, researchers, scholars and graduate students of entrepreneurship and strategic management and related topics will be certainly interested in a book that tries to address, for the very first time, in a systematic fashion the notion of entrepreneurial ecosystems as well as delving into entrepreneurial ecosystems emergence, dynamics and management. On the other hand, practitioners, managers and consultants will find in the book conceptual tools and a wealth of practical examples, besides some intriguing experimental evidence, that will trigger innovative ways of thinking about and building ecosystem and startup strategies.

Accordingly, since the book provides in-depth examples, hints, principles and techniques about entrepreneurial ecosystems, it might help a fair number of individuals to recognize and assess the imperative needed to take into account when considering the ecosystem option, both in a local and virtual fashion, in today's business world.

The book is mainly for a graduate and postgraduate student audience. Nonetheless, it may provide particularly significant reading for advanced undergraduate courses and seminars. As mentioned previously, given its pioneering and original flavor the book can be a main text for a range of newly designed and launched courses on ecosystems and startup strategies that seem of remarkable appeal or even increasingly required by a range of audiences today. In addition, it may be supplementary or complementary reading to a range of academic and non-academic or post-experience courses (both basic and advanced) in "entrepreneurship", as well as in "strategic management".

As the book's writing style is easily accessible to various kinds of readership, the book may be used in MBA courses and in other graduate and postgraduate courses on entrepreneurial ecosystem and startup strategies since, as indicated, it seems particularly well suited for newly developed courses in these areas. In addition, since it is unlocking an entirely new entrepreneurship subfield, the book can also be a fertile base for running executive education initiatives.

Finally, since it offers an array of intriguing practical implications, we envision that the book will be particularly appealing to a range of practitioners, such as entrepreneurs, executives, consultants and policy makers.

1.5   STRUCTURE OF THE BOOK

The volume features nine chapters dedicated to the study of entrepreneurial ecosystems and the diffusion of startups: this introduction, seven core chapters and a concluding chapter. All the chapters are original in nature since they have been specifically written by their authors for this editorial effort. The book's structure essentially responds to the criterion of easy reader comprehension and accessibility. The chapters follow a rational order beginning with an overview of the literature to in-depth analysis of intriguing cases of entrepreneurial ecosystems that are industry-specific, city-specific or region-specific, to the effective design of an entrepreneurial ecosystem and discussion of a methodology to assess the latitude of a startup incubator.

Chapter 2 by Anna Minà and Giovanni Battista Dagnino is entitled "Mapping entrepreneurial ecosystems inquiry: a content analysis of the analysis of the literature and its implications". The chapter underscores that awareness of the business ecosystem and the intellectual ferment it has generated, especially in the last decade, motivate the need to develop a systematic overview of the existing literature on ecosystems. The authors develop a content analysis of existing studies on ecosystems to grasp the main features and key elements that epitomize an ecosystem and then to untangle the boundary conditions around which firms can extend their entrepreneurial visions matched with strategic thinking within the ecosystem.

Chapter 3 by Llewellyn Thomas, Dmitry Sharapov and Erkko Autio is entitled "Linking entrepreneurial and innovation ecosystems: the case of AppCampus". It contributes to recent work examining entrepreneurs who participate in multiple ecosystems simultaneously by investigating the mechanisms and outcomes of the AppCampus initiative, a three-year project aimed at leveraging and enhancing the entrepreneurial ecosystem around Aalto University and the Windows Phone innovation ecosystem. The chapter reviews the characteristics of innovation and entrepreneurial ecosystems, and provides an analysis of the Windows Phone ecosystem and the Aalto entrepreneurial ecosystem. It illustrates the AppCampus initiative, clarifying each of its components and how these are linked to the Windows Phone innovation and Aalto University entrepreneurial ecosystems. The authors then discuss the effects that AppCampus has had on these ecosystems and future directions for leaders of entrepreneurial and innovation ecosystems.

Chapter 4 by Nicolai Foss and Jacob Lyngsie is entitled "Antecedents of firm-level entrepreneurship: how organizational design coordinates and controls the firm's entrepreneurial ecosystem". In this chapter, the authors propose a framework to understand how organizational design fosters those behaviors that aggregate firm-level entrepreneurial outcomes in an entrepreneurial ecosystem (that is, engaging in new markets, securing new sources of inputs, and realizing organizational, process and product innovations). The proposed framework links organizational design, intra-firm entrepreneurial behaviors and firm-level entrepreneurship. This responds to the requisite to fill a specific research gap in the literature: in fact, the entrepreneurship literature has tended to ascribe entrepreneurial capacity and outcomes either to individuals that start up new ventures or have located such capacity and outcomes at the level of firms.

Chapter 5 by Vincenzo Butticè and Massimo G. Colombo is entitled "Industry specificity and the effect of internal social capital in reward-based crowdfunding". The chapter shows that while the crowdfunding literature has highlighted the role of social capital developed within the platform (internal social capital) in determining the success of a funding campaign, prior studies have failed to emphasize that industry specificity may influence this effect. The chapter fills this gap by dissecting how social capital influences the funding of products belonging to different industries. Using a dataset of 34,121 projects launched on the Kickstarter online platform during the year 2014, the authors found that the internal social capital effect varies by industries and is stronger in magnitude when the industry is characterized by high demand uncertainty and task complexity. Overall, these findings contribute to a better understanding of the role of social capital in the phase known in venture capital studies as early stage financing.

Chapter 6 by Alison Rieple, Jonathan Gander, Paola Pisano, Adrian Haberberg and Emily Longstaff is entitled "Accessing the creative ecosystem: evidence from UK fashion design micro enterprises". The chapter examines the impact of the UK fashion design micro enterprises ecosystem on the practices of fashion designers. This ecosystem includes what is termed a socially "sympathetic infrastructure" (Pratt, 2002) and nodes: a mix of social spaces, meeting points, public areas such as markets and streets, as well as sources of inspiration such as museums and art galleries. The authors scrutinize the extent to which creative micro enterprises, such as fashion designers, access external resources to compensate for their putative internal deficiencies. In doing so, they build on a typology of apparel designers and test whether its combination of market and peer-based orientations explains the behavior of their sample. They also detect resource nodes: physical sites where actors in a design ecosystem may encounter one another and the material objects that are there, exchange ideas, give and receive emotional support and arrive at a shared understanding of design memes. Finally, the authors investigate the role of creative micro enterprises in the transmission of symbolic knowledge and the negotiation of shared meanings, and how different types of designers may use these in various ways.

Chapter 7 by Emanuele Parisi, Angelo Miglietta and Dario Peirone is entitled "Business incubators and entrepreneurial networks: a methodology for assessing incubator effectiveness and performance". The chapter maps the incubator's perimeter, underscoring the role of connector and activation centers of entrepreneurial ecosystems, thereby setting the theoretical framework for a model of incubator assessment whereby success drivers are derived from global best practices. This framework aggregates and harmonizes the effectiveness of incubation activities in given perimeters, thereby helping investors to better allocate private and public resources, and offers insights to government that may be useful in addressing national public policies.

Chapter 8 by Elias Carayannis and Mike Provance is entitled "Towards 'skarse' entrepreneurial ecosystems: using agent-based simulation of entrepreneurship to reveal what makes regions tick". The chapter starts by formulating and simulating the life cycle of knowledge-driven ventures that can be viewed as the exercise of real options under regimes of risk and uncertainty that are modeled in the form of "happy accidents", namely, strategic knowledge serendipity, arbitrage and acquisition events that punctuate the process of the venture's life cycle. The authors found that the timing, selection and sequencing of key decisions regarding new venture formation and evolution are contingent in a non-linear manner on the breadth and depth as well as the quality and density of the network structure of the business and technology ecosystem within which a venture is situated. Up to a certain point of cultivating and nurturing the new firm's socio-economic network, the costs outweigh the benefits, but with an abrupt about-face once a critical mass in the scale, scope and quality of this socio-economic network or business and technology ecosystem is attained, the benefits start outweighing and exponentially exceeding the costs. The implications for technology entrepreneurs, regional economic development managers and policy makers are apparent: fathom the nature and dynamics of their own regional business and technology ecosystem and aim to enter the market (as an entrepreneur) when the ecosystem appears to be close to its critical mass of maximum likelihood knowledge serendipity and arbitrage ("happy accidents") events, as well as aim to help the ecosystem reach its maximum "happy accident" likelihood state as sustainably and fast as possible and become in this manner a skarse-enabled entrepreneurial ecosystem (Carayannis, 2008). In this context, strategic public-private partnerships and networks, as well as risk capital, serve as key pillars of sustainable and accelerated economic development. Through the use of a simulation, the chapter supports arguments regarding localized spillover of knowledge and agglomeration of new ventures within innovation-intensive regions, but only after new ventures have acted independently to create formal networks that acquired knowledge from more distant regions. Further analysis demonstrates the substantial influence that institutions have on the formation of new ventures. Institutions that increase the diversity of knowledge flows make positive impacts on the survival of new ventures and the sustainability of entrepreneurship in a region, while heterogeneity-reducing institutions (such as ones that replicate existing knowledge or produce standardized knowledge) impede the progress of new venture formation at firm and regional levels.

Finally, the concluding chapter focuses on a few key conditions epitomizing a healthy entrepreneurial ecosystem. Drawing on a complex adaptive system approach to entrepreneurial ecosystems evolution, we call for a dynamic approach to entrepreneurial ecosystems to grasp how they emerge, maintain vitality, and deteriorate. This condition may proffer helpful groundwork to develop a value-based theory of entrepreneurial ecosystems that may allow us to understand entrepreneurial ecosystems evolutionary paths and governance systems and mechanisms.

REFERENCES

Applegate, L., Meyer, A., and Varley, T. (2017). *Rising from the Ashes: The Emergence of Chicago's Entrepreneurial Ecosystem.* Harvard Business School Case 9-817-061.

Autio, E., Nambisan, S., Wright, M., and Thomas, L.D.W. (2015). Entrepreneurial ecosystems. *Strategic Entrepreneurship Journal.* Special Issue Call for Papers. Available at: onlinelibrary.wiley.com/store/10.1002/(ISSN)1932-443X/asset/hom epages/SEJ-Entrepreneurial_Ecosystems.pdf?v=1&s=4548d7b62c28292b826ef7 d74eae7bfcd396f34a&isAguDoi=false.

Boutillier, S., Carré, D., and Levratto, N. (2016). *Entrepreneurial Ecosystems.* Hoboken, NJ: Wiley.

Carayannis, E.G. (2008). Knowledge-driven creative destruction, or leveraging knowledge for competitive advantage. *Industry and Higher Education*, **22**(6).

Cinici, M.C. and Baglieri, D. (2016). (Not) energizing ecosystems through a large firm's inventor network: lessons from Italy. In H. Wang and Y. Liu (eds), *Entrepreneurship and Talent Management from a Global Perspective.* Cheltenham, UK and Northampton, MA, USA: Edward Elgar Publishing, pp. 227–50.

Colombo, M., Dagnino, G.B., Lehman, E., and Salmador, M. (2015). The governance of entrepreneurial ecosystems. *Small Business Economics: An Entrepreneurship Journal.* Special Issue Call for Papers.

Financial Times Lexicon (2017). Definition of entrepreneurial ecosystem. Available at: lexicon.ft.com/Term?term=entrepreneurial%20ecosystem. Accessed 29 April 2017.

Isenberg, D. (2014). What an entrepreneurship ecosystem actually is. *Harvard Business Review online.* Available at: hbr.org/2014/05/what-an-entrepreneurial-ecosystem-actually-is. Accessed 5 May 2017.

Levie, J., Autio, E., Reeves, C. et al. (2014). Assessing regional innovative entre-preneurship ecosystems with the global entrepreneurship and development index: the case of Scotland. Available at: https://www.enterpriseresearch.ac.uk/ wp-content/uploads/2014/03/REAPScotlandGEMconfV13-Autio.pdf.

Mason, C. and Brown, R. (2014). Entrepreneurial ecosystems and growth oriented entrepreneurship. OECD, Paris. Available at: http://www.oecd.org/cfe/leed/Entre preneurial-ecosystems.pdf. Accessed 4 May 2017.

Minà, A., Dagnino, G.B., and Ben-Letaifa, S. (2016). Competition and cooperation in entrepreneurial ecosystems: a life-cycle analysis of a Canadian ICT ecosystem. In F. Belussi and L. Orsi (eds), *Innovation, Alliances and Networks in High-tech Environments.* Abingdon, UK: Routledge, pp. 65–81.

Pratt, A. (2002). Hot jobs in cool places. The material cultures of new media product spaces: the case of south of the market, San Francisco. *Information, Communication and Society*, **5**(1), 27–50.

Senor, D. and Singer, S. (2011). *Start-up Nation: The Story of Israel's Economic Miracle.* New York: Twelve.

Spigel, B. (2017). The relational organization of entrepreneurial ecosystems. *Entrepreneurship Theory and Practice*, **41**(1), 49–72.

Stangler, D. and Bell-Masterson, J. (2015). *Measuring an Entrepreneurial Ecosystem*. Kaufmann Foundation. Available at: http://www.kauffman.org/~/media/kauffman_org/research%20reports%20and%20covers/2015/03/measuring_an_entrepreneurial_ecosystem.pdf.

Startup Genome and Telefónica Digital (2012). *Startup Ecosystem Report 2012*. Available at: http:// www.clustermapping.us/resource/startup-ecosystem-report-2012. Accessed 5 May 2017.

2. Mapping entrepreneurial ecosystems inquiry: a content analysis of the analysis of the literature and its implications

Anna Minà and Giovanni Battista Dagnino

2.1 INTRODUCTION

Management scholars have conventionally conceived the firm as if it were located in an isolated world, in which you have to win over your competitors and to make them fail (Brandenburger and Nalebuff, 1996). The underlying assumption was that firms develop stand-alone strategies, competing with each other to achieve competitive advantage over their rivals (Porter, 1980). As a result, for more than two decades scholars have argued that firms should count solely on their own resources, knowledge, and capabilities to face the aggressive pressures coming from the environment and achieve superior competitive advantages vis-à-vis their rivals (Barney, 1995; Peteraf, 1993; Teece et al., 1997).

In a turbulent and hypercompetitive business world (D'Aveni, 1994; D'Aveni et al., 2010; Ilinitch et al., 1996), firms actually find it difficult to compete effectively in the way predicated by the previous contention. Because of the increase in the breadth of knowledge, capabilities, and resources required to sustain a firm's competitiveness and innovativeness, a single autonomous firm usually falls short of being in the position to tackle, the novel challenges coming from the environment (Dagnino et al., 2015; Dussauge et al., 2000). This condition occurs especially in knowledge-intensive industries (Baum et al., 2000).

To overcome the difficulties related to challenges spreading from the changing business world, scholars have emphasized the importance for firms to develop strategic alliances with other firms, in order to deal with the technological uncertainty in their surrounding environment (Faulkner, 1995; Folta, 1998; Park et al., 2002), enter into new markets and industries (Dussauge et al., 2000; Gulati et al., 2000), and exploit new business opportunities (Garcia-Canal et al., 2002). Under this convention, "you don't have to blow out the other fellow's light to let your own shine" (Brandenburger and Nalebuff, 1996, p. 5). However, with few exceptions (Afuah, 2000; Afuah and Baharam, 1995), while focusing on alliance partnerships most strategy and entrepreneurship research has not until recently given much importance to the role of other actors (such as complementors and suppliers) and their interdependence for achieving competitive advantage.

Drawing from biology, in the early 1990s it was Moore (1993) who pioneered the concept of "business ecosystem", intended as a cluster of interrelating actors (e.g., firms, universities, scientific parks, customers, and so on) that coexist in a common setting and evolve together in their knowledge, resource pools, and roles (Iansiti and Levien, 2004b; Lusch and Nambisan, 2015; Moore, 1993). Later, scholars have shown additional interest in business ecosystems (Adner and Kapoor, 2010; Iansiti and Levien, 2004b; Kapoor and Lee, 2013; Moore, 1996, 2006; Zahra and Nambisan, 2012) and "how business ecosystems replace standalone products and organizations are required to manage their innovation process" (Dedehayir and Makinen, 2011, p. 627), as well as orient entrepreneurial development.

The attention given to business ecosystems and the intellectual ferment it has generated in the last decade underscore the value to develop a systematic overview of the literature in order to systematize the state of the art on business ecosystems. To this aim, in this chapter we develop a content analysis of existing studies on ecosystems. We intend to identify the main features and key elements that characterize an ecosystem, and, hence, to unravel under what boundary conditions firms can develop their entrepreneurial insights coupled with strategic thinking within the ecosystem.

The chapter is structured in nine sections. Section 2.2 offers a closer look of the definitions of business ecosystem. Section 2.3 illustrates the methodological choices that inform the study. By developing a content analysis, Section 2.4 unravels the main themes of ecosystems literature and, drawing on this preliminary exploration, advances a map for guiding a systematic overview of literature. Sections 2.5 to 2.8 then carefully delve deeper into the main elements identified in the map. Finally, we underscore the main gaps in ecosystems research and single out the key challenges for future inquiry.

2.2 BUSINESS ECOSYSTEMS IN MANAGEMENT STUDIES

"Business ecosystems as networks of actors engaged in joint value crea-tion consist of both highly interdependent business actors, dependent on each other for survival, and more detached but still critical parties such as regulators and policy-makers" (Overholm, 2015, p. 14). The concept of ecosystem draws on the Greek word οιχος (= environment) and συστημα (= system), and so means "home system". From an etymological perspec-tive, therefore, the term ecosystem has generally been adopted to refer to the biological community of organisms that interact with each other in a well-defined environmental context (Willis, 1997).

During the 1990s, the term ecosystem emerged in management stud-ies and therefore turned into *business ecosystem* (Mars et al., 2012). Specifically, Moore (1993) moved from the idea that firms, as biological organisms, should not be conceived of as isolated members of a specific industry, but as part of a business ecosystem that crosses a variety of industries (Moore, 1993, p. 76). The concept of business ecosystem is intended as the setting in which clusters of firms, founders, resource providers, complementary innovators, governments and other institutions interact with each other and combine and recombine knowledge and resources to create products, to develop technologies and, more generally, to create shared value (Iansiti and Lieven, 2004b; Kanter, 2012; Moore, 1996; Zahra and Nambisan, 2012).

However, the increasing use of the ecosystem concept has opened up debates on the appropriateness of adopting the biological metaphor of the firm. Among them, Penrose (1995) has argued how unfitting it is to use the biological analogy for interfirm relationships, because this may lead to deterministic implications. Other authors support the idea that the ecosystem analogy is a "way of organizing related ideas, not as a literal analogy to an energy transfer chain in the natural world" (Li and Garnsey, 2014, p. 770).

Actually, the business ecosystem is a *meta-organization* composed of resources and competences provided by complementary actors that coop-erate and, sometimes, compete with each other for value creation (Adner and Kapoor, 2010; Iansiti and Levien, 2004b; Moore, 1993, 1996). This implies that, within an ecosystem, the firm's competitive advantage depends on its ability to put together its resources and competences, and resolve its own internal challenges, as much as on the ability of the other firms in the ecosystem to resolve their own internal challenges as well (Adner and Kapoor, 2010).

2.3   RESEARCH METHODOLOGY

While a systematic analysis of the main literature on business ecosystems would be certainly beneficial, we realize that presenting a comprehensive map of this literature seems a rather challenging task. In such a perspective, the use of quantitative methods of scrutiny appear more appropriate to both navigate a large number of studies and uncover the underlying structure of the literature (Duriau et al., 2007). In fact, a content analysis of the literature allows us to reduce large amounts of "text into fewer content categories" (Weber, 1990, p. 12). In such a way, it is possible to produce manageable pieces of data in isolated patterns, link them, and gain insights (Weber, 1990). Therefore, we content analyze articles on ecosystems in order to pinpoint the key features of the ecosystem construct and the interrelationships among the most influential studies in this research stream (Duriau et al., 2007; Erdener and Dunn, 1990).

2.3.1   Content Analysis

Content analysis is a "methodological measurement applied to text (or other symbolic material)" (Sharpiro and Markoff, 1997, p. 14) that permits "replicable and valid inferences from data to their context" (Krippendorf, 1980, p. 403; 2004, p.18). This method has been "applied by multiple researchers over large volumes of data thereby increasing the reliability of a study" (Sonpar and Golden-Biddle, 2008, p. 800). Content analysis has received wide application in business studies, for instance, to review studies on dynamic capabilities (Di Stefano et al., 2010) and to observe the evolution of the concept of strategic management (Nag et al., 2007).

We adopt the content analysis method to disentangle the *dominant* and *emerging* themes in ecosystems literature. Specifically, we first draw on frequency counts to develop a keyword. Then, we develop the grouping procedure so that "different people should code the same text in the same way" (Weber, 1990, p. 12). We follow Weber's (1990) coding protocol and discuss our data sample, our coding scheme in terms of the different units of analysis that characterize the studies in the sample, and the rules used for coding (Carley, 1993).

2.3.2   Data Sample

The concept of ecosystem has been used in several disciplines such as biology, sociology and, more recently, in strategic management and entrepreneurship studies. Similarly, it has been applied at various levels of inquiry, such as individuals, biological organisms, and firms (Iansiti and Levien,

2004b; Moore, 1993). In this chapter, we explicitly focus on the strategic management and entrepreneurship research area. In this perspective, we make two methodological choices. First, the Social Science Citation Index (SSCI) database informs our study. Second, our analysis considers articles published in the two-decade period spanning from January 1985 to June 2015 to develop our data sample. Since the ecosystem concept in management studies dates back to the second part of the 1980s, the right truncation year fixed in 1985 appears to be consistent.

In order to encompass all the studies on ecosystems, we proceeded to run a Boolean exploration inserting the term "ecosystem*" in the topic of each article (that comprises the research title, keywords, and abstract). We then treated the initial sample by applying the following selection criteria: (a) research domain: social sciences; (b) research area: management; (c) document type: articles (hence, we ruled out proceedings, reviews, and editorials); (d) language: English. This process reduced the sample to 240 studies. Our preliminary observation was that the interest in ecosystem is well reflected in the volume and scope of scientific research, along with the growth of academic literature on this topic.

Nonetheless, as mentioned previously, our focus is mainly on the most impactful and central studies, in terms of their ability to influence the advancement of the fields of strategic management and entrepreneurship. In this perspective, we limited our sample of analysis by considering the outlets of publication: those journals with a five-year impact factor of at least 2 as reported by ISI in 2014. The main idea is that the higher impact factor denotes a higher quality standing of academic journal (Podsakoff et al., 2005). Actually, the five-year impact factor is credited as an appropriate parameter to assess journal influence in the scientific debate on the basis of a quantitative citation-based measure (Garfield, 1979). Such choice reduced our sample to 154 studies.

A straightforward inspection of the data sample shows that papers are quite different in their approach to ecosystems. The term has been extensively adopted in different settings and has hence assumed different meanings depending on the context in which it has been applied. Since this study focuses on grasping the state of the art of existing studies on ecosystems as defined by Moore (1993), we underlined the following procedure: the two authors of this chapter and an additional panel comprising two post-doctoral university fellows using yes/no coding ranked all the abstracts of the articles selected. The goal of this procedure was to exclude the articles related to corporate social issues or environmental green activities. In these issues, the adoption of the concept of ecosystem is related to the management of the land, water and, more generally, living organisms. Furthermore, we also excluded reviews of books, which are considered of little use in this kind of research. This process further reduced the overall number of the papers selected to 97 studies.

2.3.3   Compilation Steps

We apply content analysis to articles' keywords. This represents a specific application of the content analytical method that uses word patterns with the aim of relating the underlying relationships between such words and the ideas emerging from them (Duriau et al., 2007). By leveraging the advantages of keyword content analysis, we attempt to unravel the core of the ecosystem literature and the main content-oriented features underlying the literature.

To proceed with the keyword analysis, we considered the keywords of the papers as chosen by the authors. However, we acknowledge that not all journals ask authors to identify keywords. Accordingly, we observed that only 68 papers out of 97 provided authors' keywords. When the keywords provided by authors were missing, we adopted the keywords provided by ISI Thompson Reuters. When even these keywords were missing, we content analyzed the abstracts and considered the most adopted words emerging from them. Specifically, we found that, as concerns 17 papers out of 29 (97 minus 68), we adopted the keywords provided by ISI Thompson Reuters, whereas as regards 12 papers out of 29, we content analyzed the abstracts and independently counted the most repeated words, starting from the ones that appeared in the abstract at least three times.

Once we had built all the keywords for all the papers included in the analysis, we performed a preliminary examination of the data and identified the most explored concepts related with ecosystem (Hancy et al., 1998). Then, we clustered the keywords into specific thematic areas. Our goal was to create "a group of words with similar meaning and connotations" (Weber, 1990, p. 37) that evocate the same underlying concept. Finally, each of the authors of this chapter independently grouped the keywords into thematic areas, to circumvent reciprocal influences and shared thoughts about the conceptual map. Having identified the key features to form a checklist, we worked together iteratively to compare our views and reach a shared representation of the thematic areas.

Table 2.1   Overall number of the keywords grouped into thematic areas

Number of Keywords	Thematic Areas
55	Ecosystem Architecture
38	Digital Communication and Technology
26	Industry Conditions, Evolution and Challenges
38	Actors
69	Firm Concept
46	Performance
27	Business Ecosystem
35	Innovation Ecosystem
12	Entrepreneurial Ecosystem
14	Service Ecosystem

2.4   AN OVERVIEW OF ECOSYSTEM RESEARCH

2.4.1   Unraveling the Main Themes of the Ecosystem Literature: a Content Analytical Approach

Table 2.1 reports the overall number of the keywords grouped into thematic areas. The overall number of words included in this study is 360. The words are listed on the basis of the number of times in which each keyword is repeated. As reported in Table 2.1, the majority of keywords (55) have been clustered in the thematic area called "ecosystem architecture", since they explicitly refer to the setting in which the interdependencies among firms are related to the structure of the ecosystem.

Then, 38 keywords have been clustered in the thematic area labeled "digital communication and technology", since they refer to concepts related to technological innovation, the adoption of information and communication technology, and the digital activities therein; 26 keywords have been clustered in the thematic area labeled "industry conditions, evolution and challenges", since they explicitly refer to the evolution of industry and the environmental turbulence that have characterized the competitive arena, leading to the formation of the ecosystem (El Sawy et al., 2010); 38 keywords have been clustered in the thematic area labeled "actors", since they identify the players that are involved in the ecosystem.

Sixty-nine keywords explicitly refer to the firm concept. Among them, we identify three main clusters, each one referring to a specific thematic area: (a) the firm's resources and capabilities (i.e., absorptive capacity, dynamic, organizational and downstream capabilities, intellectual property, exploitation, and ambidexterity) (33); (b) the firm's business model (6); and (c) the firm's strategy (30). This latter cluster includes strategies that firms adopt within the ecosystem (i.e., strategic alliances, joint ventures, M&As, and partnerships). Forty-six keywords have been clustered in the thematic area called "performance", whereas 88 keywords explicitly refer to the ecosystem concept. Among them, we identify four main clusters, each one referring to a specific thematic area: (a) business ecosystem (27); (b) innovation ecosystem (35); entrepreneurial ecosystem (12); and (d) service ecosystem (14).

2.4.2   Pathway of Analysis

Drawing on the results of the content analysis previously extracted and illustrated, we systematize the thematic areas based on the underlying links existing among them. Using the categories that emerged from the content analysis, we advance a conceptual map that detects the ecosystems literature and considers the following main features: (a) *antecedents* of ecosystems; (b) *actors and structures of ecosystems*, with a special emphasis on the role of firm strategies, resources and business models; (c) *variety of ecosystems*; and (d) *performance at both firm and ecosystem levels*.

Moving from the first left-hand side rectangle of Figure 2.1, we locate the antecedents of ecosystems. Specifically, they include the *industry conditions* that drive the emergence and formation of ecosystems, with a specific emphasis on the *role of digital, communication, and technology* that have significantly impacted on the firm's choices to interact with the other actors of the ecosystem.

In the second rectangle of Figure 2.1, we find the *actors and structures* that support the activity of the ecosystem. Among them, particular emphasis is devoted to firm features, such as firm strategies, resources, and capabilities. Based on their business models, firms in the ecosystem interact with each other with the aim of achieving a competitive advantage and contributing to the performance of the overall ecosystem (Adner and Kapoor, 2010).

The third rectangle of Figure 2.1, located in the right-hand side of the figure, includes *variety of ecosystems*. As comes to light from the analysis of the literature, it is possible to identify three different kinds of ecosystem, each with specific characteristic traits and scope of inquiry: (a) innovation ecosystem; (b) entrepreneurial ecosystem; and (c) service ecosystem.

Finally, we locate the *performance* of the overall ecosystem, as well as performance of the actors involved in it. Each player of the ecosystem intends to act with the aim of getting high performance, as well as improving the performance of the other members of the ecosystem as a whole.

In the next section, we shall explore the content of each specific rectangle

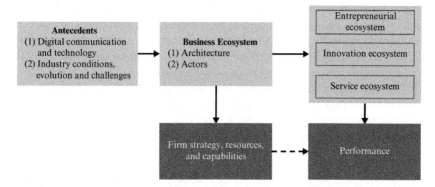

Figure 2.1   A representation of business ecosystem literature

that collectively shapes an organized map of the literature on ecosystems. We shall start from the definition of the ecosystem and its constituent elements, as concerns the actors involved and the structures supporting it. Then, we identify the kinds of ecosystems as they have been developed in the literature and the features that characterize them. Finally, we shall consider the antecedents and the performance of ecosystems.

2.5   ANTECEDENTS OF ECOSYSTEMS

The key driver supporting the emergence and formation of an ecosystem is related to the rapid and unpredictable *challenges surrounding industry evolution* (Best, 2015; Meyer et al., 2005; Wareham et al., 2014). Accordingly, volatility of market demand (Autio et al., 2013; Oriani and Sobrero, 2008), speed originating from technological change that makes the current know-how obsolete (Folta, 1998; Muller and Yogev, 2006; Walker and Weber, 1984), globalization processes (Singer, 2006), industry convergence (Basole, 2009; Meyer et al., 2005), and aggressiveness of competitive behavior are the key industry conditions driving the emergence and formation of an ecosystem, and significantly affect firms' competitive advantage in the ecosystem (Singer, 2006).

Among them, *technological, digital, and communication evolution* are the most crucial aspects motivating firms to interact with each other within an ecosystem setting (Cusumano and Gawer, 2002; Gawer, 2014; Gawer and Cusumano, 2014). While, on the one hand, technological and digital platforms may support the firm's interconnectedness and favor easier communication and knowledge sharing (Eaton et al., 2015; Iansiti and Levien, 2004b; Woodard et al., 2013), technological and digital challenges, on the other hand, may result in questions about the firm's ability to forecast and adapt to changes in the ICT environment (Kallinikos et al., 2013). Furthermore, even if firms have pre-emptively forecasted the evolution in the technological environment well and made significant investments (and divestments), some uncertain outcomes still exist (Kapoor and Furr, 2015). These uncertain outcomes are mainly due to two main aspects: (1) that markets may not accept such changes (Kapoor and Furr, 2015); and (2) that other rivals may be faster in introducing technologies that may be accepted by the market and may thus lead the firm to achieve a competitive advantage over the other competitors.

When firms are new entrants in an industry, they are more likely to develop relationships with several players that are embedded in a specific competitive arena (Teece, 2007), and choose the "technologies with higher technical performance and for which key complementary assets are available in the ecosystem" (Kapoor and Furr, 2015, p. 416). This choice would allow them to better handle the technological challenges stemming from the interactive competitive arena.

In a nutshell, since firms strive to achieve a competitive advantage, being embedded in an ecosystem makes possible a continuous reconfiguration of the resources, knowledge, and technological capabilities of the focal firm, as well as of the whole firm cluster (Kapoor and Furr, 2015).

2.6 ACTORS AND ARCHITECTURE OF ECOSYSTEMS

Two main elements characterize ecosystems: (a) actors and (b) structures or architectures that support their emergence and development.

Actors operate inside the boundaries of an ecosystem affecting their ability to appropriate the return on their investments by means of mixing competition and cooperation, or operating coopetition (Brandenburger and Nalebuff, 1996; Iansiti and Levien, 2004b; Teece, 2007). First, market customers are crucial members of the ecosystem for which firms produce goods and services (Moore, 1996). Second, in creating opportunities and facing challenges, the members of the upstream and downstream supply chain and firms that produce mutually complementary and substitutable products or services (Clarysse et al., 2014) are involved in the value creation process of the ecosystem. Finally, policy-makers and institutions are the ones in the position to develop norms and rules that can have a significant impact on the overall ecosystem, determining its overall growth, success, decline, or dissolution.

As firms develop their strategies within an ecosystem, they assume different roles, depending on the purpose of their actions and their position within the business ecosystem (Iansiti and Levien, 2004a). To this aim, Iansiti and Levien (2004b) provided a classification of the four main roles that firms may develop through their actions inside the ecosystem: (1) keystone players; (2) dominators; (3) niche players; and (4) hub landlords.

Keystone players are the protagonists of a business ecosystem. Typically, they are in the position to control the highest number of relationships that occur among the ecosystem's actors, as well as to favor the formation of connections among them. The benefits of being a keystone player are twofold. First, keystone players can decide whether (or not) to make connections between and among the members of the ecosystem in which there may be structural holes (Iansiti and Levien, 2004a). In this sense, they can exert greater influence over other ecosystem actors and take advantage from such position, even without necessarily being the largest firm in the ecosystem. Second, by leveraging their relative centrality in the ecosystem, keystone players may exert control over the combination and recombination of idiosyncratic and unsubstitutable resources and knowledge that they leverage to create value within the ecosystem.

Dominators are actors whose purpose is to take advantage from their position to exploit the value created within the business ecosystem. Different from keystone players, they offer a limited contribution to the creation of value by the ecosystem, since their strategies are focused uniquely on appropriating what has been previously created by other actors of the ecosystem rather than providing substantial governance to the ecosystem (Iansiti and Levien, 2004b).

Niche players represent the actors that produce the greatest amount of value within the ecosystem. However, since they operate in a niche, they can exert the least influence in the overall ecosystem network vis-à-vis keystones and dominators.

Finally, *hub landlords* represent the actors that aim at extracting "as much value as possible from an ecosystem or ecosystem domain without integrating forward or control[ling] it" (Iansiti and Levien, 2004b, p. 113). In essence, they recognize that the ecosystem has potential to grow and create value indirectly, but they are not interested in integrating forward to control it. The only activity they are interested in is to capture the maximum value out of the ecosystem for them. In doing so, hub landlord make the ecosystem unstable and therefore give the least contribution to value.

Regarding the architecture of the ecosystems, initially scholars approaching the study of ecosystems conventionally focused on the supply chain that was typically conceived of as the underlying infrastructure of the ecosystem (Li and Garnsey, 2014). Actually, the evolution of technological and digital industries paved the way to the formation of technological platforms (Tiwana et al., 2010; Wareham et al., 2014; Xu et al., 2010). Examples of technological and digital platforms abound today and are becoming the dominant model for software-based ecosystems (Ceccagnoli et al., 2012; Iyer et al., 2006). Firefox browser, Apple's iPhone operating system (iOS) (Maglio and Spohrer, 2013), and Facebook represent intriguing cases of technological platforms, each one characterized by a keystone player (i.e., Google and Apple) (Iansiti and Levien, 2004b) that has a pivotal role in orchestrating all the firms in the ecosystem and thereby affecting their long-term survival (Gawer, 2014; Leten et al., 2013; Weiss and Gangadharan, 2010).

Since the early 2000s, the management literature has approached platforms as markets that "mediate transactions across different customer groups" (Gawer, 2014, p. 1240). In this vein, platforms have been conceived as instrumental to actors interacting within "two-sided markets" (Rochet and Tirole, 2003). Accordingly, two-sided markets are "markets involving two groups of agents interacting via platforms where one group's benefit from joining a platform depends on the size of the other group that joins the platform" (Armstrong, 2006, p. 668).

Scholars have also posited that the way firms are organized "to manage complementary activities in the ecosystem" (Kapoor and Lee, 2013, p. 274) matters in terms of their commitment to invest in new technologies within the ecosystem. Since alliances allow easier coordination in commercializing new products, in this perspective Mitchell and Singh (1996) found that firms that pursue strategic alliances are more likely to survive than the one pursuing the strategic choice of developing arm's-length relationships. Similarly, Kapoor and Lee (2013) recognized that firms in alliance ecosystems are more oriented toward investing in new technologies with partners also being complementors rather than with other non-partner firms in arm's length relationships.

2.7   VARIETY OF BUSINESS ECOSYSTEMS

In his landmark contribution, Moore (1993) highlighted three main elements underlying the concept of business ecosystem: (a) firms cooperatively and competitively interact with each other to develop *innovations*; (b) by interacting with each other, firms create and discover *entrepreneurial opportunities* (Alvarez and Barney, 2007); (c) actors in the ecosystem draw on their resources and capabilities to share "institutional logics and mutual value creation through service exchange" (Lusch and Vargo, 2014, p. 161; Vargo and Lusch, 2014).

Correspondingly, by content analyzing the literature on business ecosys-

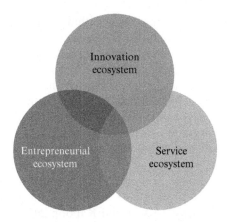

Figure 2.2   A representation of the interrelation among innovation ecosystem, entrepreneurial ecosystem and service ecosystem

tem, we are able to identify groups of scholars that focus on each of the three types of business ecosystem (i.e., innovation ecosystem, entrepreneurship ecosystem, and service ecosystem) as they emerge from Moore's contribution (1993). This partition is presented for the sake of simplicity of analysis and improved appreciation of the literature. However, we should also acknowledge that such typologies are strictly interrelated and, most of the time, difficult to separate. Therefore, they may be straightforwardly represented as intersectional sets in set theory (Figure 2.2). In the following subsections, we review extant studies on the business ecosystem by focusing on, respectively, the innovation ecosystem, entrepreneurial ecosystem, and service ecosystem.

2.7.1   Innovation Ecosystem

The rapid development of information technologies and the significant reduction of coordination costs among firms have contributed to make innovation ecosystems the core element through which firms develop their growth strategies in several industries (Adner, 2006). Innovation ecosystems represent "collaborative arrangements through which firms combine their individual offerings into a coherent, customer-facing solution" (Adner, 2006, p. 2). Specifically, within the boundaries of a business ecosystem firms "co-evolve [actors'] capabilities around a new innovation" (Moore, 1993, p. 76). This means that firms reciprocally interact with each other, applying their specialized knowledge and skills with the aim of developing new products and services, thereby satisfying the needs of their customers.

Moore (1993) emphasizes that being within a business ecosystem affects the firm's innovation capability. "The success of an individual innovation, however, is often dependent on the success of other innovation in the firm's external environment" (Adner and Kapoor, 2010, p. 310). As a consequence, it is not sufficient to consider whether the focal firm is able to "fully resolve its internal innovation challenges" (Adner and Kapoor, 2010, p. 307), but it becomes even more crucial to understand whether the other members of the ecosystem in which the focal firm is embedded are able to "resolve their own innovation challenges as well" (Adner and Kapoor, 2010, p. 307). In this perspective, "if they work, ecosystems allow firms to create value that no single firm could have created alone" (Adner, 2006, p. 2) and they also allow firms to face "the innovation challenges that reside in the firm's environment" (Adner and Kapoor, 2010, p. 308). Consistent with this idea, Vargo et al. (2015) argue that technological innovations are usually shaped by institutional processes (that include maintenance, disruption, and change) within an ecosystem.

2.7.2 Entrepreneurial Ecosystem

Within a business ecosystem, we see an "iterative process of trying out innovative ideas and discovering which solutions are attractive to customers" (Moore, 1993, p. 79). In such a perspective, the business ecosystem plays an important role for innovation. However, this process also leads to the formation of new ideas and "entrepreneurial scene . . . from which the market can ultimately select the fittest offering" (Moore, 1993, p. 79). When an ecosystem is characterized as having an entrepreneurial spirit (i.e., it is an entrepreneurial ecosystem), actors "simultaneously create opportunities that spill over to others and discover opportunities already created by others" (Overholm, 2015, p. 14).

Entrepreneurial ecosystems represent the setting in which there is a pool of "individual elements – such as leadership, culture, capital markets, and open-minded customers – that combine in complex ways" (Isenberg, 2010, p. 43). This type of ecosystem is made by actors that have a strong entrepreneurial orientation (Alvarez and Barney, 2010; Lumpkin and Dess, 1996) and entrepreneurial thinking. Taken together, these aspects allow firms to get access to external resources and achieve benefits stemming from the combination and recombination of such resources and competences (Autio et al., 2014; Burgelman, 1983; Hitt et al., 2001; Li and Garnsey, 2014).

The actors of an entrepreneurial ecosystem develop dependency among each other and "like biological species", they "share their fate with each other" (Iansiti and Levien, 2004a, p. 69). Accordingly, actors of the entrepreneurial ecosystem are involved in a double activity. On the one hand, they are prone to interact with other actors with whom they can achieve the quantity and quality of information they need as well as resources and competences. On the other hand, they experience a sense of *reciprocity* (Li and Garnsey, 2014). However, with their decisions, resources, and actions, government, universities, research parks, and financial institutions can exert a crucial role in developing an environmental context that may favor an entrepreneurship spirit (Isenberg, 2010; Spilling, 1996).

The environmental context is, thus, a crucial aspect that encourages entrepreneurial opportunities that should be properly selected by entrepreneurs. Accordingly, "a critical endeavor for entrepreneurs is to identify and select appropriate opportunities relating to what product or service" (Overholm, 2015, p. 14), as well as in new opportunities in international markets (Zander et al., 2015). In this vein, the ecosystem bears a central responsibility. Actually, "opportunity creation and discovery can be distributed among a community of entrepreneurs as a business ecosystem grows through collective efforts" (Overholm, 2015, p. 23). Furthermore, "strategic thinking and the entrepreneurial activities in an ecosystem influence one another in a cycle that perpetuates and even sparks innovation" (Zahra and Nambisan, 2012, p. 219).

While traditional approaches to entrepreneurship focus on traits and circumstances in which entrepreneurs create and discover new opportunities, the concept of entrepreneurial ecosystem shifts the analytical focus by considering that opportunities can be created and discovered within an entrepreneurial ecosystem, "where entrepreneurial efforts are distributed" (Overholm, 2015, p. 15). They "are more likely to succeed when they mobilize support by offering reciprocal returns to those who help them realize opportunities" (Li and Garnsey, 2014, p. 763).

In this perspective, the ecosystem is the setting in which strategic and entrepreneurial thinking emerges and, in turn, affects the creation and discovery of new entrepreneurial opportunities (Minà and Dagnino, 2016). Such individual characteristics are the foundation of the "entrepreneurial insight" (Zahra and Nambisan, 2012) that makes firms capable of both adapting and transforming as the forces of competition change, and "simultaneously creating and discovering opportunities while creatively and profitably exploiting other opportunities" (Zahra and Nambisan, 2012, p. 219).

2.7.3 Service Ecosystem

Quite recently, scholars have shown a growing interest in the services surrounding the ecosystem. The service ecosystem represents "a relatively self-contained, self-adjusting system of mostly loosely coupled social and economic (resource-integrating) actors connected by shared institutional logics and mutual value creation through service exchange" (Lusch and Nambisan, 2015, p. 162; Lusch, 2011). Actors are mainly loosely coupled to underline that they can freely enter into and exit from the interactions with the other actors to co-create value. They therefore "self-adjust" their behaviors in order to quickly respond to the needs of the market (Luch and Vargo, 2014).

Digital technology has significantly contributed to the easier sharing of information among actors. Concepts such as service-dominant logic (henceforth S-D logic) and service ecosystems have emerged in correspondence with the development of the digital era and the increased need for "service systems involving highly distributed, heterogeneous, and resource-integrating actors" (Eaton et al., 2015, p. 217). S-D logic and service ecosystem are strictly interrelated concepts since they both draw on the idea that the value creation process occurs through the integration, exchange, and application of resources stemming from various stakeholders. Specifically, S-D logic emphasizes "the processes of serving rather than on the output in the form of a product offering that is exchanged" (Lusch and Nambisan, 2015, p. 156). It provides a "more-holistic and dynamic lens for understanding value creation, and thus, innovation" (Vargo et al., 2015, p. 3; Vargo and Lusch, 2011). This more holistic lens differs from the traditional view of innovation, for which value is seen as mainly developed by firms (i.e., the producers of innovation). Similarly, service ecosystems imply that innovation is the collaborative recombination of resources and competences shared by loosely coupled economic and social actors that create value through social exchange (Lusch and Nambisan, 2015). As concerns service ecosystems, a challenge emerges when there exists cognitive distance among actors, meaning that they fall short of developing a common/shared perspective about the surrounding environment. Under this circumstance, it is crucial to develop and maintain a shared view among cognitively distant actors, thereby implementing a "service platform" based on resources that facilitate smooth interaction among them.

2.8   OUTCOMES OF ECOSYSTEMS

Being a fundamental part of an ecosystem implies that actors and architectures profoundly affect the processes of value creation at both the firm level and the ecosystem level (Teece, 2010; Van Der Borgh et al., 2012). Since they are strongly related to each other "through a logic of ecological interdependence" (Shrivastava, 1995, p. 118), ecosystem actors consequently depend on one another for the ecosystems' overall effectiveness and survival. Actors are thus expected to promote their own interest and, at same time, the overall health of the ecosystem (Li, 2009).

First, business ecosystems should make it easier to *achieve competitive advantages* for the firms involved in the ecosystem (Clarysse et al., 2014). This occurs thanks to the combination and recombination of resources, knowledge, and competences. In this vein, an intriguing measure of the performance of an ecosystem is its robustness. Participation in an ecosystem is more effective when members are allowed to seize opportunities and to grow and achieve long-term competitive advantage. This condition explains the relevance of considering "the survival rates of ecosystem members, either over time or relative to comparable ecosystems" (Iansiti and Levien, 2004a, p. 73).

Second, ecosystem performance should be appraised on the basis of the interdependence that facilitates the development of new technologies and innovations (Kapoor and Lee, 2013; Moore, 1996; Zahra and Nambisan, 2012). Specifically, ecosystem performance symbolizes the ecosystem's "ability to consistently transform technology and other raw materials of innovation into lower costs and new products" (Iansiti and Levien, 2004a, p. 72). This is the main element concerning productivity that emerges within the ecosystem through the continuous interactions of its actors.

Third, ecosystem performance should be evaluated through considering how interdependences among actors facilitate the emergence of an entrepreneurial context (Overholm, 2015; Pitelis, 2012). On the one hand, ecosystems play a role in managing technological and market uncertainties (Larson, 1992). On the other hand, they cultivate niches of new functions and services that develop diversity (Iansiti and Levien, 2004b; Wareham et al., 2014) as the condition that assures the combination and recombination of entrepreneurs' insights (Garnsey et al., 2008).

Finally, to benefit from an ecosystem, firms need an entrepreneurial and coopetitive mindset, as well as coopetitive business models (Zott and Amit, 2013), resources, knowledge, and capabilities (Gnyawali et al., 2008). Firms are more likely to achieve advantages from inclusion in the ecosystem if they harbor an entrepreneurial orientation, adopt a proactive strategy, organize an excellent pool of valuable resources, and are able to manage the tensions inherent in mixing cooperation and competition (Gnyawali et al., 2008).

2.9   IMPLICATIONS AND CONCLUSION

In this chapter, by developing a content analysis of extant research on business ecosystems, we have gained an understanding of several points that concern the features of this emerging stream in strategic management and entrepreneurship. First, we extracted a map depicting the antecedents of ecosystems, actors and structures that support their emergence and development, the variety of ecosystems, and the performance of ecosystems. Second, on the basis of Iansiti and Levien (2004b), we provided a classification of the four roles that firms may activate within the ecosystem: keystone players; dominators; niche players; and hub landlords. Third, we depicted the main characteristics of three important types of business ecosystem: innovation ecosystem, entrepreneurial ecosystem, and service ecosystem.

Our analysis of ecosystems has three key implications that may aid the advancement of studies on business ecosystems in management. First, the chapter sheds light on the possibility of achieving comprehensive representation (and general understanding) of the literature on business ecosystems by means of mapping the area of study using ecosystem antecedents, actors and structures, variety, and performance. Second, by originally decomposing the main business ecosystems literature into three typologies (i.e., innovation ecosystem, entrepreneurship ecosystem, and service ecosystem), the chapter opens a window on how it is possible to reorganize the current literature on the basis of these three types of business ecosystems.

Finally, since ecosystems may enable firms to create value that no single firm could create alone (Adner, 2012), this study draws managers' attention to the increasing significance of looking at whole business ecosystems as the center of their efforts, rather than at single firms or alliance, if they wish to build a solid competitive advantage. The core of the message is that by recognizing the rapidly emerging role of ecosystems in an increasingly interdependent world, managers will realize that firms may fail when they only focus on their innovations, while strategically overlooking the ecosystems on which their achievement is bound to.

Inevitably, as any research effort, this chapter has some limitations. The first limitation concerns the content analysis that may require additional research, possibly performed using complementary quantitative bibliometric methods (such as meta-analysis, coupling analysis, author citation analysis, webometric analysis, and social network analysis) to achieve more consistency and validity. In addition, since this chapter is centered on business ecosystems literature, it has inevitably overlooked overlapping areas and improvement that may come from interaction with other important technology management literatures.

We believe that to gain in both stability and reliability, the emerging area of ecosystems should look at matching, trade, and the interplay with germane literatures. It will look at the role of network effects in creating value by means of ecosystems that function as platforms (Cennamo and Santalo, 2013), platform leaders (Gawer and Cusumano, 2008); and the role of technological transitions, when, for instance, competing technologies and the ecosystems in which they are embedded challenge the option between ecosystem emergence, ecosystem extension, and ecosystem termination in the passage between the old and the new technology; as well as the study of the ways to overcome the tensions in the dual nature, both cooperative and competitive, of business ecosystems that are characterized simultaneously by information sharing and joint action among complementors and by competitive challenges in their quest for joint value creation (Kapoor, 2014).

REFERENCES

Adner, R. (2006). Match your innovation strategy to your innovation ecosystem. *Harvard Business Review*, **84**(4), 98–109.

Adner, R. (2012). *The Wide Lens: A New Strategy for Innovation*. New York: Penguin Books.

Adner, R. and Kapoor, R. (2010). Value creation in innovation ecosystems: How the structure of technological interdependence affects firm performance in new technology generations. *Strategic Management Journal*, **31**(3), 306–33.

Afuah, A. (2000). How much do your co-opetitors' capabilities matter in the face of technological change? *Strategic Management Journal*, **21**(3), 387–404.

Afuah, A.N. and Bahram, N. (1995). The hypercube of innovation. *Research Policy*, **24**(1), 51–76.

Alvarez, S.A. and Barney, J.B. (2007). Discovery and creation: Alternative theories of entrepreneurial action. *Strategic Entrepreneurship Journal*, **1**(1–2), 11–26.

Alvarez, S.A. and Barney, J.B. (2010). Entrepreneurship and epistemology: The philosophical underpinnings of the study of entrepreneurial opportunities. *Academy of Management Annals*, **4**(1), 557–83.

Armstrong, M. (2006). Competition in two-sided markets. *RAND Journal of Economics*, **37**(3), 668–91.

Autio, E., Dahlander, L. and Frederiksen, L. (2013). Information exposure, opportunity evaluation, and entrepreneurial action: An investigation of an online user community. *Academy of Management Journal*, **56**(5), 1348–71.

Autio, E., Kenney, M., Mustar, P., Siegel, D. and Wright, M. (2014). Entrepreneurial innovation: The importance of context. *Research Policy*, **43**(7), 1097–108.

Barney, J.B. (1995). Looking inside for competitive advantage. *Academy of Management Executive*, **9**(4), 49–61.

Basole, R.C. (2009). Visualization of interfirm relations in a converging mobile ecosystem. *Journal of Information Technology*, **24**(2), 144–59.

Baum, J.A., Calabrese, T. and Silverman, B.S. (2000). Don't go it alone: Alliance network composition and startups' performance in Canadian biotechnology. *Strategic Management Journal*, **21**(3), 267–94.

Best, M.H. (2015). Greater Boston's industrial ecosystem: A manufactory of sectors. *Technovation*, **39–40**, 4–13.

Brandenburger, A.M. and Nalebuff, B. (1996). *Co-opetition.* London: HarperCollinsBusiness.

Burgelman, R.A. (1983). A process model of internal corporate venturing in the diversified major firm. *Administrative Science Quarterly*, **28**(2), 223–44.

Carley, K. (1993). Coding choices for textual analysis: A comparison of content analysis and map analysis. *Sociological Methodology*, **23**, 75–126.

Ceccagnoli, M., Forman, C., Huang, P. and Wu, D.J. (2012). Cocreation of value in a platform ecosystem: The case of enterprise software. *MIS Quarterly*, **36**(1), 263–90.

Cennamo, C. and Santalo, J. (2013). Platform competition: Strategic trade-offs in platform markets. *Strategic Management Journal*, **34**(11), 1331–50.

Clarysse, B., Wright, M., Bruneel, J. and Mahajan, A. (2014). Creating value in ecosystems: Crossing the chasm between, knowledge and business ecosystems. *Research Policy*, **43**(7), 1164–76.

Cusumano, M.A. and Gawer, A. (2002). The elements of platform leadership. *MIT Sloan Management Review*, **43**(3), 51–8.

D'Aveni, R. (1994). *Hypercompetition: Managing the Dynamics of Strategic Management*. New York: The Free Press.

D'Aveni, R.A., Dagnino, G.B. and Smith, K.G. (2010). The age of temporary advantage. *Strategic Management Journal*, **31**(13), 1371–85.

Dagnino, G.B., Levanti, G., Minà, A. and Picone, P.M. (2015). Interorganizational network and innovation: A bibliometric study and proposed research agenda. *Journal of Business & Industrial Marketing*, **30**(3/4), 354–77.

Dedehayir, O. and Makinen, S.J. (2011). Measuring industry clockspeed in the systemic industry context. *Technovation*, **31**(12), 627–37.

Di Stefano, G., Peteraf, M. and Verona, G. (2010). Dynamic capabilities deconstructed: A bibliographic investigation into the origins, development, and future directions of the research domain. *Industrial and Corporate Change*, **19**(4), 1187–204, doi:10.1093/icc/dtq027.

Duriau, V.J., Reger, R.K. and Pfarrer, M.D. (2007). A content analysis of the content analysis literature in organization studies: Research themes, data sources, and methodological refinements. *Organizational Research Methods*, **10**(1), 5–34.

Dussauge, P., Garrette, B. and Mitchell, W. (2000). Learning from competing partners: Outcomes and durations of scale and link alliances in Europe, North America and Asia. *Strategic Management Journal*, **21**(2), 99–126.

Eaton, B., Elaluf-Calderwood, S. and Sorensen, C. (2015). Distributed tuning of boundary resources: The case of Apple's iOS service system. *MIS Quarterly*, **39**(1), 217–43.

El Sawy, O.A., Malhotra, A., Park, Y. and Pavlou, P.A. (2010). Seeking the configurations of digital ecodynamics: It takes three to tango. *Information Systems Research*, **21**(4), 835–48.

Erdener, C.B. and Dunn, C.P. (1990). Content analysis. *Mapping Strategic Thought*, 291–300.

Faulkner, D. (1995). *International Strategic Alliances: Co-operating to Compete.* Maidenhead: McGraw-Hill.

Folta, T.B. (1998). Governance and uncertainty: The tradeoff between administrative control and commitment. *Strategic Management Journal*, **19**(11), 1007–28.

Garfield, E. (1979). Is citation analysis a legitimate evaluation tool? *Scientometrics*, **1**(4), 359–75.

Garnsey, E., Lorenzoni, G. and Ferriani, S. (2008). Speciation through entrepreneurial spin-off: The Acorn-ARM story. *Research Policy*, **37**(2), 210–24.

Gawer, A. (2014). Bridging differing perspectives on technological platforms: Toward an integrative framework. *Research Policy*, **43**(7), 1239–49.

Gawer, A. and Cusumano, M.A. (2008). How companies become platform leaders. *MIT Sloan Management Review*, **49**(2), 28–35.

Gawer, A. and Cusumano, M.A. (2014). Industry platforms and ecosystem innovation. *Journal of Product Innovation Management*, **31**(3), 417–33.

Gnyawali, D., He, J. and Madhavan, R. (2008). Co-opetition: Promises and challenges. In C. Wankel (ed.), *21st Century Management: A Reference Handbook*, pp. 386–99. Thousand Oaks, CA: Sage Publications.

Gulati, R., Nohria, N. and Zaheer, A. (2000). Strategic networks. *Strategic Management Journal*, **21**(3), Special Issue: Strategic Networks (March), 203–15.

Haney, W., Russell, M., Gulek, C. and Fierros, E. (1998). Drawing on education: Using student drawings to promote Middle School improvement. *Schools in the Middle*, **7**(3), January–February, 38–43.

Hitt, M., Ireland, R., Camp, M. and Sexton, D. (2001). Strategic entrepreneurship: Entrepreneurial strategies for wealth creation. *Strategic Management Journal*, **22**, 479–91.

Iansiti, M. and Levien, R. (2004a). *The Keystone Advantage: What the New Dynamics of Business Ecosystems Mean for Strategy, Innovation, and Sustainability.* Cambridge, MA: Harvard Business Press.

Iansiti, M. and Levien, R. (2004b). Strategy as ecology. *Harvard Business Review*, **82**(3), 68–78.

Ilinitch, A.Y., D'Aveni, R.A. and Lewin, A.Y. (1996). New organizational forms and strategies for managing in hypercompetitive environments. *Organization Science*, **7**(3), 211–20.

Isenberg, D. (2010). The big idea: How to start an entrepreneurial revolution. *Harvard Business Review*, **88**(6), 40–50.

Iyer, B., Lee, C.H. and Venkatraman, N. (2006). Managing in a "small world ecosystem": Lessons from the software sector. *California Management Review*, **48**(3), 28–47.

Kallinikos, J., Aaltonen, A. and Marton, A. (2013). The ambivalent ontology of digital artifacts. *MIS Quarterly*, **37**(2), 357–70.

Kanter, R.M. (2012). Enriching the ecosystem. *Harvard Business Review*, **90**(3), 140–147.

Kapoor, R. (2014). Collaborating with complementors: What do firms do? In R. Adner, J.E. Oxley and B.S. Silverman (eds), *Collaboration and Competition in Business Ecosystems (Advances in Strategic Management)*, Vol. 30, pp. 3–25. Bingley, UK: Emerald.

Kapoor, R. and Furr, N.R. (2015). Complementarities and competition: Unpacking the drivers of entrants' technology choices in the solar photovoltaic industry. *Strategic Management Journal*, **36**(3), 416–36.

Kapoor, R. and Lee, J.M. (2013). Coordinating and competing in ecosystems: How organizational forms shape new technology investments. *Strategic Management Journal*, **34**(3), 274–96.

Krippendorff, K. (1980). *Content Analysis: An Introduction to its Methodology.* London: Sage Publications.

Krippendorff, K. (2004). *The Semantic Turn: A New Foundation for Design*. Boca Raton, FL: CRC Press.

Larson, A. (1992). Network dyads in entrepreneurial settings: A study of the governance of exchange relationships. *Administrative Science Quarterly*, **37**(1), 76–104.

Leten, B., Vanhaverbeke, W., Roijakkers, N., Clerix, A. and Van Helleputte, J. (2013). IP models to orchestrate innovation ecosystems: IMEC, a public research institute in nano-electronics. *California Management Review*, **55**(4), 51–64.

Li, J.F. and Garnsey, E. (2014). Policy-driven ecosystems for new vaccine development. *Technovation*, **34**(12), 762–72.

Li, Y.R. (2009). The technological roadmap of Cisco's business ecosystem. *Technovation*, **29**(5), 379–86.

Lumpkin, G.T. and Dess, G.G. (1996). Clarifying the entrepreneurial orientation construct and linking it to performance. *Academy of Management Review*, **21**(1), 135–72.

Lusch, R. and Vargo, S. (2014). *Service Dominant Logic. Premises, Perspectives, Possibilities*. Cambridge: Cambridge University Press.

Lusch, R.F. (2011). Reframing supply chain management: A service-dominant logic perspective. *Journal of Supply Chain Management*, **47**(1), 14–18.

Lusch, R.F. and Nambisan, S. (2015). Service innovation: A service-dominant logic perspective. *MIS Quarterly*, **39**(1), 155–75.

Maglio, P.P. and Spohrer, J. (2013). A service science perspective on business model innovation. *Industrial Marketing Management*, **42**(5), 665–70.

Mars, M.M., Bronstein, J.L. and Lusch, R.F. (2012). The value of a metaphor: Organizations and ecosystems. *Organizational Dynamics*, **41**(4), 271–80.

Meyer, A.D., Gaba, V. and Colwell, K.A. (2005). Organizing far from equilibrium: Nonlinear change in organizational fields. *Organization Science*, **16**(5), 456–73.

Minà, A. and Dagnino, G.B. (2016). In search of coopetition consensus: Shaping the collective identity of a relevant strategic management community. *International Journal of Technology Management*, **71**(1–2), 123–54.

Mitchell, W. and Singh, K. (1996). Survival of businesses using collaborative relationships to commercialize complex goods. *Strategic Management Journal*, **17**(3), 169–95.

Moore, J.F. (1993). Predators and prey – a new ecology of competition. *Harvard Business Review*, **71**(3), 75–86.

Moore, J.F. (1996). The death of competition. *Fortune*, **133**(7), 142.

Moore, J.F. (2006). Business ecosystems and the view from the firm. *The Antitrust Bulletin*, **51**(1), 31–75.

Muller, E. and Yogev, G. (2006). When does the majority become a majority? Empirical analysis of the time at which main market adopters purchase the bulk of our sales. *Technological Forecasting and Social Change*, **73**(9), 1107–20.

Nag, R., Hambrick, D.C. and Chen, M.J. (2007). What is strategic management, really? Inductive derivation of a consensus definition of the field. *Strategic Management Journal*, **28**(9), 935–55.

Oriani, R. and Sobrero, M. (2008). Uncertainty and the market valuation of R&D within a real options logic. *Strategic Management Journal*, **29**(4), 343–61.

Overholm, H. (2015). Collectively created opportunities in emerging ecosystems: The case of solar service ventures. *Technovation*, **39–40**, 14–25.

Park, S.H., Chen, R.R. and Gallagher, S. (2002). Firm resources as moderators of the relationship between market growth and strategic alliances in semiconductor start-ups. *Academy of Management Journal*, **45**(3), 527–45.

Penrose, E.T. (1995). *The Theory of the Growth of the Firm*. Oxford: Oxford University Press.

Peteraf, M.A. (1993). The cornerstones of competitive advantage: A resource-based view. *Strategic Management Journal*, **14**(3), 179–91.

Pitelis, C. (2012). Clusters, entrepreneurial ecosystem co-creation, and appropriability: A conceptual framework. *Industrial and Corporate Change*, **21**(6), 1359–88.

Porter, M.E. (1980). *Competitive Strategy: Techniques for Analyzing Industries and Competitors*. New York: The Free Press.

Rochet, J.C. and Tirole, J. (2003). Platform competition in two-sided markets. *Journal of the European Economic Association*, **1**(4), 990–1029.

Shapiro, G. and Markoff, G. (1997). Methods for drawing statistical inferences from text and transcripts. In C.W. Roberts (ed.), *Text Analysis for the Social Sciences*, pp. 9–31. Mahwah, NJ: Lawrence Erlbaum Associates.

Shrivastava, P. (1995). Ecocentric management for a risk society. *Academy of Management Review*, **20**(1), 118–37.

Singer, J.G. (2006). Systems marketing for the information age. *MIT Sloan Management Review*, **48**(1), 95–6.

Sonpar, K. and Golden-Biddle, K. (2008). Using content analysis to elaborate adolescent theories of organization. *Organizational Research Methods*, **11**(4), 795–814.

Spilling, O.R. (1996). The entrepreneurial system: On entrepreneurship in the context of a mega-event. *Journal of Business Research*, **36**(1), 91–103.

Teece, D.J. (2007). Explicating dynamic capabilities: The nature and microfoundations of (sustainable) enterprise performance. *Strategic Management Journal*, **28**(13), 1319–50.

Teece, D.J. (2010). Business models, business strategy and innovation. *Long Range Planning*, **43**(2), 172–94.

Teece, D.J., Pisano, G. and Shuen, A. (1997). Dynamic capabilities and strategic management. *Strategic Management Journal*, **18**(7), 509–33.

Tiwana, A., Konsynski, B. and Bush, A.A. (2010). Platform evolution: Coevolution of platform architecture, governance, and environmental dynamics. *Information Systems Research*, **21**(4), 675–87.

Van Der Borgh, M., Cloodt, M. and Romme, A.G.L. (2012). Value creation by knowledge-based ecosystems: Evidence from a field study. *R&D Management*, **42**(2), 150–69.

Vargo, S.L. and Lusch, R.F. (2011). It's all B2B . . . and beyond: Toward a systems perspective of the market. *Industrial Marketing Management*, **40**(2), 181–7.

Vargo, S.L. and Lusch, R.F. (2014). Inversions of service-dominant logic. *Marketing Theory*, **14**(3), 239–48.

Vargo, S.L., Wieland, H. and Akaka, M.A. (2015). Innovation through institutionalization: A service ecosystems perspective. *Industrial Marketing Management*, **44**, 63–72.

Walker, G. and Weber, D. (1984). A transaction cost approach to make-or-buy decisions. *Administrative Science Quarterly*, **29**(3), 373–91.

Wareham, J., Fox, P.B., Cano, G. and Josep, L. (2014). Technology ecosystem governance. *Organization Science*, **25**(4), 1195–215.

Weber, R.P. (1990). *Basic Content Analysis*, No. 49. Beverley Hills, CA: Sage.

Weiss, M. and Gangadharan, G.R. (2010). Modeling the mashup ecosystem: Structure and growth. *R&D Management*, **40**(1), 40–49.

Willis, A.J. (1997). Forum. *Functional Ecology*, **11**(2), 268–71.

Woodard, C.J., Ramasubbu, N., Tschang, F.T. and Sambamurthy, V. (2013). Design capital and design moves: The logic of digital business strategy. *MIS Quarterly*, **37**(2), 537–64.

Xu, X., Venkatesh, V., Tam, K.Y. and Hong, S.J. (2010). Model of migration and use of platforms: Role of hierarchy, current generation, and complementarities in consumer settings. *Management Science*, **56**(8), 1304–23.

Zahra, S.A. and Nambisan, S. (2012). Entrepreneurship and strategic thinking in business ecosystems. *Business Horizons*, **55**(3), 219–29.

Zander, I., McDougall-Covin, P. and Rose, E.L. (2015). Born global and international business: Evolution of a field of research. *Journal of International Business Studies*, **46**(1), 27–35.

Zott, C. and Amit, R. (2013). The business model: A theoretically anchored robust construct for strategic analysis. *Strategic Organization*, **11**(4), 403–11.

3. Linking entrepreneurial and innovation ecosystems: the case of AppCampus

Llewellyn D.W. Thomas,* Dmitry Sharapov and Erkko Autio

3.1 INTRODUCTION

In the 20 years since it was first coined (Moore, 1993), the term "ecosystem" has become increasingly prominent in the strategy and entrepreneurship literatures. In the strategy literature, the concept usually underpins studies looking at the dynamics of competition and collaboration in co-specialized technology-intensive settings (Adner & Kapoor, 2010; Autio & Thomas, 2014; Iansiti & Levien, 2004). In the entrepreneurship literature, the use of the term is more varied: it has been used by practitioners and researchers in reference to entrepreneurship policy portfolios (Wessner, 2005), regional clusters of entrepreneurs and specialized resources (Autio et al., 2017; Kenney & Von Burg, 1999), and even national systems of entrepreneurship (Acs et al., 2014). Common to both innovation and entrepreneurial ecosystems is the idea that organizations seldom operate in perfectly competitive markets characterized by arms-length transactions and head-to-head competition between firms producing substitutable products, but rather, in network structures composed of co-specialized organizations that play complementary roles to co-create value.

Despite the increasing interest in entrepreneurial and innovation ecosystems, there is little research that has considered the interactions between these two types of ecosystems, and extant work of this kind has tended to investigate entrepreneurship in the context of innovation ecosystems. For instance, Zahra and Nambisan (2011) consider how new ventures play complementary roles that keep innovation ecosystems vibrant and competitive. Taking a more cognitive turn, Zahra and Nambisan (2012) consider how strategic thinking and entrepreneurial activities can frame, revise and transform an innovation ecosystem. Furthermore, Nambisan and Baron (2013) consider how entrepreneurs within an ecosystem need to balance the goals and priorities set by ecosystem leaders with the goals and priorities of their own new venture. These papers have provided useful insight into the entrepreneurial dynamics within an innovation ecosystem. They do not directly consider the interactions between the entrepreneurial ecosystems in which these new ventures are launched and the innovation ecosystem in which they operate, however. This is an important omission in light of recent work suggesting that entrepreneurs can benefit from being embedded in multiple ecosystems (De Cock et al., 2015; Kulchina, 2016).

The purpose of this chapter is to investigate the mechanisms and outcomes of an explicit attempt to link an entrepreneurial ecosystem with an innovation ecosystem. To do so, we consider the case of AppCampus, a three-year project that aimed to both leverage and enhance both the entrepreneurial ecosystem around Aalto University, and the Windows Phone innovation ecosystem. Managed by Aalto University in Finland, who covered operating costs of around €3 million, it was funded by €9 million each from Microsoft and Nokia. AppCampus was a qualified success for both the Windows Phone ecosystem and the Aalto entrepreneurial ecosystem. For the Windows Phone ecosystem, AppCampus was not only successful in attracting developers; these developers also released apps that were of higher quality than the application market average. For the Aalto entrepreneurial ecosystem, AppCampus not only attracted funding, facilitated the launch of many new ventures locally, educated entrepreneurs, and provided additional depth of experience and personnel, but it also enhanced the legitimacy of both the Aalto entrepreneurial ecosystem as well as Aalto University itself, leading to further connections between the Aalto entrepreneurial ecosystem and other entrepreneurial and innovation ecosystems.

This is an interesting case study, as Aalto University already had an emergent entrepreneurial ecosystem, with a successful student-run accelerator, university entrepreneurship courses, a technology transfer office and vibrant entrepreneurial culture. This culture was exemplified by the annual SLUSH conference, the largest gathering of entrepreneurs, venture capital and press in Northern Europe. In contrast, the Windows Phone, having been launched to good reviews in previous years, was having difficulty attracting developers and building momentum for its ecosystem. Thus, the decision to link the two begins to shed some light on the question of how a successful entrepreneurial ecosystem can assist a struggling innovation ecosystem.

The main contribution of this chapter is to describe and explain the unique ecosystem-linking mechanism that AppCampus represents. Due to its dual roles within both the innovation and entrepreneurial ecosystem, the components that comprise AppCampus – its strategic focus, funding structure, program package (the services that are offered to participants), a selection process and alumni relations (Clarysse et al., 2015) – offer interesting insights into how innovation and entrepreneurial ecosystems can be fruitfully linked. We also contribute by detailing the lessons this initiative has for the leaders of entrepreneurial ecosystems who wish to leverage existing innovation ecosystems, as well as for the leaders of innovation ecosystems who wish to leverage entrepreneurial ecosystems for their benefit.

In what follows, we first briefly review the characteristics of both innovation and entrepreneurial ecosystems. We then outline our case study research methodology. This is followed by an analysis of both the Windows Phone ecosystem and the Aalto entrepreneurial ecosystem. We then detail the AppCampus initiative itself, explaining each of its components and how they linked both innovation and entrepreneurial ecosystems. We describe the outcomes of AppCampus for both the Aalto entrepreneurial ecosystem and the Windows Phone innovation ecosystem. We conclude with a discussion of the lessons AppCampus holds for both entrepreneurial and innovation ecosystem leaders.

3.2 ENTREPRENEURIAL AND INNOVATION ECOSYSTEMS

The notion of an "ecosystem" has proven to be an attractive metaphor to describe a range of interactions and inter-linkages between multiple organizations. The most common conceptualization of the notion of a "business ecosystem" was first proposed by Moore (1993), who used the term to describe the set of organizations and consumers that surround a focal organization, and which contribute to its performance. In their influential book, Iansiti and Levien (2004) conceptualized the ecosystem as loose networks of suppliers, distributors, outsourcing firms, makers of related products or services, technology providers and others that both affect, and are affected by, the creation and delivery of the focal organization's own offerings. Even more broadly, an ecosystem can be considered to include the community of organizations, institutions and individuals that impact the focal organization, such as customers, competitors, complementors, suppliers, regulatory authorities, standard-setting bodies, the judiciary, and educational and research institutions (Teece, 2007).

Underpinning all of these ideas is the realization that organizations seldom operate in perfectly competitive markets characterized by arms-length transactions and head-to-head competition, but in network structures composed of co-specialized organizations that play complementary roles to co-create value. This insight that the context matters has been adopted by both entrepreneurship and strategy scholars, and called *entrepreneurial ecosystems* and *innovation ecosystems*, respectively.

3.2.1   Entrepreneurial Ecosystems

Entrepreneurial ecosystems refer to the human, financial and professional resources and institutional environment which support and nurture new ventures in a specific geographic location (Autio et al., 2018; Graham, 2014; Isenberg, 2010). Referring to the systemic nature of entrepreneurship (Spilling, 1996; Van de Ven, 1993), research on entrepreneurial ecosystems is being driven by the increasing realization of the importance of context when considering entrepreneurship (Autio et al., 2014; Autio et al., 2018; Levie, 2014; Pitelis, 2012). This realization is based on the insight that startups emerge and grow not only because of heroic, talented and visionary individuals (entrepreneurs), but also because the startups are located in a network of private and public players which nurture and sustain them. Recent work has suggested that entrepreneurs can benefit from being embedded in multiple entrepreneurial ecosystems by exploiting differences in resource costs between ecosystems (Kulchina, 2016) and by overcoming resource scarcity in one ecosystem through accessing the needed resources in another (De Cock et al., 2015).

The entrepreneurial ecosystem consists of the human, financial and professional resources that an entrepreneur requires, and an institutional environment in which government policies encourage and safeguard entrepreneurs (Isenberg, 2010). Ecosystems can have many components, including the existence of prior ventures, a patent system, a culture tolerating failure, incubators, grant programs and investments by business angel and/or venture capitalists (Isenberg, 2010; Spigel, 2017). These resources and institutional environment interact, influencing the formation and eventual trajectory of startups, as well as potentially the economy as a whole (Spilling, 1996; Van de Ven, 1993). How these resources and the institutional environment are expressed is unique to the particular locale – there is no universal template that can be used for an entrepreneurial ecosystem (Isenberg, 2010).

Entrepreneurial ecosystems are increasingly vital to the success of national entrepreneurship initiatives (Acs et al., 2014; Drexler et al., 2014; Moore, 1993; Napier et al., 2012). Entrepreneurial ecosystems drive social and economic development through enabling access to markets, human capital and funding and finance for startups. In terms of access to markets, given the heterogeneity of startups in relation to their anticipated timing and magnitude of their initial revenues, having access to sustainable revenues at some stage is a central aspect of every economy's social and economic development (Foster et al., 2013). In terms of human capital, entrepreneurial ecosystems with a greater depth of skilled employees create a more hospitable environment for the scaling of early-stage companies. Furthermore, entrepreneurial ecosystems drive social and economic benefits through connecting startups with potential investors (Radojevich-Kelley & Hoffman, 2012), as well as accelerating the time horizon for reaching key milestones, including time to raising of venture capital, exit by acquisition and achievement of customer traction (Hallen et al., 2014; Winston-Smith et al., 2013).

3.2.2 Innovation Ecosystems

Innovation ecosystems refer to a network of interconnected organizations that are linked to or operate around a focal firm or a platform (Adner & Kapoor, 2010; Autio & Thomas, 2014). A defining characteristic of innovation ecosystems is that they are dynamic and purposive value-creating networks in which the participants co-create value (Adner & Kapoor, 2010; Ceccagnoli et al., 2012). In order to facilitate value co-creation, the relationships in an ecosystem efficiently move information, innovations and resources around the network (Adner, 2012; Iyer et al., 2006). The movement of information, innovations and resources is not constrained to a given locality, with value co-creation independent of the physical locations of the ecosystem participants.

Innovation ecosystems are typified by a system-level goal of value co-creation through synergistic outputs (Gulati et al., 2012; Lusch & Nambisan, 2015), explicitly and holistically considering the role of complementary asset providers in value creation and appropriation (Jacobides et al., 2006; Teece, 1986). The dynamics of value co-creation mean that opportunities enabled by ecosystems are not necessarily equally distributed amongst participants (Adner & Kapoor, 2010; Burt, 2004; Ceccagnoli et al., 2012). The hub firm or platform within an innovation ecosystem provides a coordination role (Cusumano & Gawer, 2002; Nambisan & Sawhney, 2011) and often are at the center of multi-sided markets where value creation is driven by both direct and indirect positive network externalities underpinned by shared technological standards and co-specialization (Katz & Shapiro, 1985, 1986).

Ecosystem participants embed themselves in a complex set of network relationships, combining their individual offerings into a coherent, customer-facing solution, and in the process co-creating value that would not be possible for a single participant alone. However, these are not the arms-length or hierarchical transactions of Williamson (1975), as the co-creation of value here relies on investments in relation-specific assets, substantial knowledge exchange, and non-market governance mechanisms without the participants becoming integrated into a single organization (Wareham et al., 2014). In particular, involvement in an ecosystem can increase the likelihood of investing in new technologies (Kapoor & Lee, 2013), as well as influencing technological choices, with firms trading off superior technological performance for the availability of complementary assets (Kapoor & Furr, 2015). Due to their embeddedness in the network, each ecosystem participant is symbiotic to and co-evolves with other participants. Symbiosis and co-evolution in ecosystem contexts means that each participant of the ecosystem ultimately shares the fate of the network as a whole, regardless of that individual participant's strength or power.

3.3   METHOD

This research is based on a single case study, giving the researchers the opportunity to understand the phenomenon of interest in depth. The AppCampus case meets the four criteria proposed by Pettigrew (1990) for selecting a subject for study. First, the phenomenon under investigation is transparently observable; the access granted to researchers by the organizational members has meant that the competitive challenges and operational activities are clearly visible. Second, AppCampus is a "polar type", in the sense that it represents one-of-a-kind initiative at the time of writing (although similar initiatives have started to emerge). Third, Aalto and AppCampus have high experience levels of the phenomenon under study, as the activities under investigation are within their area of purview. Finally, extensive access was granted to not only Aalto and AppCampus personnel, but also to the sponsoring firms (Nokia and Microsoft), as well as to other members of the ecosystem.

Data was collected from many sources and analyzed using standard techniques. In order to gain the level of detail and sophistication required, all evidence was triangulated (Pettigrew, 1990; Yin, 1984). Following established practice, we allowed data analysis to overlap with data collection. This overlap enhanced data collection flexibility and allowed us to adjust data collection to probe emergent themes or take advantage of unexpected opportunities (Eisenhardt, 1989). Examples of adjustments carried out include adding questions to the interview protocol and adding data sources. The evidence guiding our insights was drawn from several sources:

1. *Semi-structured interviews with AppCampus employees.* We conducted 56 semi-structured interviews with 14 key informants who developed and operated the AppCampus program. These informants included the founders, managers, functional specialists and support staff in AppCampus. The interviews were carried out by two of the authors working together, and were recorded and transcribed.

2. *Semi-structured interviews with Aalto University, Nokia and Microsoft employees.* We conducted 15 semi-structured interviews with five key informants from Aalto University, Nokia and Microsoft who were associated with the AppCampus initiative. These informants included those who were responsible for the establishment and ongoing monitoring of the initiative. The interviews were carried out by two of the authors working together, and were recorded and transcribed.

3. *Semi-structured interviews with developer teams participating in AppCampus.* We conducted 46 semi-structured interviews with members of developer teams participating in AppCampus. These interviews were carried out by one of the authors, and were recorded and transcribed.

4. *Informal discussions.* We had many informal conversations with those involved or participating in AppCampus. These ranged from brief exchanges to long talks over lunch. We talked with every employee of AppCampus, as well as with a substantial number of the application development teams. These informal conversations provided a cross check on what the interviewees said and what they actually do, countering bias that may result from selective retrieval of information.

5. *AppCademy attendance.* We observed four "AppCademy" events, where a selection of the funded teams are flown to Aalto University in Helsinki to undertake a two- to four-week intensive coaching session. These events included extensive coaching and training in branding and positioning, design and user experience excellence, development, monetization, marketing, communications and much more.

6. *Other meetings.* We attended a number of key strategy, planning and operational review meetings at Aalto and AppCampus. We also attended a number of open days and celebrations, such as birthday parties, where Aalto University and AppCampus were presented to a wide variety of external guests.

7. *Archival materials about Aalto University, AppCampus, Nokia and Microsoft.* We gathered archival material from both online and physical sources, which provided both current and historical facts, including strategy and review documents, memos and operational reports. These were examined both prior to and during the field work period. A protocol was developed to ensure that data extracted from these documents was congruent with the goals of the research.

3.4   THE ECOSYSTEM CONTEXT

Given that we are investigating the intersection of the Aalto University entrepreneurial ecosystem with the Windows Phone innovation ecosystem, we first describe each ecosystem at the time of the study.

3.4.1   Aalto Entrepreneurial Ecosystem

The Aalto entrepreneurial ecosystem is located in Espoo, a city within the metropolitan area of Helsinki, Finland's economic and political hub. Finland is a small Northern European country with developed infrastructure, highly educated and skilled workforce, and a population of about 5.5 million.[1] Finland is rated highly for the good conditions it offers for innovation and entrepreneurship, with the Nordic Growth Entrepreneurship Review 2012 ranking Finland first in the Nordic countries (Napier et al., 2012), the Innovation Union Scoreboard 2014 ranking Finland as having one of best performing innovation systems in the European Union (European Commission, 2014), and the World Economic Forum's *Global Competitiveness Report* ranking Finland as the fourth most competitive nation in the world in 2014–15 (Schwab, 2014).

Aalto University was created in 2010 as an outcome of a high-profile merger between three leading universities in Finland – the Helsinki School of Economics, the Helsinki University of Technology and the University of Art and Design Helsinki. The Aalto University School of Economics was originally established in 1904 by the business community, the Helsinki University of Technology was founded in 1849, and the University of Art and Design Helsinki was established in 1871. The goal of merging these three universities was to combine their strengths in engineering, design and business to create a new world-class university. Aalto University is seen as the flagship of a new national approach to higher education which has industry-informed research and innovation at its core.

The Aalto entrepreneurial ecosystem is located within Otaniemi, Espoo, only 20 minutes from Helsinki city center. With more than 25 research centers Otaniemi has the highest concentration of research and development (R&D) activity and represents the largest technology, innovation and business hub in Finland and in the Nordic countries. The headquarters of some of the largest Finnish companies, such as Nokia and Kone, are located near Otaniemi. The thriving Aalto entrepreneurial ecosystem is internationally recognized for its vibrancy and strength (Graham, 2014). The components that comprise the Aalto entrepreneurial ecosystem are both bottom-up and top-down, driven by both student-led initiatives and university-level programs.

Integral to the Aalto ecosystem is a vibrant student-led entrepreneurship movement originally driven by frustration with the lack of regional and university support for entrepreneurship. This student-led movement is widely viewed as the cornerstone of Aalto's emerging reputation as an entrepreneurial environment and has been the catalyst for a wider cultural change in national attitudes towards startup activities and entrepreneurship more generally (Graham, 2014). As a result of this movement, institutions such as Aalto Entrepreneurship Society and the Startup Sauna Foundation have emerged, both detailed below.

Aalto Entrepreneurship Society
Established in 2009, the Aalto Entrepreneurship Society (AaltoES) is a not-for-profit student-run society which describes itself as "the largest and most active student-run entrepreneurship society in Europe",[2] focusing on "high-tech, high growth, scalable entrepreneurship and build[ing] a leading startup ecosystem in Finland and Northern Europe". Although AaltoES operates independently of Aalto University, many of its 5,000 members are undergraduate or postgraduate students at Aalto or other Helsinki-based universities. The society organizes around 100 events each year, such as Aalto on Rails and National Day of Failure, and attracts around 10,000 participants annually. AaltoES also organizes the Summer of Startups, a two-month program to support startups emerging from the students or researcher populations. AaltoES culture is based on an open community and as a consequence most of their events are free of charge and open to anyone who wants to join their projects.

Startup Sauna Foundation
Founded by students from AaltoES in 2010 to support a functioning startup ecosystem in the region, Startup Sauna is located in Otaniemi campus of Aalto University. The Startup Sauna Foundation was founded in September 2012 by 57 individual serial entrepreneurs and investors from the community.[3] It was spun out from AaltoES to create a more structured entity to focus on the growth of regional high-growth startups, allowing AaltoES to continue to adapt and create new ways to support and nurture the entrepreneurial ecosystem. In addition to providing small grants to individuals and groups, the foundation has three key activities:

- Startup Sauna is dedicated to promoting the creation of new ventures by arranging training, events, incubator services and exchange programs. Operating bi-annually, Startup Sauna has a 1,500 square meter co-working space open for startups in Northern Europe and Russia. The highest potential teams are given the opportunity to meet with investors in Silicon Valley.

- Startup Life is an internship in an established startup anywhere in the world, open to students, postgraduates or researchers from any university. Its aim is to "get students out of the university, out of Finland to see what is possible and how startups really work".
- SLUSH Conference, founded in 2011, is one of Europe's leading startup and investor conferences. Organized every November, it brings startups in the region to meet venture capitalists and media from around the world. In 2014, representing 140 venture capital funds, more than 750 investors participated at the event.[4]

The university leadership has also been proactive in its support for the ecosystem. As well as top-down initiatives such as provision of courses and premises, they have "support[ed] but not direct[ed]" the student-led entrepreneurial movement, for example by providing public endorsement and financial help (Graham, 2014). Of note are the Aalto Center for Entrepreneurship, Aalto Start-up Center, Aalto Ventures Program, Aalto Design Factory and Open Innovation House.

Aalto Center for Entrepreneurship
The Aalto Center for Entrepreneurship (ACE) was established in 2010 on the Otaniemi campus to support the transfer and commercialization of research originating in Aalto University, through the establishment of new ventures or through industry-based licensing. ACE offers innovation evaluation, selection, commercialization and startup creation services to the whole Aalto community of researchers, staff and students, and also manages the university's intellectual property rights. In 2013, ACE processed 150 invention disclosures, 53 patent applications, and created six new companies that received more than €4 million in outside funding.[5]

Aalto Start-Up Center
Founded in 1997, the Aalto Start-Up Center is a business accelerator that operates from within Aalto University's School of Business, based in a technology park to the south of Helsinki. The Aalto Start-Up Center provides know-how in the areas of business, engineering and design through the provision of high-quality entrepreneurial training, business advisory services, a broad network of experts and office facilities. As well as supporting Rovio (the famous developer of Angry Birds), over the years the Aalto Start-Up Center has assisted in the creation of more than 2,000 new jobs in Finland.[6]

Aalto Ventures Program
The Aalto Ventures Program was established in 2012 to offer courses to Aalto undergraduate and postgraduate students to develop skills, tools and global networks that students will need to create new businesses.[7] It was developed as part of a three-year Aalto University partnership with the Stanford Technology Ventures Program.

Aalto Design Factory
The Aalto Design Factory (ADF) was established in 2008, and was modeled on the d.school at Stanford University. Bringing together the disciplines of engineering, design and business, ADF facilities include a 3,000 square meter working environment for creative work, knowledge sharing, and free interaction between Aalto students, researchers and faculty. ADF offers space reservation, machine-shop, electro-shop, and equipment loan services to assist prototyping for projects and startups. ADF also offers a number of hands-on entrepreneurship courses offered to undergraduate and postgraduate students in engineering and technology disciplines.

Open Innovation House
Open Innovation House was established within the university campus in early 2013 and is a venue for open innovation and collaboration. It hosts research centers working primarily in the information and communication technology (ICT) sector, such as the Nokia Research Centre, as well as the European ICT Labs initiative which provides space for new startup enterprises.

3.4.2 Windows Phone Ecosystem

Microsoft Corporation (commonly known as Microsoft) is the world's largest software maker by revenue,[8] and is one of the world's most valuable companies.[9] Headquartered in Redmond, Washington in the USA, it was founded by Bill Gates and Paul Allen in 1975. Microsoft dominated the personal computer operating system market with MS-DOS in the mid 1980s, followed by Microsoft Windows in the 1990s and which continues to dominate desktop operating systems today. Since the 1990s, it has increasingly diversified away from the operating system market. Today, Microsoft develops, manufactures, licenses, supports and sells computer software, consumer electronics and personal computers and services. Its best known software products are the Microsoft Windows operating systems, the Microsoft Office suite and the Internet Explorer web browser. It also has some hardware products such as the Xbox game consoles and the Microsoft Surface tablet lineup.

Windows Phone development began in 2008, when Microsoft reorganized the Windows Mobile group. Initially intended to be released in 2009, Windows Phone 7 was announced at the Mobile World Congress in Spain in February 2010 and released publicly in the USA in November in the same year. In 2011, Microsoft released Windows Phone 7.5, which added much functionality, and a minor update was released in 2012, which lowered the hardware requirements to run Windows Phone. By the beginning of 2011 there were 1.6 million devices running Microsoft OS (approximately 1.6 percent market share), while by mid 2012, Windows Phone market share had dropped to 1.3 percent in Q2 2012.[10]

In February 2011, at a press event in London, Microsoft Chief Executive Officer (CEO) Steve Ballmer and Nokia CEO Stephen Elop announced a partnership between their companies in which Windows Phone would become the primary smartphone operating system for Nokia, replacing Symbian. As part of this partnership, there was to be integration of Microsoft services with Nokia's services, as well as royalties, marketing and ad revenue sharing. The first Nokia Lumia Windows Phones, the Lumia 800 and Lumia 710, were announced in October 2011 at Nokia World 2011. At this time HTC made most of Windows Phone's sales, however due to the popularity of the Lumia phones, Nokia overtook Samsung in February 2012 and HTC a month later, to reach a 50 percent share of sales by the middle of 2012.[11]

In October 2012, Microsoft released Windows Phone 8, a new generation of the operating system, replacing its previous Windows CE-based architecture with one based on the Windows NT kernel, with many components shared with Windows 8, allowing applications to be ported between the two platforms. However, it was not possible to upgrade Windows Phone 7 devices to Windows Phone 8 due to hardware limitations. This meant that in 2013 Windows Phone 7.8 was released to include some of the features from Windows Phone 8. With the release of Lumia devices running Windows Phone 8, Nokia reached 78 percent of Windows Phone's installed base in February 2013.

Windows Phone 8 was released with much fanfare, and extensive consumer marketing activity followed on a global basis. After the release of Windows Phone 8, Gartner, a large technology analyst company, reported that Windows Phone's market share had increased to 3 percent by the end of 2012, a 124 percent increase over the same time period in 2011.[12] At the beginning of 2013 Windows Phone shipments surpassed BlackBerry shipment volume for the first time. By mid-2013, the Windows Phone held a worldwide market share of 3.6 percent, up 123 percent from the same period in 2012 and outpacing Android's rate of growth. This accounted for 10.2 percent of all smartphone sales in Europe and 4.8 percent of all sales in the USA.[13]

Alongside the consumer-focused marketing, Microsoft offered a number of services to support developers for the Windows Phone ecosystem. Microsoft had a general offering for developers, known as MSDN (Microsoft Developers Network). This service was specifically responsible for managing the firm's relationship with developers and testers, such as hardware developers interested in the operating system (OS), and software developers developing on the various OS platforms or using the API and/ or scripting languages of Microsoft's applications. Relationships with developers were maintained through web sites, newsletters, developer conferences, trade media, blogs and DVDs. Within the MSDN, from 2012 Microsoft offered support through their Windows Phone Dev Center, which provided extensive documentation, downloads and sample apps.[14] Integrated into the Windows Phone Dev Center was an online community which enabled developers to connect with Microsoft technology experts and other Windows app developers to share code samples, resources, helpful tips and answers to difficult questions. To speed up app submission, the Windows Phone Dev Center removed 3rd party app submission processes restriction some countries had, enabling developers from 180 countries to directly submit their apps into the ecosystem. In doing so, the Windows Phone Dev Center sped up the submission process, simplified the submission requirement, provided daily updating statistics, linked payments to bank accounts, and provided a managed, unlocked devices service. To access the service developers needed to pay an annual subscription, have an MSDN subscription, or through use of a promotional coupon.

Microsoft also attempted to encourage developers to create apps for the Windows Phone ecosystem, as it was well aware it needed to develop the ecosystem. In particular, it aimed to "aggressively pursue 100,000-plus apps over the first three months" and put "millions of dollars against that effort and working with publishers to get their apps live as soon as possible".[15] As well as extensive marketing within the technology press and through the MSDN blogs and Windows Phone Dev Center, it also offered bounties of $100, with developers allowed to submit up to 20 applications for a total of $2,000 in rewards.[16]

Despite this extensive support and outreach, one of the main criticisms of Windows Phone was the lack of applications when compared to iOS and Android, which not only had far more applications available, but also had more of the "must have" apps than Microsoft. This was not helped by the fact that due to the delay in the initial release, Windows Phone 7 was not compatible with earlier Windows Mobile applications, reducing the number of apps in its initial ecosystem. However, Microsoft's developer initiative programs and marketing gained attention from application developers, although some reports have indicated that developers may be less interested in developing for Windows Phone because of lower ad revenue when compared to competing platforms.[17] As of Q3 2013, an average of 21 percent of mobile developers used the Windows Phone platform, with another 35 percent stating they were interested in adopting it.[18]

Despite these apparent shortcomings, commentators were not yet writing off the potential for the Windows Phone ecosystem. At the time, Blackberry was falling further and further behind, and the relationship with Nokia was viewed as a major asset to the continued growth of the ecosystem.[19] The number of apps within the ecosystem continued to grow, with more than 145,000 available in May 2013, prompting some to forecast success for Microsoft if the Windows Phone ecosystem was able to grow.[20]

3.5   THE APPCAMPUS INITIATIVE

It was in this context that AppCampus was launched in May 2012, funded by €9 million each from Microsoft and Nokia, and managed by Aalto University in Finland, who covered operating costs of €1 million per year. AppCampus was a three-year project aiming to further leverage and enhance the entrepreneurial ecosystem around Aalto by offering grants and training to attract software application developers to the Windows Phone innovation ecosystem through a seed accelerator. In exchange for the funding and accelerator services provided, developers agreed to an exclusivity agreement requiring that the application not be released on competing smartphone platforms for a period of time after its launch for the Windows Phone platform. The available grants ranged in size from €20,000 to €70,000, and submissions went through a stringent selection process with an emphasis on application novelty and quality.

Accelerators are a type of incubator, which first became widespread in the 1980s, primarily as office space providers, housing multiple companies under the same roof. Throughout the 1990s incubators began to provide in-house business support services geared towards accelerating new firms' learning process, while throughout the 2000s they provided networking opportunities for more technology-focused startups (Bruneel et al., 2012). In general, incubators have focused on regional economic development, university technology commercialization, basic research, and the selection and support of high-potential ventures (Barbero et al., 2014).

Accelerators are a more recent phenomenon within entrepreneurial ecosystems, combining both incubation and funding aspects into a single entity.

Accelerators aim to fast-track successful venture creation by providing specific incubation services during an intensive program of limited duration (Cohen & Hochberg, 2014; Miller & Bound, 2011). The most well-known, and first, accelerator is Y-Combinator, which was established in 2005 in Cambridge, Massachusetts. By early 2015 there were more than 232 accelerators worldwide supporting more than 7,446 ventures.[21] Accelerators vary dramatically in their approaches. A "matchmaker" accelerator is typically set up by corporates, with the primary objective to match lead customers with promising startups, while an "investor-lead" accelerator receives funding from business angels, venture capital funds and corporate venture funds, with the aim of identifying promising investment opportunities (Clarysse et al., 2015). An "ecosystem accelerator" has government agencies as the main stakeholders with the explicit aim of stimulating startup technology in a region or within a specific technological domain. For instance, the Paris-based accelerator Le Camping is a non-profit organization backed by private and public partners that supports startups in the center of Paris. In contrast, Bethnal Green Ventures, based in London and funded by government agencies, helps startups developing products and services specifically for the social good. However, it is run more as a for-profit organization, taking an equity share in the startups it supports.

AppCampus was closest in nature to an ecosystem accelerator, but due to its dual role in both the Aalto entrepreneurial ecosystem and the Windows Phone ecosystem, it had some unique characteristics. These unique characteristics are a function of its ecosystem-linking role.

3.5.1   Strategic Focus

AppCampus, similar to most accelerators established by universities in entrepreneurial ecosystems, had a clear focus concerning the industry, sector and geography it targeted. The primary strategic focus was to identify, fund, develop and launch innovative startups that mobilize the Windows Phone innovation ecosystem. This link to a for-profit entity made it unique, as generally the focus of accelerators is on specific industries or sectors, rather than a particular innovation ecosystem or organization. The benefits to the local entrepreneurial ecosystem were seen to be a consequence of the success of the main focus – by supporting entrepreneurs using the operating system of Microsoft, and the handsets of Nokia, the Aalto entrepreneurial ecosystem would also benefit. This meant that AppCampus also had an explicit global remit, targeting would-be entrepreneurs around the world and enticing them to connect with the Aalto entrepreneurial ecosystem. To achieve this, AppCampus needed a distinct image, clearly differentiating itself from Microsoft and Nokia:

> We started to work on our image and tried to be young and fresh . . . And that was just to make sure that we don't prevent teams from applying, because they think we smell too much [like] corporate. That's always the antithesis of the entrepreneur because with corporate, [you get] slow, long cycles and big decision chains . . . We wanted to totally avoid that in terms of image. (Interview with Paolo Borella)

Securing support from Aalto was initially not straightforward, as there were serious concerns about whether having an organization under the university umbrella managing a significant amount of money from Microsoft and Nokia would mean a loss of independence for the university.

> It took about a year to figure out, really, how to make it so everybody could view this as a win-win . . . I've really had good access to [Microsoft and Nokia] and was able to build this thing up to be solid enough before opening it up to everybody. (Interview with Will Cardwell)

However, these concerns were overcome by emphasizing the positive impact that the program could have on Aalto's entrepreneurial ecosystem and on the Finnish economy more generally, leading to Aalto agreeing to manage the program and to support it by covering operating costs and providing office space:

> Preserving independence and academic freedom were the key issues in the beginning, but we quickly were able to create a framework where it was clear that all professors, staff members and students still had the absolute freedom to choose platforms right for them. Once this problem was solved, we then spent a lot of time working on the financial model. It was not difficult to find money in the budget for this given the scale of impact we felt we could have in terms of turning novel ideas from our Aalto community into commercially viable apps. For example, there are already several cases of projects coming out of Aalto departments and student ideas being funded. And beyond this, a significant amount of the funding is going into ideas generated in other parts of the Finnish innovation community. It is also important to understand the context that Microsoft and Nokia were going to create this program with some university partner, somewhere around the world, so we thought it was important for us to compete hard to win the competition. (Interview with Will Cardwell)

To ensure that the strategic focus met the needs of Aalto, Nokia and Microsoft, a steering board consisting of four AppCampus staff, two staff from each business partner, and an independent member, and a member of Aalto University staff met on a monthly basis to evaluate the initiative's performance to date and to discuss whether any changes were required.

3.5.2 Funding Structure

Most accelerator programs receive the major part of their working capital from shareholders, such as investors, corporates and public authorities, and an ecosystem accelerator is no different. For AppCampus, Microsoft and Nokia each provided €9 million as the main funding source. However, AppCampus also drew on the considerable non-financial resources held by these corporations, including the provision of access to relevant technological, marketing and merchandising expertise of Microsoft and Nokia for promising members of the AppCampus portfolio. In our interviews, developer teams participating in AppCampus consistently stated that this preferential access to the resources of the innovation ecosystem leaders was more valuable to them than the funding and other aspects of the program.

Alongside the payment of operational costs, Aalto University shrewdly invested in its local entrepreneurial ecosystem by providing services in kind that were of great value to the accelerator's success. AppCampus was based in the Otaniemi region, in the center of the entrepreneurial ecosystem. Its offices were large enough to provide shared working facilities for the AppCampus staff and all developer teams, with a number of different kinds of working and meeting rooms, as well as shared social spaces, and a small lecture theatre that was often used for the lectures and coaching sessions. This experience was embedded in the entrepreneurial ecosystem with all day-to-day operations carried out by AppCampus staff, who were employed by Aalto University. AppCampus also leveraged the connections that its employees had within the Aalto entrepreneurial ecosystem by convincing coaches from Startup Sauna and other initiatives to offer their services in training camps held for AppCampus developers, and by arranging for developers to meet with other members of the entrepreneurial ecosystem and participate at events such as SLUSH. Taken together, these led to a deepening of the entrepreneurial ecosystem by both the expansion of facilities on offer, and increased exposure and experience of local organizations and individuals to entrepreneurs from different entrepreneurial ecosystems.

3.5.3 Program Package

In common with more traditional accelerators, the ecosystem accelerator has investment, education and mentoring services which assist the accelerator's participants (Clarysse et al., 2015; Isabelle, 2013). However, again, particular aspects of these are unique, a product of AppCampus' ecosystem-linking role.

The *investment* service was focused on providing participants with seed investment to build and launch their offering within the innovation ecosystem. For traditional accelerators, investment generally consists of a small amount of funding in exchange for equity, averaging $22,000, with a range from $0 to $150,000 and an equity stake of typically 5–7 percent (Fehder & Hochberg, 2014). In the case of AppCampus, the primary goal was to launch as many quality startups as possible so as to "let a thousand flowers bloom". As such, the investment amount did not need to be substantial. Uniquely, it did not need to cover the full startup cost of the targeted entrepreneurs like other accelerators attempt to do, but function only to influence the cost-benefit balance of the entrepreneur in favor of the innovation ecosystem. Furthermore, the small grant amounts, ranging from €20,000 to €70,000, helped AppCampus to focus on targeting entrepreneurs in regions that were historically not targeted by ecosystem accelerators:

> While the grants we are giving may be relatively small to a developer in Silicon Valley, even a €20,000 grant can be very significant to a developer from, say, Russia, Romania, or Poland, covering salary equivalent of over 1 man-year. And these are proving to be among the strongest regions both in terms of deal flow and performance once in the program. (Interview with Will Cardwell)

In contrast to a traditional accelerator, the basic level of investment provided was "free money", that is, not dependent on an equity stake or revenue-sharing agreement. Instead, the investment was made contingent on exclusivity to the ecosystem for a particular period of time. In the case of AppCampus, this was originally set to six months exclusivity; however, after observing the speed at which mobile apps were being developed, within 12 months of launching this was reduced to three months exclusivity. This "free money" and short period of exclusivity makes participation in both ecosystems very appealing for would-be entrepreneurs, and also has the benefit that new ecosystem participants remain independent but simultaneously commit to participate in both ecosystems.

The *education* service was focused on the construction of the app offering for the innovation ecosystem and was accompanied by intensive training around such topics as branding, product management and marketing, similar to the types of education provided by traditional accelerators. Developing the local entrepreneurial ecosystem, training services were provided either by online courses or onsite through intensive courses for high-performing participants. The residential training camps of two to four weeks in length leveraged and developed the existing resources in the entrepreneurial ecosystem: The content of the training camp grew out of the experiences of several members of AppCampus staff in Startup Sauna and was delivered by different coaches, who were largely drawn from the social networks of the Aalto entrepreneurial ecosystem. An important, and unique, aspect of the training course was that it consisted of an intensive program of both technical and non-technical training on topics covering all aspects of application development as well as broader entrepreneurial skills:

> [Our program is] pretty much the same as everyone else's accelerator, [but] we've got a bit less on . . . actually, we have nothing on the company forming and the legals and the financials and that type of stuff, which a regular accelerator would cover, because these guys have to have a company [to join] . . . So that's something we don't do. But what we've added instead is the design component and the technical training . . . So that's the difference: the design, the technical training taking up a big chunk; the rest of it, same as every other accelerator out there. (Interview with Mike Bradshaw)

Similar to traditional accelerators, the AppCademy events included both demo and investor days. For those teams lucky to be in Helsinki at the time of the SLUSH conference, they were automatically entered into the "pitching" competition, with some teams performing exceptionally well.

> I think one of the teams, or two . . . no, two of the teams actually got into the Slush 20, which is like, that's really [good] . . . because they're up against like . . . these are growth entrepreneurs, and two app developers got into the Top 20, which is pretty good going. (Interview with Mike Bradshaw)

Similar to traditional accelerators, the *mentoring* service was typically provided by experienced entrepreneurs specially selected for the role. However, instead of allocating a specific mentor to a specific team based on the relevance of their expertise, all teams present at the AppCademy events had time with most mentors. This was due to the fact that all teams were working with the same platform with the goal of launching within the same ecosystem, and as such had similar mentoring requirements. For instance, some mentors specifically focused on the benefits of the Windows Phone technology.

> I make sure that everyone . . . understands all of the key benefits of the Windows Phone platform. Also, I make sure that our message to developers is clear for them, because developers have a different kind of mind-set than others. They see developer tools, communities and stuff like that as more important than the amount of customers. So I'm fine-tuning our message for them. (Interview with Teemu Tapanila)

In the case of AppCampus, while most of these entrepreneurs came from the Aalto entrepreneurial ecosystem, some members of Microsoft and Nokia's innovation ecosystems also provided mentoring on specific topics relating to how developers could best operate in and receive support from these ecosystems. Mentoring services include the introduction of participating teams to external venture capitalists to enable them to gain additional funding as required. However, emphasizing AppCampus' ecosystem-linking role, there was a subtle shift in emphasis, with the focus shifting from simply securing the next investment to securing longer term commercial success.

The *merchandising* service was focused on building momentum for the participants through "go-to-market" support. This includes distribution, localization, promotion, improvement and ecosystem optimization support before, during and after product launch. This service was truly unique due to AppCampus' ecosystem-linking role, which was only possible given the close relationship with the Windows Phone ecosystem. This support was offered to all teams, with additional support offered to those teams that showed promise:

> [We offer support to] basically all developers who have published a title from AppCampus. Of course there are variations that some teams have got more support and some teams less, but it's based on their success. So if there's a good trend in downloads, star ratings are okay, and so on, there's more reason to give a promotion. (Interview with Timo Mustanen)

The merchandising support leveraged the distribution channels of both Nokia and Microsoft to help deliver results, and developers had opportunities to meet with key people within the Microsoft and Nokia organizations through whom preferential access to these channels could be secured. Additional support was also available through other merchandising partners in particular markets. This was tailored to the individual needs of each startup:

> So, we want to make developers successful, so it could be promotion cooperation, that they promote our title. It could be that they [a merchandising partner] have their own programs for the developers. So maybe one of our developers can join that. So it's case by case ... So there's no, "it's like this", or "it's only this", but we go through the cases case by case and try to understand what they want to have and what is the best for the developer. (Interview with Timo Mustanen)

3.5.4   Selection Process

Accelerators make use of a rigorous, multistage selection process, and typically focus on teams rather than a specific entrepreneur (Miller & Bound, 2011). Ecosystem accelerators select ventures that are in a very early stage of their life cycle. AppCampus was no different here, not only explicitly selecting ideas that had not been developed within other ecosystems to date, but also insisting that the team be set up as a limited company before joining the program. This process, called "screening" for AppCampus, not only checked the composition and legal status of the team, but, aligned with the ecosystem-linking role, also ensured that the business idea aligned with the goals of the ecosystem mobilization effort, either by flatly refusing applications that did not align or by giving teams a second opportunity through specific guidance.

However, in contrast to traditional accelerators which only operate a selection process in order to gain access to the program, an ecosystem accelerator has a secondary selection mechanism which continues throughout the life of each team within the accelerator. In particular, once a team has passed the screening stage, they are then passed to "quality control" which ensures that their ecosystem solution leverages the best features and functions that the ecosystem has to offer, as well as assuring a certain level of quality and usability. Demonstrating the link between the entrepreneurial ecosystem and innovation ecosystem, AppCampus not only focused on quality apps, but also on developing the startup personnel as well:

> We want to get more of these new applications out, but we want to create new Windows Mobile developers as well, who, in the future, are able to contribute and create quality Windows Phone applications themselves without going through our processes. (Interview with Tiina Muttilainen)

In the case of AppCampus, quality control consisted of both design review and beta release milestones, and failure to meet these would mean ejection from the accelerator and non-transfer of the grant funding.

In order to ensure compliance with the quality control process, the investment was staggered depending on successful launch of the product into the ecosystem. For instance, once a team's app design was accepted, they would be transferred 30 percent of their investment amount. However, it was only once the team had completed all of the quality control stages, released an approved beta version of the application, and had been signed off by the steering board that the second tranche of investment was released. This process resulted in quality apps:

> Basically one of the coolest things is that after you have done applications with AppCampus, you know the quality. I mean, you are very good at quality at that point, and you normally don't reach that level of quality if you are an independent developer because you don't need to. (Interview with Teemu Tapanila)

3.5.5   Alumni Relations

Accelerators put a lot of emphasis on keeping close and active relations with the teams that graduate from the program, and this was also true of AppCampus. Alumni events were regular, and an active Facebook group keeps alumni teams in active contact. Although the alumni network was growing, the relationship between the innovation ecosystem and entrepreneurial ecosystem was proving problematic due to the global dispersion of the startups:

> The Alumni [network] has been growing, so we have almost 400 participants in the Facebook group, for instance . . . And I think in one sense it's successful in what it's been doing. On the other side, I kind of go almost frustrated that I see it could be much more that they can do, but it's for one reason or the other, we haven't cracked the perfect way to do it. Actually last night we . . . were talking about the network that they [another accelerator] have with the investors and among the CEOs invested in sharing or helping each other; asking for help. That I see only partly happening here with a much broader network. (Interview with Paolo Borella)

3.6   THE APPCAMPUS EFFECT

During its first year of operation, the number of staff employed by Aalto University working on the AppCampus initiative grew to 12 people. The first apps funded by the program were released to the public via the Windows Phone marketplace at the end of December 2012, with 15 available within the ecosystem by the start of June 2013, a year after their launch. AppCampus' first year of operation also saw three AppCademy training camps during which up to 20 developer teams with accepted app submissions came to Finland for a month of intensive coaching on all aspects of Windows Phone application development, as well as on more general business and entrepreneurial skills, such as pitching to investors and marketing.

3.6.1   Windows Phone Ecosystem

In its first year of operation, AppCampus received over 2,600 application submissions, 166 of which were approved for funding. At the time of its closure, over 4,298 submissions had been received from over 100 countries, with approximately €10 million invested in over 390 entrepreneurial teams. The apps produced by AppCampus teams were of significantly higher quality than the market average within the Windows Phone ecosystem, with seven times more downloads, two times higher revenue and higher user ratings.

Interviews with developer teams suggest that a significant proportion of them would not have created applications for Windows Phone without the funding and support provided by AppCampus. One reason given for this is the distrust that some developers had for Microsoft and/or Nokia, suggesting the creation of an identity for AppCampus that was distinct from its corporate sponsors was an important reason for its success in drawing such reluctant participants into Microsoft's innovation ecosystem. Reflecting on the effects of AppCampus on the Windows Phone ecosystem, a number of AppCampus employees also saw this change of developer perceptions as one of their main achievements.

3.6.2 Aalto Entrepreneurial Ecosystem

For Aalto University, AppCampus was seen as an opportunity to have a significant social impact. For instance, although AppCampus accepted teams from over 50 countries around the world, 19 percent were from its home country of Finland. It is estimated that the success of these startups in the Finnish economy created hundreds of jobs.

AppCampus also facilitated the creation of new businesses and new employment in the local area, and further developed the Aalto entrepreneurial ecosystem reputation for mentoring and acceleration of new businesses:

> So, we want to create new businesses, new companies, employing people around Aalto. So, it was a good sort of string to pull, that, okay, with AppCampus, we attract a lot of attention here. We actually have €18 million to hand out as grants, as long as the developers and companies in this area just activate themselves, and then apply. And, well, that's what has happened now. So, initially, it was, like, one third of the applications came from Finland. Now it's been going down a little bit, because the other countries are picking up . . . And, well, I think we've now made close to 100 grant decisions, totalling, I think, €2.5 million. So that's a good amount of money that has already been sunk into this ecosystem here. And so, this was the kind of a story I was telling, that, well, we will be seeing more and more, like, good-quality companies coming here, working with us, making the connection to the university on different levels, and then also, of course, not all are here or stay here. They may go somewhere else. But still, it does create the critical mass for the area, that we can really make some things happen here. And that's been, like, the theme all the time here. Like, with Start-up Sauna and Aalto Ventures Programme, and the spinoffs we create. It's really all about being sexy enough as an area so that you get the money coming here. You get the developers coming here, the entrepreneurs, coaches, all that. And we are still not there, but we are making good progress. (Interview with Tapio Siik)

> So all of this, all the things we're doing around the mentoring and acceleration, I think, we may develop a core competence about that over time, in the screening,

in kind of creative use of space. I think there are a lot of positives about it. (Interview with Will Cardwell)

A further success was the amount of money invested by the fund into the Finnish economy:

> Our message for Aalto is that we are putting a lot of this money back into our local ecosystem . . . The average grant is around €26,000 or €27,000, so if you make that estimation €30,000, we've put about €750,000 into our local ecosystem in less than a year. So that's a very positive message for us, for the Finnish community. (Interview with Will Cardwell)

AppCampus has also been successful in raising the university's profile, with the investment from Microsoft and Nokia acting as a signal of the quality of the business environment around the university and in Finland in general. This increase in the value of the university's brand may have already begun to play a role in the decisions of large ICT corporations regarding where to locate their research and development centers:

> I believe AppCampus was a significant driver in being able to show global giants, like Huawei for instance, the commitment that large companies are making to the developer eco-systems we are building around Aalto and in Finland overall. We are also seeing growing commitment from companies like Intel, Electronic Arts, and there are strong rumors of more major ICT firms opening R&D centers soon. While Nokia's commitment has always been clear, bringing in Microsoft at this level was really a major credibility signal. (Interview with Will Cardwell)

The collaboration's success to date has also proved useful for Aalto in the university's efforts to build partnerships with other universities, as in many cases it provides concrete examples of existing investment from Aalto into a developer team coming out of the target university:

> [AppCampus] is a great calling card going into the US, but also to Russia and the UK, and there are other places that we say, hey, this is effectively foreign direct investment into the markets . . . My role is partnerships with Aalto, so if I go to a Spanish university or Singaporean university I could say, hey, we've already invested €60,000 into your teams from your universities, it's a great bargaining chip to start a conversation with. I would say that is emerging, to me, as one of the critical assets for Aalto. I was just at a university that we really want to partner with a few weeks ago, and AppCampus was, you know, really strong . . . They got really excited about that immediately and in particular when I told that we'd already done one grant to their teams. And that helps us and they were then eager to talk about, you know, joint degree programmes and collaborative research and stuff like that. So I think it's good. I think the value-add to Aalto is through that channel and through this kind of local ecosystem development. (Interview with Will Cardwell)

Despite these positive contributions to the development of the Aalto entrepreneurial ecosystem, after completion of AppCampus' three-year term it seemed unlikely that Aalto would again participate in a similar program in the near future due to financial constraints imposed on the university as a result of Finland's poor economic performance post-2012.

3.7   DISCUSSION AND CONCLUSION

In this chapter we have investigated an accelerator that was designed to link the entrepreneurial ecosystem of Aalto University with the innovation ecosystem of Windows Phone. We first briefly reviewed the characteristics of both innovation and entrepreneurial ecosystems, followed by an analysis of both the Windows Phone ecosystem and the Aalto entrepreneurial ecosystem at the time of the launch of AppCampus. We then detailed the AppCampus initiative itself, explaining each of its components and how they linked both innovation and entrepreneurial ecosystems. We then discussed the range of positive outcomes that AppCampus had on both the Aalto entrepreneurial ecosystem and the Windows Phone innovation ecosystem. Taken together, the AppCampus experience holds some lessons for both entrepreneurial and innovation ecosystem leaders.

3.7.1   Lessons for Entrepreneurial Ecosystem Leaders

The case of AppCampus provides some interesting insights that leaders of entrepreneurial ecosystems can use to accelerate the development of their ecosystems. An ecosystem-spanning organization such as AppCampus that can draw on the resources of multiple entrepreneurial and innovation ecosystems can be effective not only in achieving its direct goals, but can also serve to create new connections between the ecosystems that it spans, thus strengthening them. Furthermore, such an organization can serve to legitimize the entrepreneurial ecosystem in which it is located, making it a more attractive partner for leaders of other innovation ecosystems in their acceleration efforts.

For Aalto University, having a university fund supporting nascent entrepreneurs producing such applications was a major boost to their image and standing in the list of universities having a strong impact on innovation and entrepreneurship. In addition to contributing to Aalto's social mission, AppCampus helped to establish the reputation of Aalto's entrepreneurial ecosystem as one of the most dynamic in the world, leading to numerous collaborations with other universities and major businesses being agreed over the duration of the program.

3.7.2   Lessons for Innovation Ecosystem Leaders

The case of AppCampus also holds lessons for leaders of innovation eco-systems. An ecosystem-spanning organization of this kind can supplement the resources of the innovation ecosystem leader with those embedded in the partnering entrepreneurial ecosystem, which may be particularly valuable for ecosystem leaders that are large, established organizations that lack a well-established entrepreneurial culture. For this to be the case, it is important for the ecosystem-spanning organization to be provided with the freedom to make its own operational decisions in pursuit of the goals agreed upon by its sponsor organizations. Furthermore, if the ecosystem-spanning organization is to some extent independent from its sponsoring organiza-tions, it may be able to develop its own identity which may be more positively perceived by those who the innovation ecosystem leader wants to persuade to join their ecosystem than the sponsoring organizations' own identities.

An important aspect underlying the success of AppCampus was its ability to operate largely as an entrepreneurial venture despite being a fund within Aalto University. In practice, this meant that the AppCampus team had a lot of room to make operational decisions without having to have steering board approval beforehand. It also meant that AppCampus could hire new staff members more easily than other parts of the university, allowing them to quickly put together a high-quality team by drawing on the social networks of the initial team members.

By funding an independent accelerator with its own separate identity embedded in the Aalto entrepreneurial ecosystem, Microsoft and Nokia were able to attract developers to their innovation ecosystems who otherwise would have been reluctant to participate due to their negative perceptions of these companies. Being part of the Aalto entrepreneurial ecosystem allowed AppCampus to draw on the ecosystem's considerable resources in working to achieve the goals of its funding organizations.

With all these positives, however, and while AppCampus managed to generate non-trivial momentum within the Windows Mobile ecosystem, this momentum has not been sufficient to significantly lift the Windows Mobile ecosystem in competition against the more established Android and iPhone ecosystems. This testifies to the significant lock-in advantages early ecosystem leaders can generate through user lock-in and self-reinforcing externalities that sustain the ecosystem. Thus, while AppCampus has been successful in lifting an important number of new entrepreneurial ventures into a growth trajectory, it also illustrates the importance of establishing early leadership in ecosystem competition. By the time Nokia realized the poor outlook of the Symbian system, the opportunity window was largely closed.

Even if the AppCampus initiative did not succeed in its ecosystem-strategic mission, it nevertheless illustrates how a platform-centric innovation ecosystem can feed a regionally concentrated entrepreneurial ecosystem and how the entrepreneurial ecosystem can generate important benefits for the platform-centric innovation ecosystem, which is not geographically constrained by necessity. We hope our exploration has provided ideas and insight for ecosystem practitioners and researchers alike.

NOTES

*   Corresponding author.
1. Wikipedia, https://en.wikipedia.org/wiki/Finland, accessed 23 April 2015.
2. AaltoES, http://www.aaltoes.com, accessed 20 April 2015.
3. Startup Sauna Foundation, http://www.startupsuana.com, accessed 20 April 2015.
4. SLUSH, http://www.slush.fi, accessed 23 April 2015.
5. Aalto Center for Entrepreneurship, ace.aalto.fi, accessed 20 April 2015.
6. Start-Up Center, http://www.start-upcenter.fi, accessed 23 April 2015.
7. Aalto Ventures Program, avp.aalto.fi, accessed 20 April 2015.
8. Softwaretop100, http://www.softwaretop100.org, accessed 29 June 2015.
9. YCharts, ycharts.com/companies/MSFT, accessed 29 June 2015.
10. Gartner, http://www.gartner.com/newsroom/id/1689814, accessed 29 June 2015.
11. AdDuplex, blog.adduplex.com/2013/02/windows-phone-device-stats-for-february, accessed 20 June 2015.
12. Gartner, http://www.gartner.com/newsroom/id/2335616, accessed 21 June 2015.
13. Kantar, uk.kantar.com/tech/mobile/300913-smartphone-sales-data-great-britain-and-europe, accessed 29 June 2015.
14. Windows, social.technet.microsoft.com/wiki/contents/articles/13457.windows-phone-dev-center.aspx, accessed 30 June 2015.
15. PCWorld, http://www.pcworld.com/article/2011452/microsoft-exec-windows-store-to-stock-100-000-apps-in-three-months.html, accessed 30 June 2015.
16. ArsTechnica, arstechnica.com/gadgets/2013/03/microsofts-100-per-app-bounty-is-too-much-and-not-enough, accessed 30 June 2015.
17. BGR, bgr.com/2014/01/22/microsoft-windows-phone-ad-revenue/, accessed 14 June 2015.
18. Developer Economics, http://www.developereconomics.com/reports/developer-economics-2013-q3/, accessed 24 May 2015.
19. Neowin, http://www.neowin.net/news/windows-phone-now-the-third-place-smartphone-ecosystem-as-blackberry-sinks-further, accessed 29 June 2015.
20. ZDNet, http://www.zdnet.com/article/windows-phone-hits-145000-apps-all-eyes-on-the-ecosystem, accessed 13 May 2015.
21. Seed-DB, http://www.seed-db.com, accessed 1 April 2015.

REFERENCES

Acs, Z.J., Autio, E., and Szerb, L. (2014). National systems of entrepreneurship: measurement issues and policy implications. *Research Policy*, **43**(1), 476–94.
Adner, R. (2012). *The Wide Lens: A New Strategy for Innovation*. New York: Portfolio Penguin.

Adner, R. and Kapoor, R. (2010). Value creation in innovation ecosystems: how the structure of technological interdependence affects firm performance in new technology generations. *Strategic Management Journal*, **31**(3), 306–33.

Autio, E. and Thomas, L.D.W. (2014). Innovation ecosystems: implications for innovation management. In M. Dodgson, D.M. Gann, and N. Phillips (eds), *Oxford Handbook of Innovation Management*, pp. 204–28. Oxford: Oxford University Press.

Autio, E., Nambisan, S., Thomas, L., and Wright, M. (2018). Digital affordances, spatial affordances, and the genesis of entrepreneurial ecosystems. *Strategic Entrepreneurship Journal*, **12**(1), 72–95.

Autio, E., Kenney, M., Mustar, P., Siegel, D., and Wright, M. (2014). Entrepreneurial innovation: the importance of context. *Research Policy*, **43**(7), 1097–108.

Barbero, J.L., Casillas, J.C., Wright, M., and Garcia, A.R. (2014). Do different types of incubators produce different types of innovations? *Journal of Technology Transfer*, **39**(2), 151–68.

Bruneel, J., Ratinho, T., Clarysse, B., and Groen, A. (2012). The evolution of business incubators: comparing demand and supply of business incubation services across different incubator generations. *Technovation*, **32**(2), 110–21.

Burt, R.S. (2004). Structural holes and good ideas. *American Journal of Sociology*, **110**(2), 349–99.

Ceccagnoli, M., Forman, C., Huang, P., and Wu, D.J. (2012). Co-creation of value in a platform ecosystem: the case of enterprise software. *MIS Quarterly*, **36**(1), 263–90.

Clarysse, B., Wright, M., Van Hove, J., and Pauwels, C. (2015). Understanding a new generation incubation model: the accelerator. Innovation and Entrepreneurship Department Working Paper. Imperial College Business School, London.

Cohen, S. and Hochberg, Y.V. (2014). Accelerating startups: the seed accelerator phenomenon. Available at: https://ssrn.com/abstract=2418000.

Cusumano, M.A. and Gawer, A. (2002). The elements of platform leadership. *MIT Sloan Management Review*, **43**(3), 51–8.

De Cock, R., Clarysse, B., and Andries, P. (2015). Getting the best of different worlds: multi-ecosystem leveraging. Innovation & Entrepreneurship Department Working Papers, Imperial College Business School.

Drexler, M., Eltogby, M., Foster, G., Shimizu, C., Ciesinsik, S., Davila, A., Hassan, S.Z., Jia, N., Lee, D., Plunkett, S., Pinelli, M., Cunningham, J., Hiscock-Croft, R., McLenithan, M., Rottenberg, L., and Morris, R. (2014). Entrepreneurial ecosystems around the globe and early-stage company growth dynamics. *Industry Agenda*. Geneva: World Economic Forum.

Eisenhardt, K.M. (1989). Building theories from case study research. *Academy of Management Review*, **14**(4), 532–50.

European Commission (2014). Innovation Union Scoreboard. Brussels: European Commission.

Fehder, D.C. and Hochberg, Y.V. (2014). Accelerators and the regional supply of venture capital investment. Available at: https://ssrn.com/abstract=2518668.

Foster, G., Shimizu, C., Ciesinsik, S., Davila, A., Hassan, S.Z., Jia, N., Plunkett, S., Pinelli, M., Cunningham, J., Hiscock-Croft, R., McLenithan, M., Rottenberg, L., Morris, R., and Lee, D. (2013). Entrepreneurial ecosystems around the world and company growth dynamics. *Industry Agenda*. Geneva: World Economic Forum.

Graham, R. (2014). Creating university-based entrepreneurial ecosystems. *MIT Skoltech Initiative*. Cambridge, MA: Massachusetts Institute of Technology.

Gulati, R., Puranam, P., and Tushman, M.L. (2012). Meta-organization design: rethinking design in interorganizational and community contexts. *Strategic Management Journal*, **33**(6), 571–86.

Hallen, B.L., Bingham, C.B., and Cohen, S. (2014). Do accelerators accelerate? A study of venture accelerators as a path to success. Paper presented at the Academy of Management Annual Conference, Philadelphia, PA.

Iansiti, M. and Levien, R. (2004). *The Keystone Advantage: What the New Dynamics of Business Ecosystems Mean for Strategy, Innovation, and Sustainability*. Cambridge, MA: Harvard Business School Press.

Isabelle, D.A. (2013). Key factors affecting a technology entrepreneur's choice of incubator or accelerator. *Technology Innovation Management Review*, **3**(2), 16–22.

Isenberg, D.J. (2010). How to start an entrepreneurial revolution. *Harvard Business Review*, **88**(6), 40–50.

Iyer, B., Lee, C.-H., and Venkatraman, N. (2006). Managing in a small world ecosystem: some lessons from the software sector. *California Management Review*, **48**(3), 28–47.

Jacobides, M.G., Knudsen, T., and Augier, M. (2006). Benefiting from innovation: value creation, value appropriation and the role of industry architectures. *Research Policy*, **35**(8), 1200–21.

Kapoor, R. and Furr, N.R. (2015). Complementarities and competition: unpacking the drivers of entrants' technology choices in the solar voltaic industry. *Strategic Management Journal*, **36**(3), 416–36.

Kapoor, R. and Lee, J.M. (2013). Coordinating and competing in ecosystems: how organizational forms shape new technology investments. *Strategic Management Journal*, **34**(3), 274–96.

Katz, M.L. and Shapiro, C. (1985). Network externalities, competition, and compatibility. *American Economic Review*, **75**(3), 424–40.

Katz, M.L. and Shapiro, C. (1986). Technology adoption in the presence of network externalities. *Journal of Political Economy*, **94**(4), 822–41.

Kenney, M. and Von Burg, U. (1999). Technology, entrepreneurship and path dependence: industrial clustering in Silicon Valley and Route 128. *Industrial & Corporate Change*, **8**(1), 67–103.

Kulchina, E. (2015). A path to value creation for foreign entrepreneurs. *Strategic Management Journal*, **37**(7), 1240–62.

Levie, J. (2014). The university is the classroom: teaching and learning technology commercialization at a technological university. *Journal of Technology Transfer*, **39**(5), 793–808.

Lusch, R.F. and Nambisan, S. (2015). Service innovation: a service-dominant logic perspective. *MIS Quarterly*, **39**(1), 155–75.

Miller, P. and Bound, K. (2011). *The Startup Factories: The Rise of Accelerator Programmes to Support New Technology Ventures*. London: NESTA.

Moore, J.F. (1993). Predators and prey: a new ecology of competition. *Harvard Business Review*, **71**(3), 75–86.

Nambisan, S. and Baron, R.A. (2013). Entrepreneurship in innovation ecosystems: entrepreneurs' self-regulatory processes and their implications for new venture success. *Entrepreneurship Theory and Practice*, **37**(5), 1071–97.

Nambisan, S. and Sawhney, M.S. (2011). Orchestration processes in network-cen tric innovation: evidence from the field. *Academy of Management Perspectives*, **25**(3), 40–57.

Napier, G., Rouvinen, P., Johansson, D., Finnbjornsson, T., Solberg, E., and

Pedersen, K. (2012). The Nordic Growth Entrepreneurship Review 2012, *Nordic Innovation*. Oslo: Nordic Innovation.

Pettigrew, A.M. (1990). Longitudinal field research on change: theory and practice. *Organization Science*, **1**(3), 267–92.

Pitelis, C. (2012). Clusters, entrepreneurial ecosystem co-creation, and appropriability: a conceptual framework. *Industrial & Corporate Change*, **21**(6), 1359–88.

Radojevich-Kelley, N. and Hoffman, D.L. (2012). Analysis of accelerator companies: an exploratory case study of their programs, processes and early results. *Small Business Institute Journal*, **8**(2), 54–70.

Schwab, K. (2014). *The Global Competitiveness Report 2014–2015*. Geneva: World Economic Forum.

Spigel, B. (2017). The relational organization of entrepreneurial ecosystems. *Entrepreneurship Theory and Practice*, **41**(1), 49–72.

Spilling, O.R. (1996). The entrepreneurial system: on entrepreneurship in the context of a mega-event. *Journal of Business Research*, **36**(1), 91–103.

Teece, D.J. (1986). Profiting from technological innovation: implications for integration, collaboration, licensing. *Research Policy*, **15**(6), 285–305.

Teece, D.J. (2007). Explicating dynamic capabilities: the nature and microfoundations of (sustainable) enterprise performance. *Strategic Management Journal*, **28**(13), 1319–50.

Van de Ven, A.H. (1993). The development of an infrastructure for entrepreneurship. *Journal of Business Venturing*, **8**(3), 211–30.

Wareham, J., Fox, P.B., and Cano Giner, J.L. (2014). Technology ecosystem governance. *Organization Science*, **25**(4), 1195–215.

Wessner, C.W. (2005). Entrepreneurship and the innovation ecosystem policy lessons from the United States. In D. Audretsch, H. Grimm, and C.W. Wessner (eds), *Local Heroes in the Global Village: Globalization and the New Entrepreneurship Policies*, pp. 67 –89. Boston, MA: Springer.

Williamson, O.E. (1975). *Markets and Hierarchies: Analysis and Antitrust Implications: A Study in the Economics of Internal Organization*. New York: Free Press.

Winston-Smith, S., Hannigan, T.J., and Gasiorowski, L.L. (2013). Accelerators and crowd-funding: complementarity, competition, or convergence in the earliest stages of financing new ventures. Available at: https://ssrn.com/abstract=2298875.

Yin, R.K. (1984). *Case Study Research: Design And Methods*. Beverley Hills, CA: Sage Publications.

Zahra, S.A. and Nambisan, S. (2011). Entrepreneurship in global innovation ecosystems. *AMS Review*, **1**(1), 4–17.

Zahra, S.A. and Nambisan, S. (2012). Entrepreneurship and strategic thinking in business ecosystems. *Business Horizons*, **55**(3), 219–29.

4. Antecedents of firm-level entrepreneurship: how organizational design coordinates and controls the firm's entrepreneurial ecosystem*

Nicolai J. Foss and Jacob Lyngsie

4.1 INTRODUCTION

Entrepreneurship research has long manifested an "individual-centric" tendency in which the entrepreneur's behavior is highlighted, while the contribution of complementary resources, such as members of what is effectively an entrepreneurial team, is suppressed (Foss and Lyngsie, 2014). Recent work on "entrepreneurial ecosystems" (e.g., Acs et al., 2014; Birch, 1987; Stam, 2015) does much to emphasize that entrepreneurial outcomes often result from the interplay of multiple entrepreneurial actors in a region and as influenced by prevailing institutions, policies and informal norms that define the "rules of the game" under which entrepreneurial actors interact.

In this chapter, we adopt a similar focus, but at a different level of analysis. However, by examining some of the causes of firm-level innovativeness our analysis may also be seen as constituting part of the microfoundations of the entrepreneurial ecosystem literature. Specifically, we argue that (entrepreneurial, innovative) firms manifest an internal division of entrepreneurial labor and that this division of labor is in need of coordination. This is where organizational design, the firm-specific rules of the game, is relevant.

Organizational design has received little attention in the emerging entrepreneurship literature. This is partly because of the dominant association of entrepreneurship with start-ups and entrepreneurial individuals rather than with established firms. Organizational design may seem to be of less consequence in a start-up than in established firms. The emerging strategic entrepreneurship field seeks to address the entrepreneurship of such established firms. However, while these scholars certainly highlight organization-level antecedents to entrepreneurship (e.g., absorptive capacity, various capabilities, an entrepreneurial culture; e.g., Ireland et al., 2003), explicit attention to organizational design is rare (but see Foss and Lyngsie, 2014; Foss et al., 2015; Foss et al., 2013; Kuratko et al., 2005).

This neglect is somewhat odd as there are many real-life cases of changes in organizational design causing dramatic improvements in firms' entrepreneurial capabilities. Consider, for example, the case of leading hearing aids producer, Oticon's radical change of its organizational design in 1991. Oticon (now William Demant Holding A/S) is a Danish-based world leader in the hearing aids industry (Birkinshaw and Mol, 2006; Foss, 2003; Lovas and Ghoshal, 2000). The radical decentralization initiatives undertaken by Chief Executive Officer (CEO) Lars Kolind quickly became famous for reviving Oticon's innovative and entrepreneurial capabilities, leading to the discovery and seizing of a series of opportunities in the hearing aids business. The radical change from a typical hierarchical structure to a largely self-organizing project-based structure backed up by powerful performance incentives illustrates how firms, by virtue of organizational design, can fuel innovation and entrepreneurship (Foss, 2003). Similarly, work on organizational ambidexterity increasingly points to a critical role of organizational design in successfully bringing about ambidexterity (Simsek, 2009).

In this chapter we develop a framework that can be deployed to understand how organizational design fosters those behaviors that aggregate up firm-level entrepreneurial outcomes in an entrepreneurial ecosystem (i.e., engaging in new markets, securing new sources of inputs, and realizing organizational, process and product innovations; Schumpeter, 1934). We adopt several analytical priors in setting up the framework. First, the framework assumes that there is no *direct* relation from organizational design variables to firm-level entrepreneurial outcomes; the linkages are instead mediated by individual behaviors and interaction between individuals. Second, we conceptualize the entrepreneurial process within established firms involving different entrepreneurial skills (Lazear, 2005), that is, skills (or abilities) related to discovering, evaluating, and exploiting entrepreneurial opportunities (Covin and Slevin, 1991; Ireland et al., 2003; Teece, 2007) – what may be called the firm's "division of entrepreneurial labor" (Foss and Lyngsie, 2014).

Accordingly, our overall proposition is that organizational design variables profoundly shape the acquisition, development, and organization of the focal firm's entrepreneurial skill set, and in turn the discovery, evaluation, and exploitation of entrepreneurial opportunities. As in the entrepreneurship literature, "opportunities" refer to "those situations in which new goods, services, raw materials, and organizing methods can be introduced and sold at greater than their cost of production" (Shane and Venkataraman, 2000, p. 220).

In sum, we sketch a framework that links organizational design, intra-firm entrepreneurial behaviors, and firm-level entrepreneurship. This responds to a specific research gap in the literature. The entrepreneurship literature has tended to ascribe entrepreneurial capacity and outcomes either to individuals that start up new ventures (Gifford, 1992; Kirzner, 1973; Lazear, 2005) *or* has located such capacity and outcomes at the level of firms (Hitt et al., 2001; Ireland et al., 2003). In the latter case, it is seldom made clear how firm-level capacity and outcomes emerge from intra-firm behaviors. And yet, individual employees carry the skills that underlie the discovery, evaluation, and implementation of opportunities. These skills need to be coordinated and their services need to be called forth. Whether explicitly designed for this purpose or not, organization structure and control play a key role here.

The closest "relative" of the present chapter is Ireland et al. (2003), which is also concerned with organizational antecedents of strategic entrepreneurship.[1] However, in contrast to their study we focus more specifically on organizational variables that are more directly given to managerial design (organizational structure, control systems) rather than on variables such as absorptive capacity that are much less subject to managerial influence, at least in the short run. We do not consider variables like social capital, culture, higher-order organizing principles, and so on, not because we consider them irrelevant, but rather because these are not to the same extent managerial choice variables – and we are primarily interested in how managerial choice can foster firm-level entrepreneurial outcomes.[2] A managerially relevant theory of strategic entrepreneurship should specify the "knobs" and "levers" available to managers when they wish to stimulate firm-level entrepreneurial outcomes, and the ways in which these knobs and levers exert an influence on firm-level outcomes by influencing the actions and interactions of individuals. Organizational design variables are important examples of such "knobs" and "levers."

4.2 FIRM-LEVEL ENTREPRENEURSHIP: TWO RESEARCH GAPS

4.2.1 The Individual Entrepreneur

Entrepreneurship research has traditionally addressed entrepreneurs as individuals and has, among other things, theorized how they form firms in order to exploit perceived opportunities (Foss and Klein, 2012; Knight, 1921). Entrepreneurs are individuals who deploy assets, actions, and investments in the pursuit of perceived profit opportunities in the face of uncertainty (Knight, 1921; Wennekers and Thurik, 1999). They typically believe that that they have lower information costs than other people (Casson and Wadeson, 2007), and/or possess privileged information about, for example, potential consumer preferences that are currently not being met (or that consumers have not imagined they may hold) (Knight, 1921; Mises, 1949). The mention here of "individuals" and "people" is not a coincidence: the entrepreneurship literature has overwhelmingly had an individual-centric focus, and has drawn organizations into the analysis mainly as an instrument of the entrepreneur's vision (Foss and Lyngsie, 2014; Knight, 1921; Mises, 1949; Witt, 2007); hence, the strong focus on start-ups in the literature. However, Schumpeter (1942) in a classic contribution to the literature argued that entrepreneurship may be thought of as a firm-level phenomenon. Indeed, he expressed concern about entrepreneurship becoming subordinate to the research and development (R&D) routines of the big corporation. Other scholars have supported our view that entrepreneurship can meaningfully be conceptualized at the firm level (Baumol, 1990). Strategic entrepreneurship theory broadly starts from this assertion (Ireland et al., 2001), and we link up closely with this emerging research stream.

4.2.2   Two Research Gaps

Research gap I: organizational design
Although strategic entrepreneurship is typically conceptualized at the firm level (Foss and Foss, 2008; Hitt et al., 2001; Ireland et al., 2009), little attention has been devoted to understanding how firms' organizational design can foster and coordinate entrepreneurial activities (Foss and Lyngsie, 2014).[3] Thus, a research gap exists in relation to understanding the relation, in established firms, between organizational members' entrepreneurial behavior and the firm's organizational design.[4] This may partly be caused by the focus in the entrepreneurship literature on start-ups or small firms, which makes such neglect more justifiable. However, outside new or newly established firms, there is a need to pay close attention to organizational design. For example, entrepreneurial behavior that stems from hiring, promoting, retaining, and so on particularly entrepreneurially predisposed individuals (i.e., selection and matching processes) should be separated from the effects of the organizational design itself (e.g., certain reward systems may call forth entrepreneurial initiatives even from employees that do not possess particular entrepreneurial talent

to begin with). Because this separation is largely absent in the extant literature, we know little about the relative contributions to firm-level entrepreneurship of organizational members' entrepreneurial disposition and how entrepreneurial behavior is shaped by organizational design. An important purpose of an organizational perspective is to understand the relative contributions of different variables, as well as contributions stemming from cross-variable effects.

Research gap II: the coordination of entrepreneurial actions

The need to pay closer attention to organizational design for entrepreneurship is closely intertwined with the need to better understand firms' coordination of organizational members' entrepreneurial behavior. The full entrepreneurial value chain, the discovery, evaluation and exploitation of an opportunity, may be separated into its constituent behavior components (Foss and Klein, 2010; Shane and Venkataraman, 2000). Entrepreneurs are often seen as single individuals who command all the relevant skills (Lazear, 2005), but in actuality the skills required for different entrepreneurial functions may be distributed across the organization. For example, managers on different organizational levels engage in different entrepreneurial actions to influence firm-level entrepreneurial capability (e.g., Hornsby et al., 2009).

Although the entrepreneurial value chain may be decomposed, and required skills may be dispersed across organizational members, this does not mean that its constituent behaviors are neatly compartmentalized. For example, opportunity discovery may take place anywhere in the organization and not just as a function of formalized R&D activities. While formal evaluation may be vested in certain roles or individuals, informal processes of evaluation may be quite dispersed (e.g., a middle-manager informally evaluating a salesman's proposal for changing procedures related to sales; Linder et al., 2015). Similarly, exploitation may take place at multiple loci in the organization (e.g., divisions or strategic business units (SBUs) exploiting new sources of supply, customer segments, process innovations, and so on). Distributed entrepreneurial behaviors, relying on dispersed entrepreneurial skills, require coordination. Somehow, discovery needs to be linked to evaluation, and if the latter is favorable, the discovered opportunity needs to be exploited. These issues of coordinating and motivating entrepreneurial efforts are organizational design issues.

4.3 A FRAMEWORK FOR UNDERSTANDING FIRM-LEVEL ENTREPRENEURSHIP

4.3.1 Multi-level Theory

Firm-level entrepreneurship is inherently a multi-level phenomenon, and should therefore in principle be addressed by means of multi-level theory (Klein et al., 1994; Rousseau, 1985). In the context of organizations, the purpose of multi-level theory is to "identify principles that enable a more integrated understanding of phenomena that unfold across levels in organizations" (Kozlowski and Klein, 2000, p. 7). An underlying assumption of multi-level perspectives is that most outcomes of interest are the result of a confluence of influences emanating from different levels of analysis (Rousseau, 1985). Understanding firm-level entrepreneurship requires that determinants at multiple levels and their relations be properly taken into account. Extant strategic entrepreneurship theory implicitly agrees. Thus, in an influential paper Ireland et al. (2003) build a model of strategic entrepreneurship that while not explicitly multi-level nevertheless lists determinants of firm-level entrepreneurship at different analytical levels (see also Ireland et al., 2009). Although indicating clear links between different levels, the multi-level perspective is not explicated in the model, nor does it explicitly address the role of organizational design.

The framework we propose involves explicitly accounting for entrepreneurial determinants at different levels of analysis. Conversely, if all significant determinants of entrepreneurial outcomes were placed at the firm level (e.g., in the entrepreneurial culture of the organization), and individual organizational members passively carried out activities, a mono-level model would suffice (see Stinchcombe, 1991). However, there are strong reasons to believe that individual-level heterogeneity plays an important role in mediating the influence of organizational design variables on firm-level outcomes (see Felin and Hesterly, 2007). In addition, research on corporate venturing, skunkworks, emergent strategy processes, employee entrepreneurship, and so on show that entrepreneurial initiatives may emerge from lower levels than the organizational level. Understanding how organizational design variables affect firm-level entrepreneurial outcomes requires explicitly accounting for the micro-aspects of this link.

4.3.2 Individual Actions and Interactions

While a number of the firm-level antecedents of the strategic entrepreneurship literature can be usefully employed in our argument (Covin and Slevin, 2002; Ireland et al., 2003; Zahra et al., 1999), the basic point of the proposed framework is that: antecedents of firm-level entrepreneurial outcomes only matter in so far as they influence the conditions of individual entrepreneurial action. This means that firms can deploy specific organizational design instruments to foster entrepreneurial outcomes, but that the link is composed of individual actions and interactions.

Broadly, organizational design may influence these actions and interactions in two ways. First, firms can deploy human resource management (HRM) practices related to the recruitment, hiring, rewarding, and so on of particularly entrepreneurially capable individuals. Essentially, HRM practices that increase the firm's entrepreneurial human capital. Second, organizational design can be used to structure and induce entrepreneurial behavior in such a way that organizational members' skills are matched with the constituent components of the entrepreneurial value chain (i.e., discovery, evaluation, and exploitation of opportunities). By influencing organizational members' ability, motivation, and opportunity to engage in entrepreneurial actions, organizational instruments are an important part of the creation of firm-level entrepreneurial capabilities, that is, the "systematic capacity to recognize and exploit opportunity" (Covin and Slevin, 2002, p. 311).

4.3.3   Organizational Design Factors

A substantial part of the entrepreneurship literature has explored what organizational factors may improve firm-level entrepreneurship. Ireland et al. (2009) identify what they call "pro-entrepreneurship organizational instruments" that broadly include an organic organization structure, cultural norms, reward systems, resource allocation, and firm strategy, specifically directed at promoting entrepreneurship. While these factors are all relevant to understanding firm-level entrepreneurship, we adopt a narrower focus and concentrate on more traditional organizational design variables. Specifically, we consider variables like departmentalization, job-level specialization (i.e., job descriptions), delegation of authority, rewards and procedures, practices for training, and so on of employees.

Firm-level outcome
It is widely accepted in the extant literature that entrepreneurial outcomes can take different forms, for example, engaging in new markets, new sources of inputs, and realizing organizational, process and product innovations (Schumpeter, 1934). Generally, firm-level entrepreneurial outcomes include improved competitive positioning, transformation of the firm towards new organizational forms, and transformations of markets and industries induced by firms (Covin and Miles, 1999; Ireland et al.,

2003). While the difference in entrepreneurial firm-level outcome and their wealth-creating implications are important, we do not pursue these distinctions. Instead, we mundanely assume that firms seek to create such wealth by means of their entrepreneurial capabilities.

4.3.4   Individual-level Factors of Firm-level Entrepreneurship

While recent work on strategic entrepreneurship has progressed with respect to theorizing the relation between organization-level organizational variables and entrepreneurial outcomes (e.g., Foss et al., 2015; Ireland et al., 2003), such work has not devoted much explicit attention to individual organizational members' entrepreneurial actions within firms. Yet, "In entrepreneurship, it is entrepreneurial activity that matters . . . Without action, there is no insight" (Gartner et al., 2003, p. 124).

There are several reasons why strategic entrepreneurship research stands to gain from paying more attention to activity at the individual level. First, organizational members discover, evaluate, and exploit opportunities. Interaction obviously plays a big role, but understanding interaction requires understanding individual action in the first place. Second, firms differ in terms of their entrepreneurial human capital (Felin and Hesterly, 2007). Heterogeneity by itself affects the engagement and output of entrepreneurial actions; the proper management of this diversity is therefore an important issue.

DEE: discovering, evaluating, and exploiting opportunities

Entrepreneurial actions can be divided into the discovery, evaluation, and exploitation of opportunities (Foss and Klein, 2010; Shane and Venkataraman, 2000). Research on discovery has traditionally focused on the processes and factors responsible for individuals discovering entrepreneurial opportunity. Kirzner's (1973) treatment of entrepreneurial alertness has influenced much of the present work on discovery.[5] Entrepreneurial discovery can be defined as the ability to notice hitherto undiscovered opportunities. Thus, "entrepreneurs are discoverers; they discover new resource uses, new products, new markets, new possibilities for arbitrage – in short, new possibilities for profitable trade" (Foss and Klein, 2010, p. 57). Evaluation has received less attention in the entrepreneurship literature (but see Linder et al., 2015). Nevertheless, evaluation critically determines the decision of whether or not to act on an opportunity (McMullen and Shepherd, 2005). Evaluation of an entrepreneurial opportunity involves "a comparison between the discovered opportunity and other alternatives to entrepreneurship that the entrepreneur faces" (Shane, 2000, p. 467). Hence, entrepreneurs only act upon a new opportunity if it is sufficiently profitable. Opportunity exploitation is the realization of the rent-generating potential of a new opportunity (Alvarez and Barney, 2004). In much of the entrepreneurship literature, and specifically the economics of entrepreneurship (e.g., Kirzner, 1973; Knight, 1921; Schumpeter, 1934), these three phases of entrepreneurship are not viewed as separated functions. In fact, Kirzner explicitly treats the discovery, evaluation, and exploitation of an opportunity as essentially taking place simultaneously by the same person. However, inside the established firm entrepreneurial functions may be separated and allocated across different organizational members, teams or departments. Accordingly, not only are discovery, evaluation, and exploitation conceptually separate, but in actuality different entrepreneurial functions may be undertaken by different organizational members (possibly at different organizational levels).

AMO: ability, motivation, and opportunity

Organizational design variables do not directly influence the actions of organizational members, but rather the conditions of individual action. These conditions are conceptualized using the familiar ability-motivation-opportunity framework (AMO) (Blumberg and Pringle, 1982; MacInnis et al., 1991). We use the framework to explicate how organizational design variables influence individual organizational members. Thus, actions arise from the ability to engage in different actions, the motivation the individual possess to engage in a given activity, and the opportunity to exercise action.

The conditions of individual actions have previously been explored in the entrepreneurship literature. For example, Ahuja and Lampert (2001, p. 524, emphasis added) argued that "the failure of large firms to create breakthrough inventions can be understood through either their lack of *motivation* (the economic perspective) or their lack of *ability* (the organizational perspective)." The opportunity (to act) has also been examined in entrepreneurship research, for example, network arguments have been leveraged to examine how network positions influence the decision to act upon a perceived opportunity (e.g., Aldrich and Waldinger, 1990; Burt, 1992; Tsai, 2001; Tsai and Ghoshal, 1998). More mundanely, excessive workload and unavailability of resources can eliminate the opportunity for organizational members to engage in entrepreneurial actions, despite having the right abilities and motivation.

4.4 THE DEE-AMO MATRIX

Juxtaposing the above DEE framework with the AMO framework produces a 3 x 3 matrix that maps antecedents of each entrepreneurial function in terms of individuals' ability, motivation, and opportunity. In terms of our ambition to link organizational design variables and individual entrepreneurial actions, the DEE-AMO matrix provides a needed micro-level framework. Organizational design variables matter to the extent that they influence the ability, motivation, and opportunity of individual organizational members to engage in entrepreneurial actions, and the matrix maps this influence.

4.4.1   Discovery Actions

The motivation to engage in discovery actions is influenced by the firm's use of intrinsic and/or extrinsic motivators. The motivation of individuals to engage in entrepreneurial activities has received significant attention in the entrepreneurship literature (e.g., Dess et al., 2003; Zahra et al., 1999). Rewards are generally taken as having a positive influence on entrepreneurial motivation (Block and Ornati, 1987; Sathe, 1989; Sykes and Block, 1989), although the relative effect of extrinsic and intrinsic motivators remains an under-researched area in the entrepreneurial literature. While the entrepreneurship literature does not appear to present conclusive evidence regarding the effect of different motivators on entrepreneurial actions inside firms, the creativity literature more unequivocally suggests that non-financial, intrinsic motivators will have a positive effect on individuals' motivation to discover (Amabile, 1993).

Entrepreneurship research addressing the opportunity to act entrepreneurially has often done so in terms of networks (Burt, 1992); thus, serving a brokering role between different networks may be a position that is particularly attractive from the point of view of discovering new opportunities. This position allows the centrally placed agent to engage in arbitrage (Kirzner, 1973) or to link different bodies of knowledge, resulting in Schumpeterian new combinations (Fleming, 2001; Schumpeter, 1934). Within firms, efforts to stimulate opportunities for individuals to engage in discovery actions are created by R&D labs, job rotation, and knowledge-sharing programs. R&D investments are not just investments in deepening skill levels (i.e., individuals' ability) in R&D, they are also investments in improving opportunities for discovery (Cohen and Levinthal, 1990). Individuals discover opportunities related to information they already possess (Amabile, 1997; Shane, 2000; Shane and Venkataraman, 2000; Venkataraman, 1997). Thus, acquiring new information about resource uses is a fundamental ability for engaging in entrepreneurial discovery (Casson and Wadeson, 2007).

Because knowledge is made up of an individual's idiosyncratic experiences, the ability to engage in discovery differs between organizational members. This difference has been examined in the entrepreneurship literature with respect to founders of new firms (e.g., Davidsson and Honig, 2003; Lazear, 2005). For example, Lazear (2005) argues that entrepreneurs who start new firms are more likely to be jacks-of-all-trades than specialists exactly because starting an entrepreneurial venture requires different kinds of skills. However, because firms have access to a heterogeneous set of entrepreneurial labor within their organization, they can coordinate specialist skills in discovery, evaluation, and exploitation of opportunities. Moreover, firms' organizational designs will influence the development of ability; for example, high levels of specialization constrain the breadth of work experiences, resulting in a narrower development of ability.

4.4.2 Evaluation Actions

Evaluation involves judgment of an opportunity in terms of systematically imagining and assessing the possible outcomes that may result from exploiting an opportunity (Shackle, 1979), and identifying the costs and benefits associated with different outcomes. It involves evaluating the set of complementary investments that are needed to realize the opportunity (Teece, 1986).

Evaluation leads to the confirmation (or not) that the perceived opportunity is indeed worth pursuing based on the available knowledge and information. It involves a good deal of refinement of the discovered opportunity and concrete thinking about the investments that are required to transform a loose, perhaps largely tacit, idea into a concrete, exploitable project. In this process, motivation is typically linked closely to cognition. For example, Busenitz and Barney (1997, p. 15) argue that a "higher level of confidence is likely to encourage (motivate) an entrepreneur to take action." However, confidence may also be a matter of overconfidence that will tend to make individuals overly optimistic in their initial evaluations, and only reluctantly (if at all) incorporate additional, perhaps contrary, information (Busenitz and Barney, 1997). Motivation may also result from decision-makers assigning higher probability of success to their own projects compared with competing projects (Cooper et al., 1988) (i.e., a contribution bias).

Yet, the actual process of evaluation ranges from highly analytical tools, such as real options analysis (McGrath, 1999), to processes mainly based on rules of thumb or hunches. The danger of cognitive biases and blinders is particularly acute at this entrepreneurial stage. Shane and Venkataraman (2000, p. 222) argue that "even if a person possesses the prior information necessary to discover an opportunity, he or she may fail to do so because of an inability to see new means-ends relationships." Relatedly, it has been shown empirically that entrepreneurs generally rely more heavily on heuristics than non-entrepreneurial managers (Busenitz and Barney, 1997), and those organizational members who engage in evaluation behaviors have been found to rely on heuristics because of time pressure (Shepherd and DeTienne, 2005). Examples of cognitive properties that positively relate to individuals engaging in entrepreneurial actions are seeing opportunities in situations in which others tend to see risks (Sarasvathy et al., 1998), being less prone to counterfactual thinking, less likely to experience regret over missed opportunities, and less susceptible to inaction inertia (Baron, 2000).

4.4.3　Exploitation Actions

Exploiting an opportunity entails bringing together the required resources in order to capture the value of the opportunity (Foss and Foss, 2008; Rumelt, 1987; Teece, 1986). This may lead to various outcomes (e.g., new products, processes or ventures); however, realizing opportunities usually requires complementary investments.

Following Knight (1921), Foss and Klein (2005) argue that realizing an opportunity often requires that the entrepreneur starts a firm which entails investing in assets and (often, but not necessarily) hiring employees. However, entrepreneurs by no means need to integrate the whole value chain to realize opportunities: Often the services of necessary complementary assets can be acquired through markets or alliances (Teece, 1986). Within a firm, individual organizational members' ability to exploit new opportunities depend on whether they control and/or can gain access to critical complementary resources. In order for an individual to secure resources, she must be capable of successfully championing the new opportunity. As such, individual organizational members must attract firm resources to the specific opportunity. This requires abilities relating to synthesizing and integrating information (Hornsby et al., 2002), in order to match the firm's overall resource availability with that needed to exploit the new opportunity. As Dess and Lumpkin (2005, p. 149) note, "champions are especially important after a new project has been defined but before it gains momentum." Hence, in a firm setting product champions play an important entrepreneurial role by scavenging for resources and encouraging others to take a chance on promising new ideas. In other words, capturing value from a new opportunity requires that individuals have the ability to perceive availability of resources for entrepreneurial activities in order to encourage experimentation and risk taking (Hornsby et al., 2002).

Conventionally, the expectation of future profits is crucial in motivating entrepreneurs to engage in exploitation of opportunities (Alvarez and Barney, 2005; Hornsby et al., 2002; Kirzner, 1973; Shepherd and DeTienne,

2005). In line with the championing role performed by individuals engaged in exploitation, prior research also suggests that resource availability, flexibility, and decision-making speed all positively influence exploitation (Covin and Slevin, 2002). In particular, time availability has been argued to be important in generating entrepreneurial outcomes (Stopford and Baden-Fuller, 1994; Sykes and Block, 1989). Traditionally, slack resources are also generally accepted as encouraging entrepreneurial activity (Zahra, 1996). For example, reward and resource availability are taken as principal determinants of entrepreneurial behavior by middle- and first-level managers (Hornsby et al., 2002).

4.5 ORGANIZATIONAL DESIGN AND FIRM-LEVEL ENTREPRENEURSHIP

4.5.1 Organizational Design Variables

In this section, we apply the DEE-AMO framework to forward how organizational design variables can be deployed to influence the ability, motivation, and opportunity of individuals to engage in the discovery, evaluation, and exploitation of opportunities, leading to firm-level entrepreneurial outcomes.

A large body of work on organizational design has identified a set of key variables along which organizational structure – that is, the "relatively enduring allocation of work roles and administrative mechanisms that creates a pattern of interrelated work activities" (Jackson and Morgan, 1982, p. 81) – can be characterized (e.g., Burns and Stalker, 1961; Burton and Obel, 2004; Galbraith, 1974; Miller and Dröge, 1986). These include (job and unit) specialization (with an implied allocation of decision rights, i.e., authority), and coordination by means of (workflow) formalization,[6] rules and targets, and other elements of planning. However, as Ouchi (1977) clarified, structure does not automatically translate into control and organizational design and therefore encompasses governance mechanisms for monitoring and evaluating inputs and outputs and rewarding behaviors. In the following, we discuss organizational structure and control seriatim.

4.5.2 Organizational Structure and the AMO-DEE Framework

Discovery
The aspect of organizational structure that is routinely invoked in discussions of whether organizational forms foster or inhibit initiative and dynamism is almost certainly formalization. This aspect of structure has been

argued by different authors to have opposing attitudinal effects, depending on whether it is seen as constraining or enabling (see Adler and Borys, 1996 for a summary). In the context of stimulating discovery, the effect of formalization is likewise ambiguous: on the one hand, formalized work processes may leave little opportunity for the experimentation or even tinkering that can foster discovery; on the other hand, formalization – by making activities and their relations explicit – may enable such experimentation (Foss, 2001).

However, such arguments presuppose that organizational members have the decision rights to experiment with firm resources within certain more or less narrowly circumscribed decision domains. If the organization is extremely specialized, so that members have very narrow task portfolios, individuals effectively hold narrowly circumscribed decision rights (Foss, 2001; Jensen and Meckling, 1992). Wider job description or a broadening of the task portfolios of organizational members (or functions) translate into broader rights to use firm resources in certain more or less specified ways. Broadening also provides more opportunities to engage in discovery activities. Discovery is often prompted by combining knowledge from different domains (Fleming, 2001), and an individual that holds a more diverse task portfolio will be provided with more such opportunities. In terms of ability, wider job descriptions imply that members will need a broader skill portfolio, which has also been found to correlate positively with discovery (Lazear, 2005).

Firms may wish to delegate more discretion in terms of decision rights to employees in order to stimulate their motivation to engage in discovery activities. Delegation has often been linked to intrinsic motivation, particularly in the context of complex tasks that require creativity in problem-solving (e.g., Hill and Amabile, 1993) and in the context of certain types of sharing/helping behavior (e.g., knowledge sharing; Osterloh and Frey, 2000) that antecede the discovery of new ways of combining knowledge (Cohen and Levinthal, 1990). Mintzberg (1983, p. 97) argues that "[I]n general creative and intelligent people require plenty of room to manoeuvre," and Osterloh and Frey (2000, p. 543) point out that delegation "raises the perceived self-determination of employees and therewith strengthens intrinsic motivation," leading to an increase in creativity in the pursuit of goals. This reasoning prompts clear linkage between key organizational design variables (prominently, specialization and decentralization) and organizational members' ability, motion, and opportunity to engage specifically in opportunity discovery.

Evaluation

Sah and Stiglitz (1985) argue that organizational structure has a direct and systematic bearing on the probability of acceptance/rejection of what they call "projects," that is, new proposals and initiatives. With respect to ability, the starting point is that individuals are bounded rational in the specific sense that they commit type I and II errors, that is, they may mistakenly reject a good project and mistakenly accept a bad project. This property can be ascribed to organizational units as well. Increasing the ability (i.e., reducing bounds on rationality) of individual decision-makers reduces the incidence of type I and II errors. Sah and Stiglitz further argue that organizations can be ordered on a continuum from "polyarchies" to "hierarchies." In a polyarchy, a project is only rejected if all organizational units reject it; in a hierarchy, a project is only accepted if all units accept the project. Thus, organizational structures are literally structures of evaluation. In a sense, the polyarchy provides few opportunities for project rejection, while the hierarchy provides many. It is intuitive that polyarchies will (therefore) accept more projects (but also more bad projects) than hierarchies will. It is similarly intuitive that the choice between hierarchies and polyarchies is determined by the relative importance of avoiding type I and type II errors, respectively. Thus, a hierarchy should be adopted if it is important to avoid type II errors (e.g., procedures for drug approval). Polyarchies and hierarchies are obviously extreme ideal types. However, the same logic applies to the broad spectrum of hybrid designs that exist in between these two extreme types (Christensen and Knudsen, 2010).

In terms of opportunity evaluation, a firm characterized by a high degree of (job, unit, and functional) specialization corresponds to Sah and Stiglitz's hierarchy. In such a firm, new discovered opportunities will typically directly affect multiple jobs, units, and functions and evaluation will have to be undertaken by multiple parties, cascading up the corporate hierarchy. Moreover, given a high degree of specialization, abilities are deep rather than broad. This likely increases the incidence of type I and type II errors, as organizational members have less understanding of those opportunities that involve multiple jobs, units, and functions.

Exploitation

Opportunities become realized when resources are committed to exploiting an idea (e.g., an organizational or managerial innovation, new production processes, new products, new markets, and so on) that emerged in the discovery phase and survived the evaluation phase. The traditional vertically integrated and highly specialized industrial firm with a dedicated R&D lab has been argued to be a highly efficient setting for exploiting opportunities within a largely linear and "closed" innovation process (Chandler, 1990;

Teece, 1992). Generally, firms in the exploitation phase need to mobilize complementary assets (production, sales, marketing, and so on) in a focused manner (Teece, 1986). And when exploitation efforts involve close coordination of activities in the value chain, firms that possess these assets in-house may possess an advantage relative to firms that need to access the services of complementary assets by means of market or hybrid arrangements (e.g., Teece, 1986, 1993). Thus, Schoonhoven et al. (1990) found that upstart firms that had R&D, production, and marketing services in-house performed better in terms of first product introduction than upstarts that had only a subset of these services in-house.

Increasingly, innovation involves co-creation with external parties (Chesbrough, 2003), multiple technological disciplines (Brusoni et al., 2001), and multiple feedback loops in the innovation process (Teece, 1992). However, exploitation of opportunities still calls for hierarchy and centralized decision-making, even in firms that only occupy a few stages of the value chain. Jansen et al. (2006) found that formalization and "connectedness" (essentially, informal communication across functions) were important antecedents of exploitative efforts (see also Foss et al., 2015). Formalization aids codification of new knowledge and connectedness is instrumental in disseminating such new knowledge in-house, furthering exploitation (Cohen and Levinthal, 1990; Zander and Kogut, 1995). Thus, organizational structure, especially if characterized by formalization and centralized decision-making, clearly relates to enhanced exploitation activity.

4.5.3   Organizational Control and the AMO-DEE Framework

Organizational control can broadly be defined as processes and administrative apparatus by which managers can direct attention to, motivate, and encourage organizational members to act in ways that further organizational goals and objectives (Ouchi, 1977). In line with previous entrepreneurship research (e.g., Alvarez and Barney, 2005; Mahnke et al., 2007; Zahra, 1996), we frame organizational control in line with Ouchi's (1980) influential categorization of organizational controls into market, bureaucratic, and clan control, and inquire how such controls can be deployed to positively influence organizational members' entrepreneurial behavior. Conceptualization of the different control mechanisms has previously been established in the entrepreneurship literature. Firms using market control rely on the price mechanism to evaluate opportunities and outcomes (Floyd and Lane, 2000), benefitting from its superior incentive properties and autonomous adaptation (Foss, 2003). The use of bureaucratic control entails a high reliance on standardized behavior and performance assessments, implemented through rules and procedures (Cardinal, 2001). Clan control uses traditions to convey information while relying on members' organizational identity, common culture, and goal congruence to solve exchange problems (Alvarez and Barney, 2005; Floyd and Lane, 2000).

In general, individuals will engage in entrepreneurial activities if the payoff from doing so is higher than the payoff from regular employment (Douglas and Shepherd, 2000). However, as entrepreneurial actions become embedded in an organization, the payoff from entrepreneurship changes as income changes from entrepreneurial rent to remuneration (Jones and Butler, 1992). From an agency perspective, Jones and Butler (1992) examine how this change affects individual organizational members' motivation to engage in entrepreneurial actions (specifically, opportunity discovery), and argue that this change generally reduces motivation, because the employee is less of a residual claimant than an independent entrepreneur. Because of information asymmetries coupled with "uncertainty in environmental, organization, or task conditions" and "different risk preferences [and/or] opportunism" (Jones and Butler, 1992, p. 736), firms cannot perfectly mimic market incentives (see also Foss, 2003). However, there are other means of organizational control than rewards available to the firm.

4.5.4 Discovery

Organizational members engage in discovery actions under uncertainty (Casson and Wadeson, 2007). The future outcome of entrepreneurial actions cannot be probabilistically determined (or it would be prohibitively costly to do so), either by the individual organizational member or by top management. This means that actions are not contractible, although management can of course influence search efforts. Because discovery typically involves serendipity, tacit knowledge, flashes of insights, and so on, a high degree of information impactedness characterizes discovery actions (Williamson, 1975). These properties of discovery actions compromise hierarchy and market mechanisms in the control of discovery actions. Jones and Butler (1992) argue that because it is nearly impossible to monitor and evaluate individuals engaged in discovery actions, they will tend to behave in a morally hazardous way unless they are allocated ownership rights, or if other organizational control than markets and hierarchies are used. Specifically, they invoke goal congruence induced by clan organization or ownership as a potential solution to latent agency problems connected to discovery actions (see also Alvarez and Barney, 2005 for a similar argument).

Clan control may also influence the ability to engage in discovery actions. The alignment of organizational members and firm interest reduces the opportunity to act opportunistically, and instills trust. Thus, clan-based control may increase the incentive to undertake firm-specific investments that may result in further discovery actions (Alvarez and Barney, 2005). Finally, organizational control influences the opportunity to engage in discovery actions. Market-like, high-powered incentives may reduce employees' willingness to share knowledge and interact in ways that promote the combination of knowledge. In contrast, clan control, by emphasizing shared goals and identity, promotes knowledge sharing and knowledge combining behaviors (Nahapiet and Ghoshal, 1998). Juxtaposing organizational control mechanisms and opportunity discovery illustrates that market and bureaucratic control are detrimental to organizational members' ability, opportunity, and motivation. Whereas control based on shared goals and identity (i.e., clan control) promotes entrepreneurial behavior focused on discovery.

4.5.5 Evaluation

The primary purpose of the entrepreneurial firm "is to solve transaction difficulties associated with the inability to know the value of an exchange at the time that exchange is commenced" (Alvarez and Barney, 2005, p. 788; Foss and Klein, 2005). Thus, entrepreneurial firms arise because of the market's inability to accurately evaluate the entrepreneur's idea. In this regard, organizational control can be used to enable individual organizational members to evaluate uncertain opportunities. That is, because new opportunities are novel, firms must deploy administrative apparatus in order to refine (maybe even codify) these ideas into workable projects given the firm's strategy, resources, and structure (Kuratko et al., 2005). Bureaucratic control relies on formalization of actions and managerial fiat in order to monitor and direct the actions of organizational members (Ouchi, 1980). Thus, formalized evaluation actions increasingly enable comparison of alternatives. Deploying objective and formalized evaluation of discoveries increases the opportunity that individuals can compare, and rank, different opportunities. In addition, formalization enables monitoring of individual organizational members' evaluation activity.

Evaluation outcomes are related to the inherent quality (e.g., expected value) of the discovered opportunity. An opportunity may receive a negative evaluation because the opportunity is of low quality or because the evaluation activity was erroneously performed – resulting in a wrongful rejection of a high "quality" opportunity (type II errors may also take place). Bureaucratic controls are used to formalize evaluation actions, separating the action from the opportunity (Ouchi, 1980), thereby increasing the determinability of whether rejection/acceptance of an opportunity was due to erroneous evaluation. Moreover, formalization embeds necessary interpretative processes inside the organization itself (Teece, 2007). Thus, formalized evaluation actions reduce vulnerability to turnover among key organizational members. Yet, replacing market-like high-powered incentives with formal bureaucratic rules and controls can negatively affect the ability to engage in evaluation actions. Exercising managerial fiat requires that sufficient information is available (Williamson, 1985). Conveying such information under bureaucratic control requires setting up and maintaining an explicit information apparatus at non-trivial cost (Ouchi, 1977). At lower levels of formalization, rules and standards act as guidelines enabling individual organizational members to more objectively evaluate opportunities. Yet, excessive formalization and/or standardization may impede organizational members' engagement in evaluation actions by substituting the deliberate assessment of new opportunities with routine performance. For example, highly formalized information flows can increase the probability that new opportunities will be negatively evaluated if they do not fit the status quo (Thompson, 1967).

4.5.6 Exploitation

The measurability of exploitation actions as well as the outcomes of such actions increases the closer an opportunity moves to being fully realized (Aghion et al., 2008; Holmström, 1989). For example, in the case of opportunities involving new products, realizing the opportunity implies the deployment of assets in the actual production, marketing, and sale of the product (Teece, 1986). The desired actions by organizational members are in principle known and the main organizational problems are how to motivate organizational members to engage in these actions and coordinating these in the exploitation of the opportunity. This suggests a ranking of organizational control mechanism where market-like and bureaucratic controls dominate clan-based control in terms of opportunity exploitation.

4.5.7 The Separation of Entrepreneurial Functions and Individual Actions

Discovery, evaluation, and exploitation actions must all be undertaken by individual organizational members in order to produce firm-level entrepreneurial outcomes. However, different individuals, possibly dispersed across the organization, can perform these actions. Entrepreneurial actions, at least conceptually, are undertaken in a sequential fashion, starting with the discovery of a new opportunity. The latter outcome is contingent on each action resulting in a positive outcome and the allocation of resources to the entire process. However, who and at what organizational level these actions are in practice undertaken is not necessarily dictated by their sequential ordering. For example, prior knowledge critically relates to discovery actions but is also dispersed across the entire organization; thus, discovery cannot be deterministically placed within the firm. Instead, who engages in discovery actions largely depends on the sought after outcome (Shane, 2000). Discovery actions can be undertaken by all organizational members endowed with the "right" prior knowledge, or in Burgelman's (1983) terminology represent "spontaneous initiatives" at different hierarchical levels. Indeed, our framework suggests that firms' organizational design predisposes specific individuals or groups to engage in discovery.

The sequential nature in which entrepreneurial actions are undertaken assists in a clearer placement of evaluation and exploitation actions within organizations. In regards to evaluation, organizational members must have authority to accept or reject development of the discovered opportunity. In a traditional hierarchy, such authority is conveyed by placing actions at a higher organizational level. However, the argument of our framework is that the specific positioning of evaluation actions will be determined by firms' organizational design. Typically, evaluation actions are undertaken by middle management (e.g., Bartlett and Ghoshal, 1993), as their position within the organization allows them to gather/evaluate new opportunities from inside and outside the firm. In terms of exploitation actions, the key action of allocating firm resources indicates that top management will be strongly engaged in this action (Kuratko et al., 2004).

4.6 CONCLUSIONS

Strategic entrepreneurship combines the focus on opportunity-seeking of the entrepreneurship field with the focus on advantage-seeking of strategic management. Most contributions to the field have adopted a mono-level focus; specifically, dependent as well as independent variables have been placed (and data collected) at the firm level. Moreover, traditional organizational design variables have not been highlighted as entrepreneurial antecedents. Adopting a micro-focus emphasizing individual (entrepreneurial) actions and organizational design's influence on sourcing, coordinating, and leveraging individuals' entrepreneurial skills, we built a framework that delineates how firms can deploy administrative apparatus to foster entrepreneurial outcomes.

For the sake of simplicity, we have only directly considered two analytical levels. However, strategic entrepreneurship typically involves more levels. Moreover, the subject of this volume, entrepreneurial ecosystems, addresses a high level of aggregation. Hence, expanding the framework to encompass more levels (e.g., the team/project/group level) is both possible and warranted. More explicit account needs to be taken of individual heterogeneity. Indeed, "entrepreneurial opportunities exist primarily because different agents have different beliefs about the relative value of resources" (Alvarez and Busenitz, 2001, p. 756), and such different beliefs stem not just from access to different information, but also from different interpretive frameworks, background knowledge, and so on, in short, they are rooted in heterogeneity (Felin and Zenger, 2009). The presented framework does not directly address idiosyncratic personal traits. However, this does not mean that organizational members are treated as a homogeneous mass (Felin and Hesterly, 2007). We acknowledge that organizational members are indeed heterogeneous, and emphasize that firm-level entrepreneurship can only be rendered fully intelligible as the actions and interactions of individuals. Although important headway has been made in matching distinct entrepreneurial actions with organizational factors (e.g., Block and Ornati, 1987; Hornsby et al., 2009), the focus continues to be how firms can create an overall pro-entrepreneurship architecture. However, such pro-entrepreneurship architecture is not "a unique organizational form but an internal environment or organizational context exhibiting certain attributes that individually and collectively encourage entrepreneurial behavior" (Ireland et al., 2009, p. 30). We presently know very little about how individual entrepreneurial actions and interactions can be brought forth by unique effects of organizational design. The presented framework takes a first step in trying to delineate *how* organizational design elements affect different entrepreneurial actions through their influence on the motivation, opportunity, and ability of individuals to engage in discovery, evaluation, and exploitation of opportunities.

NOTES

* We thank, without implicating, Richard Burton, Haiyang Li, Stefan Linder, Bo Nielsen, and particularly Nils Stieglitz for comments on earlier versions of this chapter.
1. We also build on Foss and Lyngsie (2014) and Foss (2012). Additionally, Foss et al. (2013), Foss and Lyngsie (2015), and Linder et al. (2015) may be seen as attempts to empirically implement the framework described in this chapter.
2. Social capital, culture, and so on may moderate the relation between managerial choice variables and firm-level entrepreneurial outcomes (e.g., Ireland et al., 2009). However, we disregard this possibility here.
3. Various literatures on corporate renewal and radical transformation, innovation versus exploration, radical learning, and so on have a bearing on firm-level entrepreneurship

(see Ireland et al., 2009). However, these learning-driven stories usually do not address organizational design variables.

4. An emerging literature on business models has, however, begun to tackle this issue (Amit and Zott, 2001; Teece, 2007).
5. For debate on whether discoveries are "created" or "discovered" see, for example, Alvarez and Barney (2007) and Klein (2008).
6. Formalization refers to the degree to which communications and procedures in an organization are written (Daft, 1986).

REFERENCES

Acs, Z.J., Autio, E., and Szerb, L. (2014). National systems of entrepreneurship: measurement issues and policy implications. *Research Policy*, **43**, 476–94.

Adler, P. and Borys, B. (1996). Two types of bureaucracy: enabling and coercive. *Administrative Science Quarterly*, **41**, 61–89.

Aghion, P., Dewatripont, M., and Stein, J.C. (2008). Academic freedom, private-sector focus, and the process of innovation. *RAND Journal of Economics*, **39**, 617–35.

Ahuja, G. and Lampert, C.M. (2001). Entrepreneurship in the large corporation: a longitudinal study of how established firms create breakthrough inventions. *Strategic Management Journal*, **22**, 521–43.

Aldrich, H. and Waldinger, R. (1990). Ethnicity and entrepreneurship. *Annual Review of Sociology*, **16**, 111–35.

Alvarez, S.A. and Barney, J.B. (2004). Organizing rent generation and appropriation: toward a theory of the entrepreneurial firm. *Journal of Business Venturing*, **19**, 621–35.

Alvarez, S.A. and Barney, J.B. (2005). How do entrepreneurs organize firms under conditions of uncertainty? *Journal of Management*, **31**, 776–93.

Alvarez, S.A. and Barney, J.B. (2007). Discovery and creation: alternative theories of entrepreneurial action. *Strategic Entrepreneurship Journal*, **1**(1–2), 11–26.

Alvarez, S. and Busenitz, L. (2001). The entrepreneurship of resource-based theory. *Journal of Management*, **6**, 755 75.

Amabile, T.M. (1993). Motivational synergy: toward new conceptualizations of intrinsic and extrinsic motivation in the workplace. *Human Resource Management Review*, **3**, 185–201.

Amabile, T.M. (1997). Entrepreneurial creativity through motivational synergy. *Journal of Creative Behavior*, **31**, 18–26.

Amit, R. and Zott, C. (2001). Value creation in e-business. *Strategic Management Journal*, **22**(6–7), 493–520.

Baron, R.A. (2000). Counterfactual thinking and venture formation: the potential effects of thinking about "what might have been." *Journal of Business Venturing*, **15**, 79–91.

Bartlett, C.A. and Ghoshal, S. (1993). Beyond the M-form: toward a managerial theory of the firm. *Strategic Management Journal*, **14**, 23–46.

Baumol, W.J. (1990). Entrepreneurship: productive, unproductive, and destructive. *Journal of Political Economy*, **98**, 893–921.

Birch, D. (1987). *Job Creation in America*. New York: Free Press.

Birkinshaw, J. and Mol, M. (2006). How management innovation happens. *MIT Sloan Management Review*, **47**, 81–8.

Block, Z. and Ornati, O.A. (1987). Compensating corporate venture managers. *Journal of Business Venturing*, **2**, 41–51.

Blumberg, M. and Pringle, C.D. (1982). The missing opportunity in organizational research: some implications for a theory of work performance. *Academy of Management Review*, **7**, 560–69.

Brusoni, S., Prencipe, A., and Pavitt, K. (2001). Knowledge specialization, organizational coupling, and the boundaries of the firm: why do firms know more than they make? *Administrative Science Quarterly*, **46**, 597–621.

Burgelman, R.A. (1983). Corporate entrepreneurship and strategic management: insights from a process study. *Management Science*, **29**, 1349–64.

Burns, T. and Stalker, G.M. (1961). *The Management of Innovation*. London: Tavistock.

Burt, R.H. (1992). *Structural Holes: The Social Structure of Competition*. Chicago, IL: University of Chicago Press.

Burton, R.M. and Obel, B. (2004). *Strategic Organizational Diagnosis and Design: The Dynamics of Fit*. New York: Springer.

Busenitz, L.W. and Barney, J.B. (1997). Differences between entrepreneurs and managers in large organizations: biases and heuristics in strategic decision-making. *Journal of Business Venturing*, **12**, 9–30.

Cardinal, L.B. (2001). Technological innovation in the pharmaceutical industry: the use of organizational control in managing research and development. *Organization Science*, **12**, 19–36.

Casson, M. and Wadeson, N. (2007). The discovery of opportunities: extending the economic theory of the entrepreneur. *Small Business Economics*, **28**, 285–300.

Chandler, A. (1990). *Scale and Scope*. Cambridge, MA: Harvard University Press.

Chesbrough, H. (2003). *Open Innovation: The New Imperative for Creating and Profiting from Technology*. Cambridge, MA: Harvard Business Press.

Christensen, M. and Knudsen, T. (2010). Design of decision-making organizations. *Management Science*, **56**, 71–89.

Cohen, W.M. and Levinthal, D.A. (1990). Absorptive capacity: a new perspective on learning and innovation. *Administrative Science Quarterly*, **35**, 128–52.

Cooper, A., Woo, C., and Dunkelberg, W. (1988). Entrepreneurs' perceived chances for success. *Journal of Business Venturing*, **3**, 19–108.

Covin, J.G. and Miles, M.P. (1999). Corporate entrepreneurship and the pursuit of competitive advantage. *Entrepreneurship Theory and Practice*, **23**, 47–63.

Covin, J.G. and Slevin, D.P. (1991). Entrepreneurship: critical perspectives on business and management. *Entrepreneurship Theory and Practice*, **16**, 7–25.

Covin, J.G. and Slevin, D.P. (2002). The entrepreneurial imperatives of strategic leadership. In M.A. Hitt, R.D. Ireland, S.M. Camp, and D.L. Sexton (eds), *Strategic Entrepreneurship: Creating a New Mindset*, pp. 309–27. Oxford: Blackwell.

Daft, R.L. (1986). *Organization Theory and Design*, Second edn. St. Paul, MN: West.

Davidsson, P. and Honig, B. (2003). The role of social and human capital among nascent entrepreneurs. *Journal of Business Venturing*, **18**, 301–31.

Dess, G. and Lumpkin, G. (2005). The role of entrepreneurial orientation in stimulating effective corporate entrepreneurship. *Academy of Management Executive*, **19**, 147–56.

Dess, G., Ireland, R.D., Zahra, S.A., Floyd, S.W., Janney, J.J., and Lane, P.J. (2003). Emerging issues in corporate entrepreneurship. *Journal of Management*, **29**, 351–78.

Douglas, E.J. and Shepherd, D. (2000). Entrepreneurship as a utility maximizing response. *Journal of Business Venturing*, **15**, 231–51.

Felin, T. and Hesterly, W.S. (2007). The knowledge-based view, nested heterogeneity, and new value creation: philosophical considerations on the locus of knowledge. *Academy of Management Review*, **32**, 195–218.

Felin, T. and Zenger, T. (2009). Entrepreneurs as theorists: on the origins of collective beliefs and novel strategies. *Strategic Entrepreneurship Journal*, **3**, 127–46.

Fleming, L. (2001). Recombinant uncertainty in technological search. *Management Science*, **47**, 117–32.

Floyd, S.W. and Lane, P.J. (2000). Strategizing throughout the organization: managing role conflict in strategic renewal. *Academy of Management Review*, **25**, 154–77.

Foss, K. (2001). Organizing technological interdependencies: a coordination perspective on the firm. *Industrial and Corporate Change*, **10**, 151–78.

Foss, K. and Foss, N.J. (2008). Understanding opportunity discovery and sustainable advantage: the role of transaction costs and property rights. *Strategic Entrepreneurship Journal*, **2**, 191–207.

Foss, N.J. (2003). Selective intervention and internal hybrids: interpreting and learning from the rise and decline of the Oticon spaghetti organization. *Organization Science*, **14**, 331–49.

Foss, N.J. (2012). Towards a theory of the entrepreneurial established firm. *Strategy Entrepreneurship*, pp. 41–77. Lund: Lund Business Press.

Foss, N.J. and Klein, P.G. (2005). Entrepreneurship and the economic theory of the firm: any gains from trade? In R. Agarwal, S.A. Alvarez, and O. Sorenson (eds), *Handbook of Entrepreneurship Research: Disciplinary Perspectives*, pp. 55–80. New York: Springer.

Foss, N.J. and Klein, P.G. (2010). Entrepreneurial alertness and opportunity discovery: origins, attributes, critique, pp. 98–120. In H. Landström and F. Lohrke (eds), *Historical Foundations of Entrepreneurship Research*. Cheltenham, UK and Northampton, MA, USA: Edward Elgar Publishing.

Foss, N.J. and Klein, P.G. (2012). *Organizing Entrepreneurial Judgment: A New Approach to the Firm*. Cambridge: Cambridge University Press.

Foss, N.J. and Lyngsie, J. (2014). The strategic organization of the entrepreneurial established firm. *Strategic Organization*, **12**(3), 208–15.

Foss, N.J., Lyngsie, J., and Zahra, S.A. (2013). The role of external knowledge sources and organizational design in the process of opportunity exploitation. *Strategic Management Journal*, **34**(12), 1453–71.

Foss, N.J., Lyngsie, J., and Zahra, S.A. (2015). Organizational design correlates of entrepreneurship: the roles of decentralization and formalization for opportunity discovery and realization. *Strategic Organization*, **13**(1), 32–60.

Galbraith, J. (1974). Organization design: an information processing view. *Interfaces*, **4**, 28–36.

Gartner, W.B., Carter, N.M., and Hills, G.E. (2003). The language of opportunity. In C. Steyaert and D. Hjorth (eds), *New Movements in Entrepreneurship*, pp. 103–24. Cheltenham, UK and Northampton, MA, USA: Edward Elgar Publishing.

Gifford, S. (1992). Allocation of entrepreneurial attention. *Journal of Economic Behavior and Organization*, **19**, 265–84.

Hill, K.G. and Amabile, T.M. (1993). A social-psychological perspective on creativity: intrinsic motivation and creativity in the classroom and workplace. pp. 400–432. In S.G. Isaksen, M.C. Murdoch, R.L. Firestien, and D.J. Treffinger (eds), *Understanding and Recognizing Creativity*. Norwood, NJ: Ablex.

Hitt, M.A., Ireland, R.D., Camp, S.M., and Sexton, D.L. (2001). Guest editors' introduction to the Special Issue. Strategic entrepreneurship: entrepreneurial strategies for wealth creation. *Strategic Management Journal*, **22**, 479–91.

Holmström, B. (1989). Agency costs and innovation. *Journal of Economic Behavior and Organization*, **12**, 305–27.

Hornsby, J., Kuratko, D., and Zahra, S.A. (2002). Middle managers' perception of the internal environment for corporate entrepreneurship: assessing a measurement scale. *Journal of Business Venturing*, **17**, 253–73.

Hornsby, J., Kuratko, D., Shepherd, D.A., and Bott, J.P. (2009). Managers' corporate entrepreneurial actions: examining perception and position. *Journal of Business Venturing*, **24**, 236–47.

Ireland, R.D., Covin, J.G., and Kuratko, D. (2009). Conceptualizing corporate entrepreneurship strategy. *Entrepreneurship Theory and Practice*, **33**, 19–46.

Ireland, R.D., Hitt, M.A., and Sirmon, D.G. (2003). A model of strategic entrepreneurship: the construct and its dimensions. *Journal of Management*, **29**, 963–89.

Ireland, R.D., Hitt, M.A., Camp, S.M., and Sexton, D.L. (2001). Integrating entrepreneurship and strategic management actions to create firm wealth. *The Academy of Management Executive*, **15**, 49–63.

Jackson, J. and Morgan, C. (1982). *Organization Theory*. Englewood, NJ: Prentice-Hall.

Jansen, J., Van Den Bosch, F.A.J. and Volberda, H.W. (2006). *Exploratory Innovation, Exploitative Innovation, and Performance: Effects of Organizational Antecedents and Environmental Moderators*. ERIM Report Series Reference No. ERS-2006-038-STR.

Jensen, M.C. and Meckling, W.H. (1992). Knowledge, control and organizational structure: parts I and II. In L. Werin and H. Wijkander (eds), *Contract Economics*, pp. 251–74. Oxford: Blackwell.

Jones, G.R. and Butler, J.E. (1992). Managing internal corporate entrepreneurship: an agency theory perspective. *Journal of Management*, **18**, 733–49.

Kirzner, I.M. (1973). *Competition and Entrepreneurship*. Chicago, IL: University of Chicago Press.

Klein, K.J., Dansereau, F., and Hall, R.J. (1994). Levels issues in theory development, data collection and analysis. *Academy of Management Review*, **19**, 195–229.

Klein, P.G. (2008). Opportunity discovery, entrepreneurial action, and economic organization. *Strategic Entrepreneurship Journal*, **2**(3), 175–90.

Knight, F.H. (1921). *Risk, Uncertainty and Profit*. Boston, MA: Houghton Mifflin Company.

Kozlowski, S.W.J. and Klein, K.J. (2000). A multilevel approach to theory and research in organizations: contextual, temporal, and emergent processes. In K.J. Klein and S.W.J. Kozlowski (eds), *Multilevel Theory, Research, and Methods in Organizations: Foundations, Extensions, and New Directions*, pp. 3–90. San Francisco, CA: Jossey-Bass.

Kuratko, D., Ireland, R.D., and Hornsby, J. (2004). Corporate entrepreneurship behaviour among managers: a review of theory, research and practice. *Advances in Entrepreneurship, Firm Emergence and Growth*, **7**, 7–45.

Kuratko, D.F., Ireland, R.D., Covin, J.G., and Hornsby, J.S. (2005). A model of middle-level managers' entrepreneurial behavior. *Entrepreneurship Theory and Practice*, **29**, 699–716.

Lazear, E.P. (2005). Entrepreneurship. *Journal of Labor Economics*, **23**, 649–77.

Linder, S., Lyngsie, J., Foss, N.J. and Zahra, S.A. (2015). Wise choices: how thoroughness of opportunity appraisal, incentives, and performance evaluation fit together. *IEEE Transactions on Engineering Management*, **62**(4), 484–94.

Lovas, B. and Ghoshal, S. (2000). Strategy as guided evolution. *Strategic Management Journal*, **21**, 875–96.

MacInnis, D.J., Moorman, C., and Jaworski, B.J. (1991). Enhancing and measuring consumers' motivation, opportunity, and ability to process brand information from ads. *Journal of Marketing*, **55**, 32–53.

Mahnke, V., Venzin, M., and Zahra, S.A. (2007). Governing entrepreneurial opportunity recognition in MNEs: aligning interests and cognition under uncertainty. *Journal of Management Studies*, **44**, 1278–98.

McGrath, R.G. (1999). Falling forward: real options reasoning and entrepreneurial failure. *Academy of Management Review*, **24**, 13–30.

McMullen, J.S. and Shepherd, D.A. (2005). Entrepreneurial action and the role of uncertainty in the theory of the entrepreneur. *Academy of Management Review*, **31**, 132–52.

Miller, D. and Dröge, C. (1986). Psychological and traditional determinants of structure. *Administrative Science Quarterly*, **3**, 539–60.

Mintzberg, H. (1983). *Structures in Fives*. Englewood Cliffs, NJ: Prentice-Hall.

Mises, L. (1949). *Human Action*. New Haven, CT: Yale University Press.

Nahapiet, J. and Ghoshal, S. (1998). Social capital, intellectual capital, and the organizational advantage. *Academy of Management Review*, **23**, 242–66.

Osterloh, M. and Frey, B. (2000). Motivation, knowledge transfer and organizational form. *Organization Science*, **11**, 538–50.

Ouchi, W.G. (1977). The relationship between organizational structure and organizational control. *Administrative Science Quarterly*, **22**, 95–113.

Ouchi, W.G. (1980). Markets, bureaucracies, and clans. *Administrative Science Quarterly*, **25**, 129–41.

Rousseau, D.M. (1985). Issues of level in organizational research: multi-level and cross-level perspectives. *Research in Organizational Behavior*, **7**, 1–37.

Rumelt, R.P. (1987). Theory, strategy, and entrepreneurship. In D. Teece (ed.), *The Competitive Challenge*, pp. 11–32. Cambridge, MA: Ballinger.

Sah, R. and Stiglitz, J. (1985). Human fallibility and economic organization. *American Economic Review*, **75**, 292–7.

Sarasvathy, D.K., Simon, H.A., and Lave, L. (1998). Perceiving and managing business risks: differences between entrepreneurs and bankers. *Journal of Economic Behavior & Organization*, **33**, 207–25.

Sathe, V. (1989). Fostering entrepreneurship in the large, diversified firm. *Organizational Dynamics*, **18**, 20–32.

Schoonhoven, C., Eisenhardt, K., and Lyman, K. (1990). Speeding products to market: waiting time to first product introduction in new firms. *Administrative Science Quarterly*, **35**, 177–207.

Schumpeter, J. (1934). *The Theory of Economic Development*, 1911, translated by Redvers Opie. Cambridge, MA: Harvard University Press.

Schumpeter, J. (1942). *Capitalism. Socialism and Democracy*. New York: Harper and Row.

Shackle, G.L.S. (1979). *Imagination and the Nature of Choice*. Edinburgh: Edinburgh University Press.

Shane, S. (2000). Prior knowledge and the discovery of entrepreneurial opportunities. *Organization Science*, **11**, 448–69.

Shane, S. and Venkataraman, S. (2000). The promise of entrepreneurship as a field of research. *Academy of Management Review*, **25**, 217–26.

Shepherd, D.A. and DeTienne, D.R. (2005). Prior knowledge, potential financial reward, and opportunity identification. *Entrepreneurship Theory and Practice*, **29**, 91–113.

Simsek, Z. (2009). Organizational ambidexterity: towards a multilevel understanding. *Journal of Management Studies*, **46**, 597–624.

Stam, E. (2015). Entrepreneurial ecosystems and regional policy: a sympathetic critique. *European Planning Studies*, **23**, 1759–69.

Stinchcombe, A.L. (1991). The conditions of fruitfulness of theorizing about mechanisms in social science. *Philosophy of the Social Sciences*, **21**, 367–88.

Stopford, J.M. and Baden-Fuller, C. (1994). Creating corporate entrepreneurship. *Strategic Management Journal*, **15**, 521–36.

Sykes, H.B. and Block, Z. (1989). Corporate venturing obstacles: sources and solutions. *Journal of Business Venturing*, **4**, 159–67.

Teece, D.J. (1986). Profiting from technological innovation: implications for integration, collaboration, licensing and public policy. *Research Policy*, **15**, 285–305.

Teece, D.J. (1992). Competition, cooperation, and innovation: organizational arrangements for regimes of rapid technological progress. *Journal of Economic Behavior and Organization*, **18**(1), 1–25.

Teece, D.J. (1993). The dynamics of industrial capitalism: perspectives on Alfred Chandler's scale and scope. *Journal of Economic Literature*, **31**(1), 199–225.

Teece, D.J. (2007). Explicating dynamic capabilities: the nature and micro foundations of (sustainable) enterprise performance. *Strategic Management Journal*, **28**, 1319–50.

Thompson, J.D. (1967). *Organizations in Action*. New York: McGraw-Hill.

Tsai, W. (2001). Knowledge transfer in intraorganizational networks: effects of network position and absorptive capacity on business unit innovation and performance. *Academy of Management Journal*, **44**, 996–1004.

Tsai, W. and Ghoshal, S. (1998). Social capital and value creation: the role of intrafirm networks. *Academy of Management Journal*, **41**, 464–76.

Venkataraman, S. (1997). The distinctive domain of entrepreneurship research. *Advances in Entrepreneurship, Firm Emergence and Growth*, **3**, 119–38.

Wennekers, S. and Thurik, R. (1999). Linking entrepreneurship and economic growth. *Small Business Economics*, **13**, 27–56.

Williamson, O.E. (1975). *Markets and Hierarchies*. New York: Free Press.

Williamson, O.E. (1985). *The Economic Institutions of Capitalism: Firms, Markets, Relational Contracting*. New York: Free Press.

Witt, U. (2007). Firms as realizations of entrepreneurial visions. *Journal of Management Studies*, **44**, 1125–40.

Zahra, S.A. (1996). Governance, ownership, and corporate entrepreneurship: the moderating impact of industry technological opportunities. *Academy of Management Journal*, **39**, 1713–35.

Zahra, S.A., Jennings, D.F., and Kuratko, D. (1999). The antecedents and consequences of firm-level entrepreneurship: the state of the field. *Entrepreneurship Theory and Practice*, **24**, 45–65.

Zander, U. and Kogut, B. (1995). Knowledge and the speed of the transfer and imitation of organizational capabilities: an empirical test. *Organization Science*, **6**, 76–92.

5. Industry specificity and the effect of internal social capital in reward-based crowdfunding

Vincenzo Butticè* and Massimo G. Colombo

5.1 INTRODUCTION

A beautiful, lush, floating pool on the banks of the Thames.[1] A film containing Orson Wells's last memories.[2] A space defense system to prevent asteroid smashes.[3] All these entrepreneurial projects share some common ground: they sought money through reward-based crowdfunding campaigns.

Reward-based crowdfunding, the practice of collecting monetary contribution from the crowd in exchange for the delivery of products or services (Belleflemme et al., 2014), is gaining more and more resonance worldwide. The growth of the phenomenon has been extraordinary. In less than five years, more than 400,000 projects have been crowdfunded and more than $5 billion have been collected through crowdfunding platforms (Crowdfunding Industry Report, 2015). This increasing economic relevance has led researchers from different fields, such as economics (Acemoglu et al., 2014), management (Mollick, 2014) and information technology (Walsh, 2014), to start studying this phenomenon.

Initial contributions have mainly focused on discriminating reward-based crowdfunding from somewhat similar phenomena, such as peer-to-peer lending (Zhang and Liu, 2012), micro-credit (Khandker, 1998) and equity crowdfunding (Agrawal et al., 2013). Concurrently, scholars have stressed that the advantages of reward-based crowdfunding go beyond the collection of capital, and also relate to collecting non-financial resources in the form of feedbacks (Agrawal et al., 2013; Colombo et al., 2015a) and social capital (Butticè et al., 2017). In this vein, reward-based crowdfunding is seen as promoting the development of new entrepreneurial ecosystems (Lambert and Schwienbacher, 2010; Frydrych et al., 2014) and favoring the diffusion of startups (Weber and Hine, 2015). This is particularly true for those individuals located in places not known for entrepreneurship, who are often excluded from traditional forms of entrepreneurial funding (Fleming and Sorenson, 2016). Crowdfunding is reported to be a way to democratize access to capital and helps startups located outside traditional venture capital hubs to emerge (Mollick and Robb, 2016). Crowdfunding also arose as a valuable source of funding for highly risky startups (Agrawal et al., 2016) and women (Mollick and Robb, 2016), both often excluded from venture capital funding. It thus seems reasonable to believe that crowdfunding may allow a more diverse spectrum of people to become entrepreneurs, and, in turn, may lead to the transformation of the entrepreneurial ecosystem (Mathews, 1997; Zacharakis et al., 2003).

Given these premises, focusing on understanding how entrepreneurs can take advantage of crowdfunding is an immediate consequence. Several recent studies have examined factors that drive entrepreneurs to succeed in collecting funding through a reward-based crowdfunding campaign. Scholars have highlighted the role of the design of the campaign (Belleflemme et al., 2014), proponents' human capital (Ahlers et al., 2014), and backers' commitment (Kuppuswamy and Bayus, 2017). Within this strand of literature, project proponents' social capital has been identified as a primary determinant of the success of the campaign. Previous works have stressed the importance of family and friends (Agrawal et al., 2011) and personal acquaintances (Mollick, 2014), showing that both direct and online contacts are relevant for collecting money. Similarly, Colombo et al. (2015b) consider social capital within the crowdfunding platform – that is, internal social capital – and document that its effect on the success of a reward-based crowdfunding campaign is even greater in magnitude compared to other forms of social capital. However, the authors underline the need for additional research that aims at verifying whether their results hold after controlling for industry specificities. The present chapter aims to fill this gap.

In particular, the chapter contributes to the current debate on the role of social capital in crowdfunding and more generally in early stage financing (Shane and Cable, 2002; Shane and Stuart, 2002; Zhang and Liu, 2012; Jonsson and Lindbergh, 2013) by analysing how internal social capital helps to attract financial contributions depending on product characteristics. Similar to Colombo and colleagues (2015b), we maintain that social capital triggers reciprocation through a feeling of mutual obligation (Coleman, 1988). However, we posit that industry specificities influence the effectiveness of this mechanism. Descriptive evidence, indeed, suggests that project proponents in eight out of ten cases finance products coming from the same industry as their own product. Therefore, when the product object of the crowdfunding campaign belongs to an industry characterized by high demand uncertainty and task complexity, it is highly likely that the proponent had financed the same kind of product in the past. In the funding of such products, repeated interactions with the other members of the community are favored. These conditions lead to the emergence of embedded relationships and make social norms of reciprocity stronger. Therefore, we expect that for these products the internal social capital has a positive effect on the probability of collecting funding that is greater in magnitude than other forms of social capital.

To test our hypothesis, we use a set of probit models on a sample of 34,121 projects launched during the first nine months of 2014 on Kickstarter. Results fully support our arguments that the effect of the proponents' internal social capital on the probability of project success changes in magnitude depending on the characteristic of the industry. In particular, social capital developed within the platform has a greater effect in industries such as Technology, Fashion Design and Videogames, characterized by high uncertainty. In addition, in line with the results of Colombo et al. (2015b), we show that the effect of internal social capital is greater than that of external social capital, independent of the industry. The chapter is organized as follows. The next section presents the conceptual background and research hypotheses. It is followed by a presentation of the data and methodology. We next illustrate the econometric models and empirical results and discuss the robustness of the estimates. The final section discusses implications for scholars and practitioners.

5.2   THEORETICAL BACKGROUND

Several studies have highlighted that project proponents' social capital, namely the sum of actual and potential resources embedded within the networks of connections (Nahapiet and Ghoshal, 1998) and available to project proponents through the contacts these networks bring (Burt, 2000), plays a prominent role in attracting financial resources during a crowdfunding campaign.

Agrawal et al. (2011), by investigating the role of geography in influencing the dynamics of success of a crowdfunding project, showed that the majority of the early backers are people with whom the proponents have social contacts including close friendships and familiar relationships. These contacts play a key role in determining the overall success of the campaign by providing an indirect clue about project quality and triggering imitating behavior. A similar result is highlighted by Ordanini and colleagues (2011) who stressed that in the initial phase of a crowdfunding campaign, contributions are primarily made by close friends of the proponents.

The literature has highlighted that online social connections also have a positive effect on the success of the crowdfunding campaign. Mollick (2014) shows that the number of Facebook friends of proponents is positively related to the number of backers. Moreover, he finds that not having a Facebook account is better than having few Facebook friends. In a similar vein, Colombo and colleagues (2015b) highlight that professional acquaintances, proxied by the number of LinkedIn connections, are positively related with early backers. In general, these studies confirm the findings of prior literature on early stage financing which stressed that social capital helps overcome the information asymmetries between emerging entrepreneurs and external investors (Shane and Cable, 2002; Jonsson and Lindbergh, 2013).

Colombo and colleagues (2015b) make a further step in examining the role of social capital for the success of a crowdfunding campaign. The authors document that social capital developed within the platform (i.e., internal social capital) has a positive effect on the probability of collecting funding and its effect is even greater in magnitude compared with other forms of social capital. According to the authors, financing others' projects leads to embedded relationships within the platform and engenders the rise of unwritten social norms of reciprocity. Therefore, in such a setting, proponents who had developed several social ties are more likely to receive monetary contributions. In this chapter, we move from this argument and acknowledge that the emergence of norms of reciprocity not only depends on the number of projects the proponents had backed in the past but is also affected by the industry in which the product belongs.

Prior research, indeed, has suggested that product specificities influence the proportion of embedded ties in a network (Jonsson and Lindbergh, 2013). Specifically, products belonging to industries characterized by higher levels of demand uncertainty and task complexity lead to repeated interactions between project proponents and backers (Jones et al., 1997). Backers, especially in the early phases of the crowdfunding campaign, offer suggestions and feedback that proponents use to improve their products and make them more suitable to customers' tastes (Colombo et al., 2015b). These repeated interactions engender greater social identification with the proponent (Moran, 2005). Thus, such products help the proponent to develop embedded relationships within the platform (Granovetter, 1992) and ultimately strengthen the norms of reciprocity across the community (Williamson, 1985; Coleman, 1988).

Demand uncertainty is generated by rapid shifts in consumer preferences and seasonality. These conditions are well exemplified in both the entertainment industry (e.g., Music), wherein it is difficult to ascertain what makes a new album a hit (Peterson and Berger, 1971), and the haute cuisine industry, where customers are always looking for novel and tasteful dishes (Rao et al., 2003; Petruzzelli and Savino, 2014). Another case in point is the fashion industry (Uzzi, 1997), where heterogeneous demand (Djelic and Ainamo, 1999), short life cycles and tremendous variety (Sen, 2008) make predicting demand a difficult task.

Task complexity, which refers to the number of different specialized inputs needed to complete a product or service (Salancik and Pfeffer, 1978), leads to repeated exchanges between the members of the community and the proponent. Industries that exhibit this feature are, with no doubt, the high-tech industry (Barley et al., 1992) and the videogames industry (Tschang, 2007).

Therefore, we expect:

H1: The magnitude of the effect of social capital on the probability of success in a crowdfunding campaign varies across industries.
H2: The effects of social capital are higher in industries characterized by higher levels of demand uncertainty and task complexity. Such industries are Music, Haute Cousine, Fashion Design, High-Tech and Games.

5.3   SAMPLE AND VARIABLE

To test the hypotheses presented in this chapter, we collected all the projects posted on Kickstarter from 1 January 2014 to 12 September 2014. Focusing on Kickstarter offers several advantages. First, the platform is the largest existing crowdfunding platform both in terms of money collected and projects financed (Colombo et al., 2015b). From its inception, about 232,000 projects have been launched in the platform at the time of writing, and of these about 85,000 have been successfully funded, collecting more than $1.73 billion.[4] Therefore, Kickstarter provides numerous, easily accessible data for examining the effects of social capital on the success of a campaign. Second, Kickstarter has a generalist target and hosts crowdfunding campaigns in a large number of categories, including art, dance and theater, fashion design, film, food, games, music, publishing and technology. This allows us to investigate the effects of both internal and external social capital on projects belonging to different industries. Third, this setting offers an ideal test-bed for empirical work. Indeed, it allows us to control for virtually all the information that backers could use at the time they took the decision on whether or not to fund the project. Finally, Kickstarter.com data have been used in several prior studies of crowdfunding (Kuppuswamy and Bayus, 2017; Mollick, 2014; Colombo et al., 2015b), making results comparable and potentially replicable.

Our unit of analysis is the crowdfunding campaign. For each of these, we collected three sets of information. First, we collected information related to the project: the number of visuals (videos plus images) contained within the project description (*ln_visuals*), the industry, the duration of the campaign (*duration*), the number of links to external websites with further information about the project (*more_information*), and the target capital of the campaign expressed in dollars (*ln_target*). When the project was expressed in currencies different from the dollar, we used a monthly average exchange rate to make all the figures comparable.

A second set of information related to the rewards offered in the campaign. Kickstarter allows the proponents to offer a wide variety of rewards besides the product presale. Several projects offer customized products, such as a videogames special edition with the main character sharing the backer's traits. Similarly, projects offer what we call "ego-boosting" types of rewards, such as including the backer's name in the film credits, and projects offering "community-belonging" types of rewards are widely diffused. The latter type of reward involves events that provide opportunities for social interaction (e.g., an invitation to a development workshop or to a launch party) and the offering of symbolic objects (e.g., a branded outfit) meant to display support for a project. We created a set of dummy variables indicating the presence of customized reward (*d_customized*), ego-boosting rewards (*d_ego*) and community rewards (*d_community*). In order to create reward variables, we ran a content analysis algorithm, based on a search of characterizing terms in the textual description of the rewards.[5] We tested the appropriateness of this methodology by running the algorithm on a test-sample of 669 projects whose rewards had been human-classified. Evaluations obtained through the algorithm were in line with the results provided by the evaluators.[6]

Finally, a third set of information relates to proponents. We coded internal social capital as represented by the number of Kickstarter projects that the proponent had financed at the time of the launch of the focal project (*int_social_capital*). This represents the degree to which a proponent had been active within the platform and is a proxy of the social connections with peers she had established in the community (Colombo et al., 2015b). Moreover, we recorded information about the number of the proponent's Facebook friends. This information is intended as a proxy of external social capital (*ext_social_capital*) and is available on the Kickstarter platform. We tend to prefer this measure of external social capital for two reasons. First, the same variable has been widely used in prior studies (e.g., Mollick, 2014; Kuppuswamy and Bayus, 2017), making our results easily comparable with extant literature. Second, the number of Facebook friends, unlike LinkedIn connections, also comprises the relationships based on kinship and friendship. These relationships play a significant role in influencing the funding dynamics (Agrawal et al., 2011) and are especially important when the product has a highly creative content (Caves, 2000), such as many of the products on Kickstarter. Information about Facebook friends was collected at the time of the project launch. Finally, we coded whether the proponent was located in the United States by means of a dummy variable (*d_USA*).

The summary statistics and definitions of the variables are shown in Table 5.1.

5.4   DESCRIPTIVE STATISTICS

Table 5.2 reports preliminary descriptive statistics by industry.

First, we report the number of crowdfunding campaigns presented in each industry. The projects belonging to the categories Film, Music, Games and Newsstand represent more than 55 percent of the overall campaigns. Projects related to Theater and Dance are rather rare (less than 4 percent of the total campaigns). Finally, projects in the categories Technology, Food, Fashion and Art each represent around 9 percent of the population.

Given that Kickstarter is an "all or nothing platform", which means that the money is cashed in by the proponent only if the capital pledged by the end of the campaign is equal to or greater than the target amount, we created a dummy variable *success* taking value 1 if the capital raised exceeds the target capital. Not surprisingly (Mollick, 2014; Colombo et al., 2015b), success is not evenly distributed between project categories.[7] Indeed, successful campaigns are more common in the categories Music, Games and Theater; while considerably lower than average in Food and Technology. Descriptive statistics on target capital reveal a peculiar feature of crowdfunding campaigns. On average, the total amount of capital that a project seeks to raise is limited ($18,451) with significant variance across projects. As discussed in previous literature, crowdfunding is a viable funding method especially addressed to projects with limited finances (Schwienbacher and Larralde, 2010). Data in the table confirm this contention. Moreover, figures reported show heterogeneity among categories. Projects belonging to Film, Music and, above all, Technology categories on average tend to ask for more capital. On the contrary, projects related either to artwork or to editorial content share the tendency to ask for less capital.

In addition, we computed the ratio between pledged and target capital to create a variable measuring the percentage of capital at closure. The distribution of this variable by industry is reported in Figure 5.1. The graphs show similarity and differences among categories. Independent from the project typology, the distribution of pledged capital follows a

Table 5.1   Variable description and summary statistics

	Obs.	Mean	St. Dev.	Min.	Max.	Variable Description
d_success	34,121	0.3103	0.4626	0	1	Dummy = 1 if pledged capital is greater or equal to target capital; 0 otherwise
int_social_capital	34,121	3.1703	10.879	0	259	Number of projects that the proponents had backed at the time of campaign launch
ext_social_capital	34,121	4.3927	7.1179	0	51.43	Number of Facebook connections/100
d_nofacebook	34,121	0.3614	0.4804	0	1	Dummy = 1 if the proponents do not have a Facebook account
duration	34,121	33.094	11.135	0	68	Duration of the campaign in days
ln_visuals	34,121	1.5676	0.9557	0.6931	5.1239	Ln(Number of pictures and videos in project description +1).
moreinfo	34,121	0.8057	0.5716	0	3.3672	Ln(Number of links external to Kickstarter provided in project description + 1)
d_US	34,121	0.7539	0.4307	0	1	Dummy = 1 if project location is in the United States; 0 otherwise
ln_target	34,121	8.4408	1.8523	0.6519	18.871	Ln(Target capital in thousand dollars)
d_ego	34,121	0.5615	0.4961	0	1	Dummy = 1 if the project has at least one reward that entails crediting the backers publicly
d_community	34,121	0.3897	0.4876	0	1	Dummy = 1 if the project has at least one reward that fosters feelings of community belonging
d_customized	34,121	0.2314	0.4217	0	1	Dummy = 1 if the project has at least one reward that offers a customized product or service

bimodal pattern.[8] Some differences exist across categories, referring to the first mode. Categories such as Technology and Food have a mode of approximately 0 percent, while other categories have a mode between 10 and 20 percent of the target capital. On the contrary, all the categories share the second mode at approximately 100 percent of the target capital.

Table 5.2 Descriptive statistics by project categories

	Technology		Food		Newsstand		Fashion and Design		Film	
Number of projects	2,772		3,308		5,827		4,418		5,289	
	Mean	St. Dev.	Mean	St. Dev.	Mean	St. Dev.	Mean	St. Dev.	Mean	St. Dev.
Success (%)	0.195	0.396	0.182	0.386	0.2943	0.456	0.294	0.456	0.358	0.479
Target capital ($)	45,323	88,587	20,396	57,297	10,220	31,602	19,082	43,547	23,293	66,525
Capital at closure (%)	1.207	16.90	0.502	3.808	0.683	4.861	1.191	49.45	0.776	13.44
Duration (days)	35.55	11.47	33.40	11.22	33.22	11.02	33.58	10.25	32.23	11.33

	Music		Games		Theater and Dance		Art and Crafts		All	
Number of projects	4,666		2,813		1,627		3,401		3,4121	
	Mean	St. Dev.	Mean	St. Dev.	Mean	St. Dev.	Mean	St. Dev.	Mean	St. Dev.
Success (%)	0.3585	0.4796	0.382	0.486	0.403	0.491	0.2959	0.456	0.311	0.463
Target capital ($)	23,293	66,525	24,886	68,776	11,653	53,119	10,380	43,280	18,451	55,222
Capital at closure (%)	0.776	13.44	5.277	92.44	1.038	15.77	0.888	8.414	1.794	86.07
Duration (days)	32.23	11.33	32.71	10.30	31.34	11.63	32.07	11.53	33.06	11.10

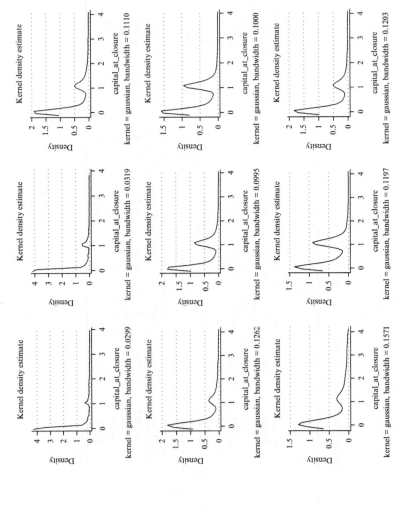

Figure 5.1   Capital at closure

Table 5.3 *Correlation matrix and VIF scores*

	1	2	3	4	5	6	7	8	9	10	11	12	VIF
1.success	1												
2.int_social_capital	0.1912*	1											01.08
3.ext_social_capital	0.1123*	0.0605*	1										01.31
4.d_nofacebook	−0.0518*	−0.0598*	−0.4649*	1									01.29
5.duration	−0.1739*	−0.0450*	−0.0135*	0.0046	1								01.06
6.ln_visual	0.2190*	0.2431*	0.0093	−0.0006	−0.0029	1							01.27
7.moreinfo	0.1872*	0.1316*	0.1622*	−0.0974*	−0.0363*	0.2743*	1						01.14
8.d_US	0.0284*	0.0668*	0.0966*	−0.0915*	−0.0069	−0.0276*	0.0211*	1					01.03
9.ln_target	−0.1345*	0.0180*	0.0348*	0.0213*	0.2117*	0.2791*	0.1533*	0.0277*	1				01.16
10.d_ego	0.0972*	0.0188*	0.0459*	−0.0348*	−0.0264*	0.1793*	0.1213*	−0.0111	0.0582*	1			01.10
11.d_community	0.0524*	0.0219*	0.0577*	−0.0385*	0.0066	0.1067*	0.1143*	0.0047	0.0907*	0.2338*	1		01.08
12.d_custom	0.0831*	0.0477*	0.0520*	−0.0434*	−0.0054	0.1764*	0.1236*	0.1104*	0.0872*	0.1503*	0.1225*	1	01.08

Notes: * p-value ≤ 0.05; VIF: variance inflation factor; mean VIF = 1.15.

Table 5.4   Results

dependent variable: success	(I) Controls	(II) Total Sample	(III) Technology	(IV) Food	(V) Newsstand
int_social_capital		0.0166***	0.0241***	0.0232***	0.0159***
		(0.001)	(0.004)	(0.004)	(0.002)
ext_social_capital		0.0195***	0.0229***	0.0017	0.0206***
		(0.001)	(0.008)	(0.006)	(0.003)
d_nofacebook		0.0703***	0.0585	−0.0674	0.0380
		(0.018)	(0.075)	(0.067)	(0.046)
duration	−0.0194***	−0.0191***	−0.0121***	−0.0208***	−0.0180***
	(0.001)	(0.001)	(0.003)	(0.003)	(0.002)
ln_visual	0.3490***	0.3169***	0.7157***	0.4387***	0.3909***
	(0.009)	(0.009)	(0.041)	(0.042)	(0.024)
moreinfo	0.3938***	0.3434***	0.2927***	0.4791***	0.3291***
	(0.014)	(0.014)	(0.063)	(0.055)	(0.036)
d_US	0.1251***	0.0684***	0.2635***	0.1827**	0.0027
	(0.018)	(0.018)	(0.072)	(0.080)	(0.045)
ln_target	−0.1782***	−0.1800***	−0.3152***	−0.1081***	−0.2153***
	(0.005)	(0.005)	(0.022)	(0.013)	(0.014)
ego	0.1475***	0.1538***	0.0144	0.0026	0.1276***
	(0.016)	(0.016)	(0.069)	(0.060)	(0.040)
community	0.0661***	0.0587***	−0.0370	0.2541***	0.0404
	(0.016)	(0.016)	(0.068)	(0.058)	(0.040)
custom	0.1107***	0.1103***	0.0233	0.2122***	0.2344***
	(0.018)	(0.018)	(0.074)	(0.067)	(0.046)
Constant	0.4705***	0.4410***	0.4007**	−0.6597***	0.5866***
	(0.042)	(0.043)	(0.199)	(0.137)	(0.122)
Observations	34,121	34,121	2,772	3,308	5,827

Notes: Standard errors in parentheses. *** $p < 0.01$, ** $p < 0.05$, * $p < 0.10$. Probit estimate.

Our data show considerably less variation in referring to the campaign duration. The typical duration of a funding campaign is one month, with 15, 45, and 60 days being other common periods. With limited variance, this result stands by industry.

5.5   RESULTS

We test our hypotheses by means of a set of probit models, wherein the dependent variable is a dummy value taking 1 if the campaign raised at least 100 percent of the target capital and 0 otherwise. Results are reported in Table 5.4. The models in columns I and II report the estimates run on the full sample, while the following columns show the estimates by industry.

(VI) Fashion/Design	(VII) Film	(VIII) Music	(IX) Games	(X) Theater/Dance	(XI) Art/Craft
0.0268***	0.0197***	0.0481***	0.0118***	0.0207***	0.0106***
(0.003)	(0.003)	(0.006)	(0.001)	(0.008)	(0.003)
0.0200***	0.0159***	0.0098***	0.0037	0.0133***	0.0151***
(0.004)	(0.003)	(0.002)	(0.006)	(0.005)	(0.004)
0.0487	0.0300	0.1739***	0.0327	0.0712	−0.0091
(0.053)	(0.046)	(0.050)	(0.063)	(0.082)	(0.058)
−0.0114***	−0.0209***	−0.0186***	−0.0167***	−0.0201***	−0.0214***
(0.002)	(0.002)	(0.002)	(0.003)	(0.003)	(0.002)
0.5590***	0.3308***	0.1974***	0.6380***	0.0615	0.3450***
(0.029)	(0.025)	(0.032)	(0.035)	(0.055)	(0.030)
0.3037***	0.1022***	0.2384***	0.2614***	0.1032	0.3806***
(0.044)	(0.035)	(0.037)	(0.058)	(0.065)	(0.046)
−0.0495	−0.0033	0.1767***	0.2371***	0.2551***	−0.0570
(0.051)	(0.044)	(0.052)	(0.063)	(0.079)	(0.056)
−0.2734***	−0.2527***	−0.1822***	−0.3172***	−0.1783***	−0.1667***
(0.016)	(0.014)	(0.017)	(0.020)	(0.027)	(0.015)
−0.0398	0.3588***	0.2027***	−0.0941	0.1373*	0.1304**
(0.046)	(0.047)	(0.041)	(0.057)	(0.071)	(0.051)
−0.0621	−0.0316	0.2531***	−0.2361***	0.1707**	0.1240**
(0.052)	(0.039)	(0.041)	(0.058)	(0.067)	(0.054)
0.0461	0.0264	0.1519***	0.2497***	0.0617	0.0718
(0.049)	(0.046)	(0.047)	(0.062)	(0.084)	(0.058)
0.5363***	1.4599***	0.7667***	0.8956***	1.1684***	0.3854***
(0.140)	(0.117)	(0.146)	(0.171)	(0.222)	(0.131)
4,418	5,289	4,664	2,813	1,627	3,401

Results in model I indicates that all control variable signs are in line with prior crowdfunding literature. As expected, the success of the campaign is negatively related with the duration and the size of the project expressed by the target capital of the campaign (Mollick, 2014). The higher the capital the project proponent is seeking, the lower the probability of success. Likewise, choosing a longer duration of the campaign reveals a proponent's lack of confidence (Mollick, 2014) and is associated with lower chances of success. The number of images and videos (*ln_visual*) included in the project description show a positive and significant coefficient. Making a video is strongly suggested by Kickstarter itself and may be regarded as a proxy of project quality (Mollick, 2014). Projects in the United States are 4.2 percent more likely to succeed (p-value < 0.01). The coefficient of *more_information*, which is a proxy of the completeness of the information provided by the project proponent, is positive and significant (p-value < 0.01). With respect to offering only the pre-purchase of the product, offering a customized product within the campaign is associated with a 3.7 percent increase in the likelihood of success. Likewise, offering rewards that foster internal motivations (Deci and Ryan, 1985) entails an increase in the likelihood of success of 4.9 percent (ego-boosting rewards) and 2.2 percent (community-belonging rewards). All these effects are significant with a confidence of 99 percent.

Let us now turn to the explanatory variables capturing proponents' social capital. As expected, when we run the estimates on the full sample (column II), both internal and external social capital are positively related with the likelihood of success. This result is in line with prior literature (Mollick, 2014; Colombo et al., 2015b). Moreover, the magnitude of the effects of both internal and external social capital is quite relevant. With all continuous covariates at their mean and dummy variables at their median value, a one-standard deviation increase of *int_social_capital* leads to a 48 percent increase (from 13.4 percent to 19.6 percent) in the likelihood of success. Likewise, the corresponding increase of *ext_social_capital*, proxied by the number of Facebook friends, entails a 28 percent (from 13.9 percent to 17.8 percent) positive shift in the chances of a project being successful. In line with prior studies, having no Facebook friends is better than having few connections on the famous social network (Mollick, 2014).

Let us now consider the estimates relating to the specific industry effect (Models III–XI). In all these models, the effect of internal social capital is positively and significantly related to the probability of success. However, the magnitude of this effect varies by industry. This supports our Hypothesis 1 that the positive effect of social capital developed within the funding platform on the likelihood of success of the campaign varies by industry. To assess the economic magnitude of internal social capital we set all continuous variables at their mean values and all dummy variables at their median value, and we computed the increase in the estimated likelihood of success engendered by a one-standard deviation increase in the independent variable (McDonald and Moffit, 1980). These results are reported in Table 5.5. The estimates show, in line with Hypothesis 2, that the effect of internal social capital is greater in industries such as Food (33 percent increase, from 11 to 15 percent), Games (32 percent increase, from 34 to 45 percent), Music (32 percent increase, from 34 to 45 percent), and Technology (30 percent increase, from 12 to 16 percent). In contrast, the magnitude of the effect of internal social capital is limited for projects belonging to the categories Theater and Dance (7 percent increase, from 39 to 42 percent) and Art and Craft (9 percent increase, from 22 to 24 percent). Surprisingly, external social capital (*ext_soc_capital*) has no significant effect in project product categories (Food and Games), in which internal social capital has a particularly strong effect. Furthermore, overall,

Table 5.5 *Marginal effect (all coefficients are significant with a confidence of 99 percent)*

		Internal Social Capital			External Social Capital		
		Margin	95% Confidence Interval		Margin	95% Confidence Interval	
II-Full Sample	At mean	0.2826338	0.2721626	0.293105	0.2826338	0.2721626	0.293105
	Plus one-sd	0.3465476	0.3334695	0.3596256	0.3311441	0.3196966	0.3425916
III-Technology	At mean	0.1288989	0.0983858	0.1594121	0.1288989	0.0983858	0.1594121
	Plus one-sd	0.1679332	0.1295491	0.2063173	0.150293	0.1174672	0.1831188
IV-Food	At mean	0.1181315	0.0949637	0.1412993	0.1181315	0.0949637	0.1412993
	Plus one-sd	0.1541294	0.1236605	0.1845984	0.1199003	0.0955961	0.1442044
V-Newsstand	At mean	0.2488393	0.2236554	0.2740231	0.2488393	0.2236554	0.2740231
	Plus one-sd	0.3090052	0.2777838	0.3402266	0.2957191	0.2675082	0.32393
VI-Fashion/Design	At mean	0.2303412	0.2035533	0.2571291	0.2303412	0.2035533	0.2571291
	Plus one-sd	0.2834354	0.2522071	0.3146636	0.265412	0.2363476	0.2944764
VII-Film	At mean	0.3580805	0.3301997	0.3859614	0.3580805	0.3301997	0.3859614
	Plus one-sd	0.4113693	0.3784544	0.4442842	0.4020392	0.3724259	0.4316525
VIII-Music	At mean	0.3539728	0.3243734	0.3835722	0.3539728	0.3243734	0.3835722
	Plus one-sd	0.4568889	0.4152101	0.4985676	0.395108	0.3626332	0.4275724
IX-Games	At mean	0.3437274	0.2985457	0.3889091	0.3437274	0.2985457	0.3889091
	Plus one-sd	0.4557887	0.4025408	0.5090366	0.350602	0.304329	0.3968749
X-Dance/Theater	At mean	0.3933222	0.3413789	0.4452654	0.3933222	0.3413789	0.4452654
	Plus one-sd	0.4262936	0.3691367	0.4834505	0.4363164	0.3823967	0.4902361
XI-Art/Craft	At mean	0.2217519	0.1944244	0.2490794	0.2217519	0.1944244	0.2490794
	Plus one-sd	0.2485557	0.2161152	0.2809963	0.2341027	0.2065849	0.2616205

the magnitude of the effect of this variable is weaker than that of internal social capital. Lastly, when we run the estimates on subsamples divided by industry, we lose the positive effect of not having Facebook friends except for the music industry.

5.6   ROBUSTNESS CHECK

Some scholars have advised caution when comparing how the effects of variables differ across groups. Allison (1999), for instance, argues that there is potential peril in cross-group comparison when doing binary regression models. Indeed, in these models, when residual variation differs across group, it produces an apparent difference in coefficients that may lead to erroneous interpretation. Mood (2010) suggests that comparing marginal effects, as we have done here, is enough to assure the validity of the interpretation. However, this solution has not been unanimously accepted by scholars because comparing marginal effects actually corresponds to estimating a linear probability model in disguise.[9] In this debate the heterogeneous choice model (also known as the location scale model) has been proposed as a superior way of dealing with the problem (Williams, 2009). To this end, we run such a model to confirm the validity of our interpretations.

Table 5.6 shows the results of the model in which the variable *"theater and dance"* has been omitted. Thus, all the results should be interpreted as relative effect compared to this baseline. Heterogeneous choice regressions provide two sets of information. First, through the set of parameters *lnsigma*, this category of models provides hints about the residual variation across groups. When *lnsigma* is significantly different from zero, it means that residual variance in the group differs from that in the baseline. In our estimates, the unexplained variance in all subsamples is significantly lower compared with the category *"theater and dance"*.

Second, as already mentioned, heterogeneous choice models allow us to make a cross-group comparison of coefficients. When the interaction terms included in the model are significant, it means that the variable of interest has either a lower or greater effect on the dependent variable compared with the baseline. Therefore, in our case, the magnitude of the effect of *internal social capital* on the success of the campaign is always greater compared with the baseline (*theater and dance*). In line with the main model, the effect of social capital is greater in the categories Music (+3.9 percent), Food (+3.5 percent), Fashion (+1.65 percent) and Technology (+1.12 percent). Therefore, these estimates further confirm both hypotheses H1 and H2.

Table 5.6   Heterogeneous choice model

Variables	(1) Model
int_soc_cap x Tech	0.0115***
	(4.65)
int_soc_cap x Food	0.0349***
	(4.93)
int_soc_cap x Film	0.0096***
	(4.19)
int_soc_cap x Music	0.0390***
	(5.62)
int_soc_cap x Newsstand	0.0111***
	(7.11)
int_soc_cap x Fashion_Design	0.0165***
	(7.55)
int_soc_cap x Art_Crafts	0.0057**
	(3.10)
int_soc_cap x Games	0.0081***
	(7.25)
ext_soc_cap x Tech	0.00807**
	(2.83)
ext_soc_cap x Food	0.0127**
	(3.15)
ext_soc_cap x Film	0.0073***
	(4.40)
ext_soc_cap x Music	0.0043***
	(3.15)
ext_soc_cap x Newsstand	0.0124***
	(6.91)
ext_soc_cap x Fashion_Design	0.0059***
	(3.41)
ext_soc_cap x Art_Crafts	0.0094***
	(4.72)
ext_soc_cap x Games	0.0037
	(1.61)
Controls	Yes
lnsigma	
Film	−1.045***
	(−10.17)
Music	−0.849***
	(−7.70)
Food	−0.774***
	(−6.33)

Table 5.6 (continued)

Variables	(1) Model
Tech	−1.458***
	(−13.48)
Newsstand	−1.071***
	(−11.23)
Fashion/Design	−1.300***
	(−13.24)
Art/Craft	−1.060***
	(−10.72)
Games	−1.331***
	(−13.03)
Constant	−1.3952***
	(0.118)

Notes: Standard errors in parentheses. *** $p < 0.01$, ** $p < 0.05$, * $p < 0.10$.

5.7 CONCLUSIONS

Crowdfunding is emerging as a powerful way to promote the diffusion of startups (Flemming and Sorenson, 2016) and ultimately to transform existing entrepreneurial ecosystems (Frydrych et al., 2014). Use of crowdfunding platforms allows fundraisers to seek money at relatively low cost (Martinez-Canas et al., 2012), thus opening new doors to access the entrepreneurial ecosystem (Carroll and Khessina, 2005). In addition to providing funding, backers also represent the initial customers' base to the fundraisers (Gerber et al., 2012). Backers contribute to the testing of completely new products (Ordanini et al., 2011) and sometimes are directly involved in the product design by becoming co-developers (Gerber and Hui, 2013). These features of crowdfunding reduce the dependence of nascent entrepreneurs on other actors in the ecosystem, such as business angels and venture capitalists (Colombo and Shafi, 2016).

Several successful startups have been funded by the crowd over the years (Ordanini et al., 2011) and new entrepreneurs residing outside regions where venture capitalists are located have emerged (Mollick and Robb, 2016). Given these results, crowdfunding has generated considerable enthusiasm among scholars (see Butticè et al., 2018, for a comprehensive review), especially regarding the investigation of how entrepreneurs succeed in collecting money from the crowd.

Following prior literature on the topic, in this chapter we focus on the determinants of success of a crowdfunding campaign. We investigate how the effect of internal social capital (viz. the social capital developed within a community) varies across different industries. We show that the positive effect of internal social capital on the success of the crowdfunding campaign varies in magnitude depending on the type of product object of the campaign. We posit that industry specificities affect the conditions under which social capital works, namely, norms of reciprocity and mutual identification (Nahapiet and Ghosal, 1998), and consequently influence the effect of social capital in attracting financial contributions. Following the extant literature (Jones et al., 1997), we claim that social capital is more relevant in industries characterized by high demand uncertainty and task complexity.

By means of econometric estimates on a sample of 34,121 projects launched on Kickstarter during 2014, we show that internal social capital has a greater effect in magnitude when the crowdfunding campaign relates to a product belonging to industries characterized by high uncertainty and task complexity such as the product categories Music, High-Tech, Games, Food and Fashion Design. Furthermore, in line with Colombo et al. (2015b), we highlight that social capital developed within the crowdfunding platform always has a greater effect compared with other forms of social capital developed outside the platform. Finally, in contrast with prior studies (Mollick, 2014), we do not find any significant positive effect of not having Facebook friends when we focus on product category estimates.

The chapter contributes to the extant knowledge in a twofold manner. First, it contributes to the nascent crowdfunding literature, showing the importance of industry specificities in influencing the effect of the determinants of success. Specifically, we show that the effects of both internal and external social capital varies in magnitude by industry. Scholars interested in investigating the crowdfunding phenomenon should carefully consider this heterogeneity when developing their models. Second, the chapter contributes to the broader debate on social capital in early stage financing (Shane and Cable, 2002). In so doing, we highlight that the effect of social capital developed within the crowdfunding platform varies by industry and is far from being negligible. We think that our results call for future investigations in order to disentangle the signaling effect of social capital from social obligation and reciprocated behavior.

This chapter has some limitations that pave the way for further research. First, in measuring internal social capital as the number of connections within the crowdfunding platform, we do not consider the strength of such ties, disregarding the cognitive dimension of social capital (Foss and

Lorenzen, 2009). Studies considering these aspects could enable a more comprehensive understanding of the role of internal social capital in favoring the success of crowdfunding projects. Second, many scholars agree that social capital, by working as a signal of ability and trustworthiness, reduces information asymmetries and, therefore, influences the ability to obtain seed capital (Shane and Stuart, 2002). However, other scholars (e.g., Jonsson and Lindbergh, 2013) show that the links between social capital and seed financing go beyond the reduction of information asymmetries (Spence, 2002) and involve mutual identification and social obligations of reciprocity. In this chapter, we are unable to distinguish the magnitude of these effects or to assess their relative importance. Third, using data from a single platform advances some caution about the generalizability of our results. Kickstarter hosts projects only from the United States. Therefore, caution should be taken in extending our findings to other countries, because the social norms governing the behavior of members in crowdfunding communities may be culturally mediated. Developing a dataset that includes crowdfunding projects from multiple platforms would allow us to observe whether our results are platform specific rather than generalizable to different contexts.

Our results have interesting implications for practitioners. Estimates broadly confirm that internal social capital is a critical resource to achieve success in a crowdfunding campaign. However, its effect varies across industry. Platform managers, interested in attracting successful projects, should consider industry specificity when developing functionalities that enable social interactions. Designing functionalities that favor a strong identification and a sense of social proximity among project proponents and backers is a crucial activity especially for platforms that host project related to music, high-tech, food and fashion design. The study also has interesting implications for proponents whose projects belong to industries characterized by high demand uncertainty and task complexity. For these proponents it is crucial to back other members' projects and grow strong social connections within the platform before launching their own campaign. Based on these arguments, it appears clear that platforms should favor interaction between entrepreneurs. In turn, these actions may potentially contribute to transform the entrepreneurial ecosystem through the emergence of a shared feeling of support. This ultimately may lead entrepreneurs to support each other in order to increase their own chances of succeeding in the crowdfunding arena.

NOTES

*   Corresponding author.
1. https://www.kickstarter.com/projects/thamesbaths/thames-baths-a-new-beautiful-lido-for-the-river-th, accessed on 15 January 2018.
2. https://www.indiegogo.com/projects/finish-orson-welles-last-film, accessed on 15 January 2018.
3. https://www.indiegogo.com/projects/help-defend-earth-against-asteroid-threats#/story, accessed on 15 January 2018.
4. https://www.kickstarter.com/help/stats?ref=footer, accessed on 15 January 2018.
5. Thus, in building, for instance, the variable *d_customized* we looked at the presence of textual descriptions containing the root "*custom*" or its synonyms. The full dictionary is available upon request to the corresponding author.
6. The results of the algorithm were concordant with those provided by the evaluators in 98 percent of the cases.
7. The null hypothesis that successful campaigns are evenly distributed among categories is rejected at conventional confidence levels (Kruskal-Wallis test: $\chi^2[8] = 488.87$).
8. The Hartigan dip statistic is always significant at a confidence of 99 percent.
9. See the stata forum for an example: http://www.statalist.org/forums/forum/general-stata-discussion/general/390061-testing-average-marginal-effects-across-samples, accessed on 15 January 2018.

REFERENCES

Acemoglu, D., Mostagir, M., and Ozdaglar, A. (2014). Managing Innovation in a Crowd. NBER Working Paper No. W19852. National Bureau of Economic Research, Cambridge, MA. Available at: http://www.nber.org/papers/w19852, accessed 26 April 2015.

Agrawal, A., Catalini, C., and Goldfarb, A. (2011). The Geography of Crowdfunding. NBER Working Paper No. W16820. National Bureau of Economic Research, Cambridge, MA. Available at: http://papers.ssrn.com/sol3/papers.cfm?abstract_id=1770375, accessed 19 June 2015.

Agrawal, A.K., Catalini, C., and Goldfarb, A. (2013). Some Simple Economics of Crowdfunding. NBER Working Paper No. W19133. National Bureau of Economic Research, Cambridge, MA. Available at: http://www.nber.org/papers/w19133, accessed 26 April 2015.

Agrawal, A.K., Catalini, C., and Goldfarb, A. (2016). Are Syndicates the Killer App of Equity Crowdfunding? *California Management Review*, **58**(2), 111–21.

Ahlers, G.K., Cumming, D., Günther, C., and Schweizer, D. (2014). Signaling in Equity Crowdfunding. Working Paper. Available at SSRN: http://papers.ssrn.com/sol3/papers.cfm?abstract_id=2161587.

Allison, P.D. (1999). Comparing Logit and Probit Coefficients Across Groups. *Sociological Methods and Research*, **28**(2), 186–208.

Barley, S.R., Freeman, J., and Hybels, R.C. (1992). Strategic Alliances in Commercial Biotechnology. In N. Nohria and R. Eccles (eds), *Networks and Organizations*, pp. 311–47. Boston, MA: Harvard Business School Press.

Belleflamme, P., Lambert, T., and Schwienbacher, A. (2014). Crowdfunding: Tapping the Right Crowd. *Journal of Business Venturing*, **29**(5), 585–609.

Burt, R.S. (2000). The Network Structure of Social Capital. *Research in Organizational Behavior*, **22**, 345–423.

Butticè, V., Colombo, M.G., and Wright, M. (2017). Serial Crowdfunding, Social Capital, and Project Success. *Entrepreneurship Theory and Practice*, **41**(2), 183–207.

Butticè, V., Franzoni, C., Rossi-Lamastra, C., and Rovelli, P. (2018). The Road to Crowdfunding Success: A Review of Extant Literature. In A. Afuah, C. Tucci, and G. Viscusi (eds), *Crowdsourcing Context and Innovation*, pp. 35–65. Oxford: Oxford University Press.

Carroll, G.R. and Khessina, O.M. (2005). The Ecology of Entrepreneurship. In Z. Acs and D. Audretsch (eds), *Handbook of Entrepreneurship Research*, pp. 167–200. New York: Springer.

Caves, R.E. (2000). *Creative Industries*. Cambridge, MA: Harvard University Press.

Coleman, J.S. (1988). Social Capital in the Creation of Human Capital. *American Journal of Sociology*, S94, 95–120.

Colombo, M.G. and Shafi, K. (2016). Does Crowdfunding Help Firms Obtain Venture Capital and Angel Finance? Evidence from Kickstarter. SSRN, accessed on 21April 2016, https://papers.ssrn.com/sol3/papers.cfm?abstract_id=2785538.

Colombo, M.G., Franzoni, C., and Rossi-Lamastra, R. (2015a). Internal Social Capital and the Attraction of Early Contributions in Crowdfunding. *Entrepreneurship Theory and Practice*, **39**(1), Special Issue: Seeding Entrepreneurship with Microfinance, 75–100.

Colombo, M.G., Franzoni, C., and Rossi-Lamastra, R. (2015b). Cash from the Crowd. *Science*, **6240**(348), 1201–2.

Crowdfunding Industry Report (2015). Available at: http://research.crowdsourcing.org/2014cf-crowdfunding-industry-report, accessed 26 April 2015.

Deci, E.L. and Ryan, R.M. (1985). The General Causality Orientations Scale: Self-Determination in Personality. *Journal of Research in Personality*, **19**(2), 109–34.

Djelic, M.L. and Ainamo, A. (1999). The Coevolution of New Organizational Forms in the Fashion Industry: A Historical and Comparative Study of France, Italy, and the United States. *Organization Science*, **10**(5), 622–37.

Fleming, L. and Sorenson, O. (2016). Financing By and For the Masses: An Introduction to the Special Issue on Crowdfunding. *California Management Review*, **58**(2), 5–20.

Foss, N. and Lorenzen, M. (2009). Towards an Understanding of Cognitive Coordination: Theoretical Developments and Empirical Illustrations. *Organization Studies*, **30**(11), 1201–226.

Frydrych, D., Bock, A.J., Kinder, T., and Koeck, B. (2014). Exploring Entrepreneurial Legitimacy in Reward-based Crowdfunding. *Venture Capital*, **16**(3), 247–69.

Gerber, E.M. and Hui, J. (2013). Crowdfunding: Motivations and Deterrents for Participation. *ACM Transactions on Computer-Human Interaction* (TOCHI), **20**(6), 34–48.

Gerber, E.M., Hui, J.S., and Kuo, P.Y. (2012, February). Crowdfunding: Why People are Motivated to Post and Fund Projects on Crowdfunding Platforms. In *Proceedings of the ACM 2012 Conference on Computer Supported Cooperative Work* (Workshop Paper), pp. 9–10. Seattle, Washington, USA, February 11–15, 2012.

Granovetter, M. (1992). Problems of Explanation in Economic Sociology. In N. Nohria and R.G. Eccles (eds), *Networks and Organizations: Structure, Form, and Action*, pp. 25–56. Boston, MA: Harvard Business School Press.

Jones, C., Hesterly, W.S., and Borgatti, S.P. (1997). A General Theory of Network

Governance: Exchange Conditions and Social Mechanisms. *Academy of Management Review*, **22**(4), 911–45.

Jonsson, S. and Lindbergh, J. (2013). The Development of Social Capital and Financing of Entrepreneurial Firms: From Financial Bootstrapping to Bank Funding. *Entrepreneurship Theory and Practice*, **37**(4), 661–86.

Khandker, S.R. (1998). *Fighting Poverty with Microcredit: Experience in Bangladesh.* Oxford: Oxford University Press.

Kuppuswamy, V. and Bayus, B.L. (2017). Does my Contribution to your Crowdfunding Project Matter? *Journal of Business Venturing*, **32**(1), 72–89.

Lambert, T. and Schwienbacher, A. (2010). An Empirical Analysis of Crowdfunding. SSRN, 1578175.

Martinez-Canas, R., Ruiz-Palomino, P., and del Pozo-Rubio, R. (2012). Crowdfunding and Social Networks in the Music Industry: Implications for Entrepreneurship. *International Business and Economics Research Journal* (Online), **11**(13), 1471–92.

Mathews, J.A. (1997). A Silicon Valley of the East: Creating Taiwan's Semiconductor Industry. *California Management Review*, **39**(4), 26–54.

McDonald, J.F. and Moffit, R.A. (1980). The Uses of Tobit Analysis. *Review of Economics and Statistics*, **62**(2), 318–21.

Meyer, J.W. and Rowan, B. (1977). Institutionalized Organizations: Formal Structure as Myth and Ceremony. *American Journal of Sociology*, **83**(2), 340–63.

Mollick, E. (2014). The Dynamics of Crowdfunding: Determinants of Success and Failure. *Journal of Business Venturing*, **29**(1), 1–16.

Mollick, E. and Robb, A. (2016). Democratizing Innovation and Capital Access: The Role of Crowdfunding, *California Management Review*, **58**(2), 72–88.

Mood, C. (2010). Logistic Regression: Why We Cannot Do What We Think We Can Do, and What We Can Do About It. *European Sociological Review*, **26**(1), 67–82.

Moran, P. (2005). Structural vs. Relational Embeddedness: Social Capital and Managerial Performance. *Strategic Management Journal*, **26**(12), 1129–51.

Nahapiet, J. and Ghoshal, S. (1998). Social Capital, Intellectual Capital, and the Organizational Advantage. *Academy of Management Review*, **23**(2), 242–66.

Ordanini, A., Miceli, L., Pizzetti, M., and Parasuraman, A. (2011). Crowdfunding: Transforming Customers into Investors through Innovative Service Platforms. *Journal of Service Management*, **22**(4), 443–470.

Peterson, R.A. and Berger, D.G. (1971). Entrepreneurship in Organizations: Evidence from the Popular Music Industry. *Administrative Science Quarterly*, **10**, 97–106.

Petruzzelli, A.M. and Savino, T. (2014). Search, Recombination, and Innovation: Lessons from Haute Cuisine. *Long Range Planning*, **47**(4), 224–38.

Rao, H., Monin, P., and Durand, R. (2003). Institutional Change in Toque Ville: Nouvelle Cuisine as an Identity Movement in French Gastronomy. *American Journal of Sociology*, **108**(4), 795–843.

Salancik, G.R. and Pfeffer, J. (1978). A Social Information Processing Approach to Job Attitudes and Task Design. *Administrative Science Quarterly*, **23**(2), 224–53.

Schwienbacher, A. and Larralde, B. (2010). Crowdfunding of Small Entrepreneurial Ventures. Available at: https://ssrn.com/abstract=1699183.

Sen, A. (2008). The US Fashion Industry: A Supply Chain Review. *International Journal of Production Economics*, **114**(2), 571–93.

Shane, S. and Cable, D. (2002). Network Ties, Reputation, and the Financing of New Ventures. *Management Science*, **48**(3), 364–81.

Shane, S. and Stuart, T. (2002). Organizational Endowments and the Performance of University Start-ups. *Management Science*, **48**(1), 154–70.

Spence, M. (2002). Signaling in Retrospect and the Informational Structure of Markets. *American Economic Review*, **92**(3), 434–59.

Tschang, F.T. (2007). Balancing the Tensions Between Rationalization and Creativity in the Video Games Industry. *Organization Science*, **18**(6), 989–1005.

Uzzi, B. (1997). Social Structure and Competition in Interfirm Networks: The Paradox of Embeddedness. *Administrative Science Quarterly*, **42**(1), 35–67.

Walsh, A. (2014). Seek!: Creating and Crowdfunding a Game-based Open Educational Resource to Improve Information Literacy. *Insights: The UKSG Journal*, **27**(1), 63–7.

Weber, M.L. and Hine, M.J. (2015). Who Inhabits a Business Ecosystem? The Technospecies as a Unifying Concept. *Technology Innovation Management Review*, **5**(5), 69–78.

Williams, R. (2009). Using Heterogeneous Choice Models to Compare Logit and Probit Coefficients Across Groups. *Sociological Methods and Research*, **37**(4), 531–59.

Williamson, O.E. (1985). *The Economic Institutions of Capitalism: Firms, Markets and Relational Contracting*. New York: Free Press.

Zacharakis, A.L., Shepherd, D.A., and Coombs, J.E. (2003). The Development of Venture-capital-backed Internet Companies: An Ecosystem Perspective. *Journal of Business Venturing*, **18**(2), 217–31.

Zhang, J. and Liu, P. (2012). Rational Herding in Microloan Markets. *Management Science*, **58**(5), 892–912.

6. Accessing the creative ecosystem: evidence from UK fashion design micro enterprises

Alison Rieple, Jonathan Gander, Paola Pisano, Adrian Haberberg and Emily Longstaff

6.1 INTRODUCTION

The influence of the ecological environment on the behaviour of organizations is a matter of considerable interest to students of economics, innovation and strategic management (Breschi and Lissoni, 2001; DeCarolis and Deeds, 1999; Feldman, 1994; Martin and Sunley, 2003; Porter, 1995, 1998a, 1998b, 2000). Researchers in the cultural industries have taken a particular interest in the place-based and clustering characteristics of creative production (Florida, 2002; Lazzeretti et al., 2008; Maskell, 2007; Maskell and Lorenzen, 2004; Mommas, 2004; Scott, 2004). Cultural knowledge and practice is place based, with, for example, urban districts providing an aesthetic context for the production of symbolic meaning represented in music, fashion, and art scenes and products (Currid, 2007; Drake, 2003; Hauge and Hracs, 2010; Scott, 1999).

In the clothing design sector, studies have identified a local production/ global distribution structure (Pratt, 2002). Creative clusters, located in major urban centres such as Milan, London, Paris and New York, contain dense agglomerations of companies participating in rich ecosystems of knowledge, resources and socio-spatial externalities of trust and belief. These create products that can be mass reproduced and distributed worldwide (Bair and Gereffi, 2001; Bathelt and Turi, 2011). Fashion designers generate an ecosystem in order to benefit from close proximity to customers, competitors and locally embedded social and cultural resources (Ashton, 2006; Drake, 2003; Dwyer and Jackson, 2003; Rantisi, 2002, 2004; Rinallo and Golfetto, 2006).

In this chapter we use factor and cluster analysis to deepen our understanding of how micro fashion design firms use ecological resources. We focus on micro enterprises for two reasons: the importance to creative small

117

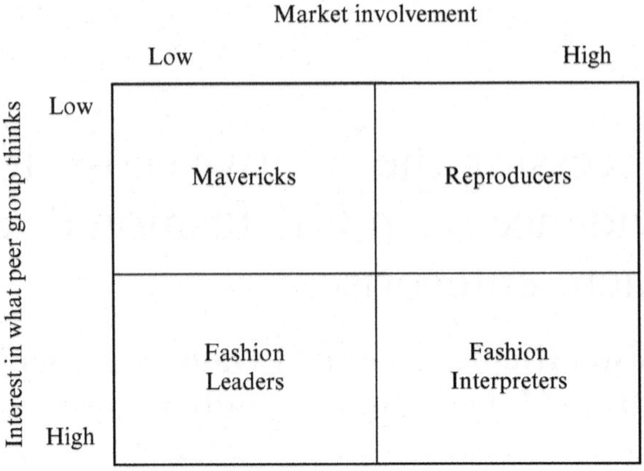

Market involvement

	Low	High
Low	Mavericks	Reproducers
High	Fashion Leaders	Fashion Interpreters

Interest in what peer group thinks

Source: Rieple and Gander (2009).

Figure 6.1   Typology of apparel designers

businesses of locally embedded resources (Grabher, 2002), and the fact that micro firms make intensive use of location-specific resources due to their limited size (Balkundi and Kilduff, 2005). What little is known about the strategic behaviour of micro enterprises points to the importance to them of supplementing their limited resources with those outside the firm, for example through personal networks (Gilmore et al., 2001) and observation and interaction with user communities (Di Maria and Finotto, 2008).

This chapter examines the impact of their ecosystem on the practices of fashion designers. This ecosystem includes what has been termed a socially sympathetic infrastructure (Pratt, 2002) and nodes: the mix of social spaces, meeting points and public areas such as markets and streets, as well as sources of inspiration such as museums and art galleries. We examine the extent to which creative micro enterprises such as fashion designers access external resources to compensate for their putative internal deficiencies. We do this by building on a typology of apparel designers (Rieple and Gander, 2009; Figure 6.1) and testing whether its combination of market and peer-based orientations explains the behaviour of our sample. We also examine resource nodes (Rieple and Gander, 2009): physical sites where actors in a design ecosystem may encounter one another and the material objects that are there (Law and Singleton, 2005), exchange ideas, give and receive emotional support and arrive at a shared understanding of design memes. We investigate their role in the transmission of symbolic knowledge and the negotiation of shared meanings, and how different types of designers may use these in different ways.

In the following sections we review the literature relating to the geography of fashion designing, and the ecological resources likely to be used during the creation of new garments. We then describe our research design and methodology, present our results and discuss the findings. Finally, we draw out implications for the study of creative production clusters.

6.2 LITERATURE REVIEW

Fashion clothing is a cultural good that conveys symbolic meaning, involves creativity in its production, and embodies some degree of intellectual property (Roodhouse, 2008; Throsby, 2004). However, clothing also has an element of functionality. It is the combination of these two aspects (Crane and Bovone, 2006; Molotch, 2002) that has led some cultural industry commentators to describe fashion designing as a hybrid (Hesmondhalgh, 2002) in which there are a number of possible strategic foci. This makes the clothing design industry an interesting one to examine in terms of the location of its inputs and design processes, and the attractiveness of certain locations for certain types of designer start-ups. Do designers need to be located close to sources of trend knowledge, such as fellow designers or customer groups, or to raw material inputs such as fabric fairs and sample houses in order to develop successful products? Conflicting evidence exists. While some researchers (e.g., Aage and Belussi, 2008) find evidence that co-located fashion designers form networks, others (Boschma and ter Wal, 2007) have found limited evidence of engagement within them.

Questioning the importance of location to the practice of designers is linked to a notable feature of fashion designing – the practice of imitation and the reworking of ideas. While intellectual property does exist in fashion designs, it is rarely enforced. Copying is obvious and pervasive and appears to be a necessary part of the construction of trends that help stabilize customer preferences and thus sales. This is likely to be particularly important for some of the types of clothing designer shown in Figure 6.1. The construction of trends – formatted products with shared qualities and symbolic values – is essential if a stable fashion market is to be produced (Bourdieu, 1984; Cappetta et al., 2006; Caves, 2000; Goldman, 1996). This mitigates uncertainty in demand, reduces the cost of production by enabling replication of production processes, and increases the effectiveness of marketing by allowing for shared themes to be employed by distributors (Mora, 2006; Ryan, 1992).

The product similarities that result from this shared use of design cues – type of material, patterns, cuts, colours, plus reproduced marketing messages and values – serves to make the product more understandable for the customer, and reduces uncertainty for the producers (Rinallo and Golfetto, 2006). However, a bandwagon approach to product development brings a danger that the resulting product is too similar to existing offers making it appear a less valuable "me too" version of the trend and increasing the need to compete on price. This is the "curious bind" as termed by Schatz (1981): products need to be familiar enough to reduce the risk of purchase and make selection easier but also novel enough to make the purchase worthwhile and avoid price-based competition. Designers therefore need to balance these twin demands of novelty and familiarity (Bianchi, 2002).

Fashion designing involves idea generation, experimentation with fabrics and other materials, cuts and themes, the making of prototypes, refinement and final decisions about production (Rieple and Gander, 2009). This process is embedded in the ecosystem in which the designer works. As some clothes are a symbolic good, certain types of designer need to join the conversation of interconnected cultural trends: social scenes expressed in performances such as live music, the wearing of "tribal" clothing, and the display of art and ideas in galleries and exhibition spaces. Since fashion trends can develop rapidly (Richardson, 1996), the benefits of being located within such an aesthetic ecology (Entwistle, 2002) are clear. Ideas can be developed within an "atmosphere" that increases the likelihood that the resulting product is interpreted and included within a trend.

The "spillacrosses" of cultural knowledge from different cultural sectors (Stolarick and Florida, 2006) mean that creative milieu are often embedded within social practices that are spatially mediated (Grabher, 2002; Lange, 2011). These dense social networks also provide a warning system against opportunistic behaviour (Banks et al., 2000). That trust can be more effectively established through face-to-face communication (F2F) (Storper and Venables, 2004), the use of which can help reduce transaction costs, is a well-established explanation for the clustering of particular economic activities. Less well accepted, but of significant importance in creative industries such as fashion designing, is the role that human contact can have on confidence and spirit. It is likely that some of the doubt that accompanies the creation of new things (Bstieler, 2005) can be reduced by F2F communication with producers experiencing similar emotions. This is a socialized view of creativity. Rather than being an individual, internalized affair, the creative act is a collective activity, the outcome of a set of relationally achieved ideas and actions (Bilton, 2007; Drake, 2003; Granger and Hamilton, 2010) – situated creativity as Belussi and Sedita (2008) describe it. In this respect, meeting spaces, such as bars and restaurants, cafes and clubs, can encourage congregation of like-minded individuals and provide a means to access support, information and encouragement.

It is important then to include designers' use of a socially sympathetic exchange infrastructure in studies of clustered cultural production.

Location in a creative milieu thus helps designers develop the appropriate aesthetic sensibility (Crane and Bovone, 2006) needed to understand what trends are forming and evolving, and offers the possibility of encouragement, often necessary during the creation of something new (Schatz, 1981). These localized creative ecologies are also connected to international marketing and distribution chains. The meaning and therefore the value of apparel designs is negotiated across this wider network of materials fairs, fashion shows and exhibition events that circulate and construct the interpretation of clothes designs and their cultural value (Rinallo and Golfetto, 2006).

6.3 METHODOLOGY

As noted in the introduction to this chapter, we selected micro-sized fashion design firms as a community that was disproportionately likely to make strategic use of local environmental resources. London, as a thriving centre for fashion and home to many such enterprises, was a natural location for this research. Earlier research by two of the chapter's authors (Rieple and Gander, 2009) had suggested a typology of designers based on two variables, responsiveness to the market and responsiveness to the opinions of other designers. Applying these two concerns, four types of designer were proposed. Designers with little concern for either market signals or the views of other designers were termed "mavericks". These designers were likely to be more interested in the novelty of their work rather than in contributing to a trend. The opposite position, designers who used imitation and tried to join successful trends that were already established in the market we called "reproducers". A third type of designer was the fashion leader; concerned with what their peers think of their designs, they are, like the maverick, interested in the novelty side of the curious bind, but also seek recognition or social capital from their peers. The final class of designer was the fashion interpreter, those who included both market signals and the judgements of their peers in their designing.

In addition to these postures towards the market and peers, our literature review revealed a number of environmental resources that designers can draw upon. These were aspects of their location that provided a socially sympathetic infrastructure (Pratt, 2002), sources of inspiration as well as nodal points where industry practitioners meet. In this study, we measured whether patterns in the use of ecosystem-based resources were a defining characteristic of certain types of designer.

We did so using the questionnaire shown in the Appendix. We assessed designers' market responsiveness through questions MR1–MR10, and their responsiveness to their peers through questions PGC1–PGC10. The designers' use of locationally based resources focused on: (a) nodes (questions RNO1–RNO10), such as sample houses (where designers lodge samples of their work for inspection by potential wholesalers or retailers), fabric fairs (where they can see samples of materials they might use in their creations), and fashion shows (such as London Fashion Week); (b) socially sympathetic infrastructure (questions RSSI1–RSSI10); and (c) sources of embedded knowledge (RK1–RK10) such as museums and galleries, other designers or fashion-conscious individuals.

Since our aim was to discover how micro-sized design businesses used resources, our sampling was purposive in identifying and making personal contact with those that had fewer than ten employees. Such firms do not appear in company indices, or registers of limited liability companies. A database of over 1,000 fashion design firms was distilled from publicly available business directories (along with a few from other public sources such as Google maps): a London-based fashion agency's 2008 directory, from participants in London Fashion Week in 2009 and 2010, and from 2011 attendees at PURE, a London-based trade show specifically aimed at smaller fashion designers. PURE regards itself as being focused on contemporary design, with a sub-set, PURE Spirit, focusing on a younger demographic. London Fashion Design Week promotes the work of leading-edge designers, again with a focus on contemporary style.

Our initial strategy was to contact firms on the database by telephone in order to filter out those that were not actually micro design firms – for example, those that were sales agencies or parts of larger firms. Those that were suitable were briefed about the research and asked to complete an online questionnaire hosted by "Qualtrics". The link to the questionnaire was emailed within 24 hours of the phone call. If the questionnaires were not completed within seven days a reminder was sent. It became clear that this was an unsuccessful way of eliciting responses, with a response rate of only 9.4 per cent, in part because of difficulties in reaching the designers themselves. In response, we administered the survey face-to-face (in a visit to the company) or by telephone. A small snowball sample, of designers who were passed a link to the survey by earlier participants, was added to those on the database. Eventually, we were able to obtain 91 usable questionnaires.

We do not therefore claim that this sample is representative of the population of apparel designers. It is limited to those designers that we could establish contact with, and is heavily skewed towards London-based firms that are at the more fashionable end of the apparel design spectrum.

6.4   DATA FINDINGS AND ANALYSIS

Table 6. 1 shows the descriptive statistics of responses to the questionnaire.

Data analysis was undertaken using SPSS software. As a first stage, exploratory factor analysis with orthogonal varimax rotations (Leiponen, 2005) was used to identify the questions from within the questionnaire that related to genuine areas of significance. Factor analysis when applied to qualitative data attempts to account for observed interrelationships of variables in terms of a small number of underlying latent dimensions (Drejer and Vinding, 2007). This initial filter served to reduce the incidence of multi-collinearity which can distort the outcomes of cluster analysis (Punj and Stewart, 1983). Inspection of the scree plot showed a point of inflection after the extraction of the eighth factor; and this eight factor model was chosen on the basis that it gave the best available set of factor eigenvalues in the range 1–2.

This set of factors enabled us to select the questions to form the basis of cluster analysis. A mix of questions relating to designer characteristics and to use of the various classes of resource were selected on the basis of the absolute value of their correlation coefficient with at least one of the eight factors being above 0.6 (Hedges, 2007). Hierarchical cluster analysis was undertaken using the retained cluster centres. The mean response by cluster members to each of those questions is shown in Table 6.2, using a scale from 1 to 100 where high scores indicate strong disagreement

Inspection of the dendrogram agglomeration and schedule showed that a three-cluster model provided the best available grouping of the 91 respondents. Each of the three clusters described below contained a reasonable number (20+) of respondents, while only 8 respondents were not allocated to any cluster.[1] The clusters categorized designers in terms of their responsiveness to the market, their responsiveness to their peers and their use of the different types of environmental resource (social spaces, inspiration places). The most relevant questions were those within the ANOVA analysis with F statistics >10 (Cohen, 1977). These are high-lighted in Table 6.2 with an asterisk.

Before we discuss the specific attributes of these clusters, it is useful to place them within the context of the overall sample. The designers who responded to our questionnaires showed, through their mean responses to Q.1 to Q.10, a relatively high regard for both fashion trends and the market place.

Designers in our sample do not design for themselves but target their design work to appeal to particular customers. All of our designers recognized the need to see their designs from a customer's viewpoint (Q.9); they wanted to ensure that their designs were aligned with market trends,

Table 6.1   Descriptive statistics

On scale 1–100. High score = strong disagreement	N	Minimum	Maximum	Mean	Std. Deviation
I design for myself not for the market	88	0.00	100.00	63.0909	28.16317
I pay little attention to current fashion trends	90	0.00	100.00	59.6667	31.69801
It's important to give customers what they want	83	0.00	100.00	18.7470	23.01847
My designs are directed at specific customer segments	83	0.00	100.00	28.2169	27.53581
I measure my success by selling large numbers of my clothes	88	0.00	100.00	44.1591	27.97079
It is important to me to not get pulled into reacting to customer demands	89	0.00	100.00	58.9326	29.28535
Consumer and market research is a useful way of understanding what I need to do	86	0.00	100.00	39.6163	30.19940
The customer is king	88	0.00	100.00	28.9545	28.11426
I think it is important to get inside the heads of my potential customers	84	0.00	100.00	29.3452	28.09643
If I think too much about what the customer wants, it stunts my creativity	83	0.00	100.00	52.5060	30.78223
I like to discuss my designs with other fashion designers	88	0.00	100.00	45.0455	33.53842
I don't care what so-called fashion design experts think	89	0.00	100.00	51.4719	31.03923
Other people's designs are a useful starting point for my own thinking	84	0.00	100.00	47.9762	30.73202
It is easy for me to think of other designers who have influenced me	83	0.00	100.00	40.9518	28.09301
I see myself as a leader in my particular field and not a follower	83	0.00	99.00	29.9157	25.00059
I enjoy being controversial	86	0.00	100.00	49.3488	32.55503
I am pleased if my fellow designers imitate my work	83	0.00	100.00	54.4819	32.44859

Table 6.1   (continued)

On scale 1–100. High score = strong disagreement	N	Minimum	Maximum	Mean	Std. Deviation
It is of no importance if my designs are out of line with what other people are doing	83	0.00	100.00	40.2048	28.69807
I regard success as the number of column inches I get in the trade press	82	70.00	100.00	59.7195	29.98776
Success to me is about creating a work of art	79	0.00	100.00	45.7595	33.67081
I see attendance at fashion shows as very important	83	0.00	100.00	38.9398	32.42866
London Fashion Week is a waste of time	84	0.00	100.00	63.2619	32.94139
To be successful you have to talk to people at fashion events	88	0.00	100.00	36.7614	29.92135
It is always interesting browsing around sample houses	88	0.00	100.00	38.1136	30.04266
I prefer to keep my designs out of sight until they are finished	85	0.00	100.00	39.4000	30.65989
Sample houses are good for getting an idea of what's going on	88	0.00	100.00	52.3977	30.33512
I get by without attending fabric or materials fairs	88	0.00	100.00	53.0909	32.84153
Fabric or materials fairs give me information I cannot get by other means	84	0.00	100.00	52.3690	31.54869
I find most of my suppliers at fabric or materials fairs	88	0.00	100.00	56.9318	34.45597
It's important to have lots of places to socialize near to where I work	84	0.00	100.00	42.4167	31.37154
I like the feel of working in a happening place	86	0.00	100.00	32.5233	30.10989
"Buzzy" places are stimulating places to work in	83	0.00	100.00	31.0602	29.85058
The area that I work in has no effect on the work I produce	85	0.00	100.00	58.5176	29.22353
I avoid ugly environments	83	0.00	100.00	44.4337	28.58244
I get strength from the area where I work	88	0.00	100.00	38.4432	29.01005

Table 6.1   (continued)

On scale 1–100. High score = strong disagreement	N	Minimum	Maximum	Mean	Std. Deviation
I don't like being surrounded by "suits"	83	0.00	100.00	49.9518	31.44911
I love working close to the kinds of people I like	84	0.00	100.00	24.5238	22.47809
I am comfortable working in any kind of neighbourhood	87	0.00	100.00	43.9195	28.07764
The good thing about where I'm based is that there are places nearby where I am unlikely to meet fellow designers	89	0.00	100.00	60.9326	30.33817
I regularly bump into people who are at the forefront of new trends	88	0.00	100.00	46.7273	30.43921
I like to be near to people who experiment with their own personal look	83	0.00	100.00	30.1325	27.27537
I never bother to talk to my neighbouring designers	83	0.00	100.00	67.6988	28.09945
Chance encounters have led to interesting projects	83	0.00	100.00	29.5542	27.16358
I work close to sources of design know-how	83	0.00	100.00	40.4819	28.74207
I get great ideas from visiting museums and galleries	83	0.00	100.00	34.9639	28.72300
I find out about trends from other designers in the area	83	0.00	100.00	63.3133	28.21474
Being located close to other designers is irrelevant to me	86	0.00	100.00	49.1395	29.86880
I find out about trends from consumers in the area	88	0.00	100.00	51.4205	30.74168
I could do my work on top of a mountain if needs be	83	0.00	100.00	49.1205	30.06108

as well as seeing themselves as leaders in their field (Q.15). We suggest that this accords with the need to create products that are familiar, and thus understandable by customers, *and* novel, containing the differences that are required for a garment to be valued as a differentiated cultural product.

As anticipated in the literature reviewed above, respondents appeared to draw strength from being in "happening" or "buzzy" environments where

Table 6.2 Final cluster centres

On scale 1–100. High score = strong disagreement	Cluster		
	1	2	3
(No. of members)	(28)	(35)	(20)
7*. Consumer and market research is a useful way of understanding what I need to do	34.39	28.60	65.95
8*. The customer is king	18.71	18.26	58.45
10. If I think too much about what the customer wants, it stunts my creativity	49.04	57.37	48.85
13*. Other people's designs are a useful starting point for my own thinking	68.61	28.46	52.00
22. London Fashion Week is a waste of time	61.61	72.43	49.55
23*. To be successful you have to talk to people at fashion events	36.39	22.51	60.55
24*. It is always interesting browsing around sample houses	45.64	22.71	55.00
26. Sample houses are good for getting an idea of what's going on	58.79	38.97	68.75
27*. I get by without attending fabric or materials fairs	79.82	50.34	18.80
28*. Fabric or materials fairs give me information I cannot get by other means	30.14	53.63	82.75
34. I avoid ugly environments	44.39	41.17	50.20
36. I don't like being surrounded by "suits"	44.21	58.09	43.75
42. I never bother to talk to my neighbouring designers	57.75	75.43	68.10
43. Chance encounters have led to interesting projects	32.93	24.51	33.65
47*. Being located close to other designers is irrelevant to me	35.11	68.14	37.35
48*. I find out about trends from other designers in the area	75.79	46.54	75.20

Notes: *Has an F score > 10 in between clusters in the ANOVA analysis.

they can encounter compatible souls (Q.31, 32, 35) and be surrounded by people who are experimental or trend-setting (Q.41). This ecology influenced their design output (Q.33). They also seemed enthusiastic about socializing with or discussing designs with their peers (Q.39/42) and allowing them to see work in progress (Q.25). This appears to suggest that working within a socially sympathetic infrastructure of meeting places, place-based sources of ideas and inspiration (Q.45) and sympathetic people (Q.37/41) aid the design process (Q.35) (Pratt, 2002). The density of such ecologies of creativity is further valued for what might be described as the increased opportunity to be lucky. All of the respondents in the sample valued the chance encounters that led to new work opportunities (Q.43), something that is increased by locating within a clustered environment.

Our data support the importance of economic as well as social capital as indications of success in fashion design. Analysis of responses to the descriptive questions (D11a–h) revealed that the majority of our sample viewed customer feedback, sales, profit and the respect of their peers as important indicators of success. Very few responses above 50 (indicating disagreement) were seen. Our expectations, on the basis of the work of Bourdieu (1984, 1993) and previous research of two of this chapter's authors (Rieple and Gander, 2009), were that the various designer types would vary in the importance they attached to these resources, but this proved not to be the case. Differences in the patterns of response between the clusters were not statistically significant.

Contrary to the expectations raised by earlier qualitative research, the responses to questions 17 and 19, indicating designer's sensitivity to what their peers were *saying* about them, were firstly more negative than positive (means of 55 and 60, respectively), and secondly, did not prove to be significant in discriminating between clusters. However, there was significant variation (chi-square test, $p = 0.02$) concerning the importance attached to that element of social capital reified in institutional awards (D11g). This is discussed within the results for the individual clusters. With these overall results in mind we now consider the discriminating characteristics of the different clusters of designers.

6.4.1   Designer Clusters

Three designer types could be discerned in our data.

C1

This cluster is attentive to market signals and customer perspectives. However, they do not include the work of their fellow designers in their design decisions and were disproportionately likely to attach low (> 50) importance to institutional awards, and hence peer validation. They place importance on fashion events and fabric fairs. We are not sure why fabric fairs are important to these designers, but speculate that it may allow them to rework established designs and themes in different colours and materials in response to their customers' wishes, while remaining largely true to their own in-house style. C1 are also interested in fashion events. Unfortunately, our questions did not discriminate between the use of these events as sources of cultural or trend knowledge and their use as promotional and marketing opportunities. Future research could usefully disaggregate these issues. Their indifference to sample houses, places where they might view work by other designers, is more clearly in line with our prediction. This attitude is reflected in responses to Q.47 and Q.48. C1 designers do not believe it is important to be near their fellow designers.

C2

As with C1, designers in cluster 2 place importance on the need to be responsive to the market and agree that the customer's voice is critical. They are, however, distinct from C1 in the importance they place on including the work of fellow designers during the creation of their designs. Designers in cluster 2 use other designers as a resource (Q.13. 47, 48), to access information about emerging trends while also incorporating market information and customer research. Members of this cluster believe that fashion shows such as London Fashion Week are important to their practice. Unlike C1 they are ambivalent about the importance of fabric fairs, suggesting that our assumption that these would be important sources of trend knowledge is not supported. They do, however, use sample houses, the places where limited runs of designs are constructed for review by designers and their clients, to access this knowledge. In sample houses, trending design features (colours, materials, cuts, and so on) can be accessed visually. Observing the work of others equips designers with information on the patterning of the market and thus allows them to participate in the design conversation (Schatz, 1981). Designers in C2 were disproportionately likely to attach high (< 30) and unlikely to attach low (> 50) importance to institutional awards, suggesting that peer approval had some weight with them.

C3

The third cluster is notable for its members' rejection of both customers and peers as useful sources of information. Designers in C3 appear detached from their ecosystem, rejecting external sources of information at fashion events and fabric fairs, and placing little importance on locally located designers.

For C3 designers, resource nodes such as sample houses or fabric fairs and proximity to their peers are irrelevant. These designers reject the importance of the customer and the benefits of networking at fashion events yet also, according to their responses to questions D11a–h, recognize the value of customer satisfaction and economic rents (profit/sales). They are mavericks who also exhibit a realism regarding the need to gather economic and social resources.

6.5   DISCUSSION AND PROPOSALS FOR FURTHER RESEARCH

In this chapter, we have furthered our understanding of the use of external resources by micro-sized apparel design firms. Through a combination of factor and cluster analysis we have identified a diversity in the population of fashion designers. We have affirmed the existence of at least three types of fashion designer and have discovered that they differ in their attitudes to their markets and their peers and in their use of external resources.

Specifically, our research suggests that a crucial difference between different types of designer lies in the types of nodes that they access. Our findings are broadly supportive of earlier research into the value that creative individuals attach to socially sympathetic infrastructure and sources of informal knowledge (Pratt, 2002; Scott, 1999, 2008). However, they offer insight into the differential use of nodes by individuals with different approaches or attitudes to design. Whether this is a form of tribal behaviour, in which like-minded individuals congregate around different nodes, such as fashion events, sample houses and fabric fairs, or whether it is a matter of different individuals accessing nodes that meet their specific information requirements is a matter for further research. This finding suggests the possibility of planners who aspire to set up creative clusters being able to fine-tune their membership through the provision of nodes that will attract a specific population.

We suggest that an element of overgeneralization may have crept into the discourse regarding cultural clusters and shared resources. For two of our three types of designer F2F communication appears to have surprisingly little practical relevance. They like meeting with their peers in appropriate social settings, but only a minority, albeit a substantial one, look to those peers for inspiration. This leads us to question whether the early writers on creative clusters (e.g., Florida, 2002; Leadbetter and Oakley, 1999) may have overstated the extent to which the clustered forms of socialization truly influenced the quality and quantity of outcomes. Certainly, the members of our C3 have more in common with that much earlier stereotype of the creative person – the solitary individual who toils alone in their studio, with only their ideas for company. Further research might be helpful in determining whether similar groupings can be observed in other creative industries, or whether the curious bind and the visual character of fashion have together led some designers to prefer being present in clusters, but not necessarily engaged in them.

One of our clusters, C2, displayed a dual focus reflective of the idea that fashion interpreters' designs need to be understandable in relation to other designs. Such designers signal the value of their designs in a market of uncertain and symbolic attributes and qualities by containing comparable as well as novel elements within their works (Cohendet and Simon, 2007; Schatz, 1981). This linking together of design qualities and themes across different designers forms a trend that is used by customers to help value the different fashion products available. The precise nature of the balance, of being part of a recognizable grouping of clothing while simultaneously being distinct, is a challenge for these designers. It is notable that this duality is observable only in this cluster, and that the designers in C1 and C3 do not seem to strongly perceive this need to position their output in this symbolic market place. This again challenges the pervasiveness of those attributes given to designers by earlier researchers.

Our findings also suggest that, even amongst firms where access to shared resources is entirely rational from an economic viewpoint, there is a substantial body of people who will eschew this. What could account for the level of detachment in design practice that characterizes C3, given that designers are working in an economic *and* social environment? We suggest that these designers may be observing a cultural industry variant of Goodhart's law (1984). This "law" observes the loss of value of a particular metric or quality of calculation that occurs when it is used as a target to inform behaviour. Mavericks recognize that success involves the accrual of economic, social and cultural capital without necessarily using these to influence how to design. Their economic performance comes from being different and avoiding isomorphic forces (DiMaggio and Powell, 1983) that may stem from focusing on customers or of using the work of other designers as an orientating device for their own design practice. We speculate that mavericks may not last in business for long, and certainly not as long as designers in C1 and C2; this tentative hypothesis remains to be tested. Micro enterprises are often run to suit the individual whims and personality traits of their principals: the extent to which this is true of creative firms could benefit from further research.

Within these groups there are some interesting anomalies and some other questions that remain to be resolved, for example the absence from our clusters of the category of Fashion Leader. This may reflect our sample of micro enterprises. Maybe they are more likely to be found in older, larger, firms. It may, however, be the case that the category does not exist.

Finally, our findings suggest that care is needed in interpreting and operationalizing the concept of social capital. In an earlier qualitative study (Gander and Rieple, 2009) two of the authors of this chapter conflated two constructs – "sensitivity to what the peer group thinks" and "peers as a discriminant between the different types of designer". Our data indicate that this needs to be refined. As already noted, our respondents did not appear sensitive to what their peers were *saying* about them, and this sensitivity did not prove to be significant in discriminating between clusters. What *was* significant was sensitivity to what their peers were *doing* – as sources of fashion inspiration or information. The character and formulation of apparel designers' relations with the social and economic resources of the clusters they inhabit contain more variation and nuance than hitherto identified.

NOTE

1. Another paper by the same authors from a different theoretical perspective (Rieple et al., 2015) reports on an alternative four-cluster model, which uses the full sample but contains one very small cluster.

REFERENCES

Aage, T. and Belussi, F. (2008). From fashion to design: creative networks in industrial districts. *Industry and Innovation*, 15(5), 475–91.
Ashton, P. (2006). Fashion occupational communities – a market-as-network approach. *Journal of Fashion Marketing and Management*, 10(2), 181–94.
Bair, J. and Gereffi, G. (2001). Local clusters in global chains: the causes and consequences of export dynamism in Torreon's blue jeans industry. *World Development*, 29(11), 1885–903.
Balkundi, P. and Kilduff, M. (2005). The ties that lead: a social network approach to leadership. *Leadership Quarterly*, 6, 941–61.
Banks, M., Lovatt, A., O'Connor, J., and Raffo, C. (2000). Risk and trust in the cultural industries. *Geoforum*, 31, 453–64.
Bathelt, H. and Turi, P. (2011). Local, global and virtual buzz: the importance of face-to-face contact in economic interaction and possibilities to go beyond. *Geoforum*, 42(5), 520–529.
Belussi, F. and Sedita, S.R. (2008). Managing situated creativity in cultural industries. *Industry and Innovation*, 15(5), 457–8.
Bianchi, M. (2002). Novelty, preferences, and fashion: when goods are unsettling. *Journal of Economic Behavior and Organization*, 47(1), 1–18.
Bilton, C. (2007). *Management and Creativity: From Creative Industries to Creative Management*. Oxford: Blackwell.
Boschma, R.A. and ter Wal, A.L.J. (2007). Knowledge networks and innovative performance in an industrial district: the case of a footwear district in the south of Italy. *Industry and Innovation*, 14(2), 177–99.
Bourdieu, P. (1984). *Distinction: A Social Critique of the Judgement of Taste*. London and New York: Routledge and Kegan Paul.
Bourdieu, P. (1993). *The Field of Cultural Production: Essays on Art and Literature*. Cambridge: Polity Press.
Breschi, S. and Lissoni, F. (2001). Knowledge spillovers and local innovation systems: a critical survey. *Industrial and Corporate Change*, 10(4), 975–1005.

Bstieler, L. (2005). The moderating effect of environmental uncertainty on new product development and time efficiency. *Journal of Product Innovation Management*, **22**, 267–84.

Cappetta, R., Cillo, P., and Ponti, A. (2006). Convergent designs in fine fashion: an evolutionary model for stylistic innovation. *Research Policy*, **35**(9), 1273–90.

Caves, R. (2000). *Creative Industries: Contracts Between Commerce and Creativity.* Cambridge, MA: Harvard University Press.

Cohen, J. (1977). *Statistical Power Analysis of the Behavioral Science.* Hillsdale, NJ: Lawrence Erlbaum Associates.

Cohendet, P. and Simon, L. (2007). Playing across the playground: paradoxes of knowledge creation in the videogame firm. *Journal of Organizational Behavior*, **605**(5), 587–605.

Crane, D. and Bovone, L. (2006). Approaches to material culture: the sociology of fashion and clothing. *Poetics*, **34**(6), 319–33.

Currid, E. (2007). *The Warhol Economy: How Fashion, Art and Music Drive New York City.* Princeton, NJ: Princeton University Press.

DeCarolis, D.M. and Deeds, D.L. (1999). The impact of stocks and flows of organizational knowledge on firm performance: an empirical investigation of the biotechnology industry. *Strategic Management Journal*, **20**(10), 953–68.

Di Maria, E. and Finotto, V. (2008). Communities of consumption and made in Italy. *Industry and Innovation*, **15**(2), 179–97.

DiMaggio, P. and Powell, W. (1983). Institutional isomorphism and collective rationality. *American Sociological Review*, **48**, 147–60.

Drake, G. (2003). "This place gives me space": place and creativity in the creative industries. *Geoforum*, **34**(4), 511–24.

Drejer, I. and Vinding, A. (2007). Searching near and far: determinants of innovative firms' propensity to collaborate across geographical distance. *Industry and Innovation*, **14**(3), 259–75.

Dwyer, C. and Jackson, P. (2003). Commodifying difference: selling EASTern fashion. *Environment and Planning D: Society and Space*, **21**(3), 269–91.

Entwistle, J. (2002). The aesthetic economy: the production of value in the field of fashion modelling. *Journal of Consumer Culture*, **2**, 317–39.

Feldman, M. (1994). *The Geography of Innovation.* London: Kluwer.

Florida, R. (2002). *The Rise of the Creative Class: and How it is Transforming Work, Leisure, Community and Everyday Life.* New York: Basic Books.

Gander, J. and Rieple, A. (2009). Product development within a clustered environment: the case of apparel design firms. *Creative Industries Journal*, **2**(3), 273–89.

Gilmore, A., Carson, D., and Grant, K. (2001). SME marketing in practice. *Marketing Intelligence Planning*, **19**(1), 6–11.

Goldman, W. (1996). *Adventures in the Screen Trade: A Personal View of Hollywood.* London: Abacus.

Goodhart, C.A.E. (1984). *Monetary Theory and Practice.* London: Macmillan.

Grabher, G. (2002). The project ecology of advertising: tasks, talents and teams. *Regional Studies*, **36**(3), 245–62.

Granger, R.C. and Hamilton, C. (2010). Re-spatializing the creative industries: a relational examination of underground scenes, and professional and organizational lock-in. *Creative Industries Journal*, **3**(1), 47–60.

Hauge, A. and Hracs, B.J. (2010). See the sound, hear the style: collaborative linkages between indie musicians and fashion designers in local scenes. *Industry Innovation*, **17**(1), 113–29.

Hedges, L. (2007). Correcting a significance test for clustering. *Journal of Educational and Behavioral Statistics*, **32**(2), 151–79.

Hesmondhalgh, D. (2002). *Cultural Industries*. London: Sage.

Lange, B. (2011). Professionalization in space: social-spatial strategies of culture-preneurs in Berlin. *Entrepreneurship and Regional Development*, **23**(3), 259–79.

Law, J. and Singleton, V. (2005) Object lessons. *Organization*, **12**(3), 331–55.

Lazzeretti, L., Boix, R., and Capone, F. (2008). Do creative industries cluster? Mapping creative local production systems in Italy and Spain. *Industry Innovation*, **15**(5), 549–67.

Leadbetter, C. and Oakley, K. (1999). *The Independents: Britain's New Cultural Entrepreneurs*. London: Demos.

Leiponen, A. (2005). Organization of knowledge and innovation: the case of Finnish business services. *Industry and Innovation*, **12**(2), 185–203.

Martin, R. and Sunley, P. (2003). Deconstructing clusters: chaotic concept or policy panacea? *Journal of Economic Geography*, **3**, 5–35.

Maskell, P. (2007). Transient inter-firm projects in creative industries: local and global search for knowledge and solutions. DRUID Summer Conference 2007 on Appropriability, Proximity, Routines and Innovation, Copenhagen, CBS, Denmark, 18–20 June.

Maskell, P. and Lorenzen, M. (2004). Firms and markets, networks and clusters: traditional and creative industries. DRUID Winter Conference Paper 2004.

Molotch, H. (2002). Place in product, *International Journal of Urban and Regional Research*, **26**(4), 665–88.

Mommas, H. (2004). Cultural clusters and the post-industrial city: towards the remapping of urban policy. *Urban Studies*, **41**(3), 507–32.

Mora, E. (2006). Collective production of creativity in the Italian fashion system. *Poetics*, **34**(6), 334–53.

Porter, M. (1995). The competitive advantage of the inner city (R. Legates, ed.), *Harvard Business Review*, **73**(3), 55–71.

Porter, M. (1998a). Location, clusters and the "new" microeconomics of competition. *Business Economics*, **33**(1), 7–17.

Porter, M. (1998b). Clusters and the economics of competition. *Harvard Business Review*, November–December, 77–90.

Porter, M. (2000). Locations clusters and company strategy. In G. Clark, M. Feldman and M. Gertler (eds), *Handbook of Economic Geography*, pp. 253–74. Oxford: Oxford University Press.

Pratt, A. (2002). Hot jobs in cool places: the material cultures of new media product spaces the case of the south of the market, San Francisco. *Information Communication and Society*, **5**(1), 27–50.

Punj, G. and Stewart, D.W. (1983). Cluster analysis in marketing research: review and suggestions for application. *Journal of Marketing Research*, **20**(2), 134–48.

Rantisi, N. (2004). The designer in the city and the city in the designer. In D. Power and A. Scott (eds), *Cultural Industries and the Production of Culture*, pp. 91–109. New York: Routledge.

Rantisi, N.M. (2002). The local innovation system as a source of "variety": openness and adaptability in New York City's garment district. *Regional Studies*, **36**(6), 587–602.

Richardson, J. (1996). Vertical integration and rapid response in fashion apparel. *Organization Science*, **7**(4), 400–412.

Rieple, A. and Gander, J. (2009). Product development within a clustered environment: the case of apparel design firms. *Creative Industries Journal*, **2**(3), 273–89.

Rieple, A., Gander, J., Pisano, P., and Haberberg, A. (2015). UK fashion designers working in micro-sized enterprises; attitudes to locational resources, their peers and the market. *Industry and Innovation*, **22**(2), 147–64.

Rinallo, D. and Golfetto, F. (2006). Representing markets: the shaping of fashion trends by French and Italian fabric companies. *Industrial Marketing Management*, **35**(7), 856–69.

Roodhouse, S. (2008). Creative industries: the business of definition and cultural management practice. *International Journal of Arts Management*, **11**(1), 16–27.

Ryan, B. (1992). *Making Capital from Culture: The Corporate Form of Capitalist Cultural Production*. Berlin: Walter de Gruyter.

Schatz, T. (1981). *Hollywood Genres, Formulas, Screenwriting and Filmmaking*. Philadelphia, PA: Temple University Press.

Scott, A. (1999). The cultural economy: geography and the creative field. *Media, Culture and Society*, **21**, 807–17.

Scott, A. (2004). The other Hollywood: the organizational and geographic bases of television-program production. *Media Culture and Society*, **26**(2), 183–205.

Scott, A.J. (2008). Resurgent metropolis: economy, society and urbanization in an interconnected world. *International Journal of Urban and Regional Research*, **32**(3), 548–64.

Stolarick, K. and Florida, R. (2006). Creativity, connections and innovation: a study of linkages in the Montréal region. *Environment and Planning – Part A*, **38**(10), 1799–817.

Storper, M. and Venables, A. (2004). Buzz: face-to-face contact and the urban economy. *Journal of Economic Geography*, **4**, 351–70.

Throsby, D. (2004). *Economics and Culture*. Cambridge: Cambridge University Press.

APPENDIX   THE QUESTIONNAIRE

Questions measured on a 100-point sliding Likert scale (strongly agree–strongly disagree) using Qualtrics online survey tool. The order of these questions was randomized and answering all questions was compulsory.

Market Responsiveness

MR1.   I design for myself not for the market
MR2.   I pay little attention to current fashion trends
MR3.   It's important to give customers what they want
MR4.   My designs are directed at specific customer segments
MR5.   I measure my success by selling large numbers of my clothes
MR6.   It is important to me to not get pulled into reacting to customer demands
MR7.   Consumer and market research is a useful way of understanding what I need to do
MR8.   The customer is king
MR9.   I think it is important to get inside the heads of my potential customers
MR10.   If I think too much about what the customer wants, it stunts my creativity

Peer Group Concern

PGC1.   I like to discuss my designs with other fashion designers
PGC2.   I don't care what so-called fashion design experts think
PGC3.   Other people's designs are a useful starting point for my own thinking
PGC4.   It is easy for me to think of other designers who have influenced me
PGC5.   I see myself as a leader in my particular field and not a follower
PGC6.   I enjoy being controversial
PGC7.   I am pleased if my fellow designers imitate my work
PGC8.   It is of no importance if my designs are out of line with what other people are doing
PGC9.   I regard success as the number of column inches I get in the trade press
PGC10. Success to me is about creating a work of art

Locational Resource Nodes

RNO1. I see attendance at fashion shows as very important

RNO2. London Fashion Week is a waste of time

RNO3. To be successful you have to talk to people at fashion events

RNO4. It is always interesting browsing around sample houses

RNO5. I prefer to keep my designs out of sight until they are finished

RNO6. Sample houses are good for getting an idea of what's going on

RNO7. I get by without attending fabric or materials fairs

RNO8. Fabric or materials fairs give me information I cannot get by other means

RNO9. I find most of my suppliers at fabric or materials fairs

Socially Sympathetic Infrastructure

RSSI1. It's important to have lots of places to socialize near to where I work

RSSI2. I like the feel of working in a happening place

RSSI3. "Buzzy" places are stimulating places to work in

RSSI4. The area that I work in has no effect on the work I produce

RSSI5. I avoid ugly environments

RSSI6. I get strength from the area where I work

RSSI7. I don't like being surrounded by "suits"

RSSI8. I love working close to the kinds of people I like

RSSI9. I am comfortable working in any kind of neighbourhood

RSSI10. The good thing about where I'm based is that there are places nearby where I am unlikely to meet fellow designers

Socially Situated and Embedded Knowledge

RK1. I regularly bump into people who are at the forefront of new trends

RK2. I like to be near to people who experiment with their own personal look

RK3. I never bother to talk to my neighbouring designers

RK4. Chance encounters have led to interesting projects

RK5. I work close to sources of design know-how

RK6. I get great ideas from visiting museums and galleries

RK7. I find out about trends from other designers in the area

RK8. Being located close to other designers is irrelevant to me

RK9. I find out about trends from consumers in the area

RK10. I could do my work on top of a mountain if needs be

Open Coded Questions

D1.   How do your designs get to market?
D2.   How many sales of a single design would you regard as a success?
D3.   How long have you been in business as a designer?
D4.   In comparison to your direct competitors, are you more or less successful?
D5.   How many employees in your firm?
D6.   How long have you been in business as a designer?
D7.   Preferred distribution channels
D8.   Designer's postcode
D9.   Where did you train as a designer?
D10.   How many sales of a single design would you regard as a success in a single year?
D11.   How do you measure your success as a designer?
      a – Respect of my peers
      b – Positive customer feedback
      c – Growth in turnover
      d – Growth in profits
      e – Growth in unit sales
      f – Profit margin
      g – Design prizes or awards
      h – Personal satisfaction with the aesthetic quality of the design

7. Business incubators and entrepreneurial networks: a methodology for assessing incubator effectiveness and performance

Emanuele Parisi, Angelo Miglietta and Dario Peirone

7.1 INTRODUCTION

The increasing awareness of entrepreneurial mechanism complexity requires specialists to analyse the impact of every agent that acts as a system variable, embedding economic, social and personal aspects (Isenberg 2011; Schwarzkopf 2016). Variables such as culture, free exchange of information, startups availability and growth capital are amongst the most important factors to drive entrepreneurial success. To this extent, business incubators play a crucial role for entrepreneurial development and their ability to address and leverage these variables marks their overall success.

The number of incubators in Europe is growing at a very significant rate, each encompassing differences pertaining to the entrepreneurial ecosystem where they operate (Chengappa et al. 2014). Italy has seen significant advancements in the birth of incubators especially between 2003 and 2009 in specific regions and districts, where their activities represent a crucial pivot for local innovation, entrepreneurship and knowledge transfer (Auricchio et al. 2013). These beneficial community spillovers lead some of them to be non-profit. Indeed, incubators can be managed privately, publicly or by mixed participation, and in spite of *for-profit* or *non-profit*, the chosen model entails different managerial approaches and targets (Chandra 2007).

Non-profit facilities may be less motivated to profit since they prioritize knowledge transfer and entrepreneurship development, whereas private or mixed participation models prioritize the pursuit of revenues (Rashid and Rashid 2012). Nowadays, most incubators are non-profit organizations. In the US, which is an innovation leader, about 90 percent of incubators are non-profit and largely dependent on public resources (Marks et al. 2009). In Italy, over one-third of all incubators rely entirely on public funds – in alignment with European tendencies where incubators are generally considered as public tools for pursuing economic policy goals (Tavoletti 2013). The rationale being that incubators promote local development, create jobs and increase the entrepreneurship rate by increasing the survival rate of startups, and their role as social safety nets in times of youth unemployment is also recognized (Rampado 2013). Despite minor private involvement, incubators are not always managed according to market logics (Chandra et al. 2007) and they are often perceived as public tools to be backed by governments. However, increasing concern about national budgets is often not conducive to objective analysis and shared rating factors. There is no harmonized assessment on the effectiveness of incubator practices in terms of profits, local development and knowledge transfer, and resources are not always clearly allocated.

In this chapter, we aim to map the incubators' perimeter, highlighting their role as connector and activation centers of entrepreneurial ecosystems, thereby setting the theoretical framework for an assessment model based on success drivers derived from global best practices. This framework can be used to aggregate and harmonize the effectiveness of incubation activities in given perimeters, helping investors to better allocate resources – whether private or public – and offering useful insights to governments in addressing national public policies.

7.2   INCUBATORS: ORIGINS AND EVOLUTIONS

Business incubators are not a new phenomenon in Europe but their numbers grew more rapidly after the second half of the 1990s, when some pioneering countries began to establish incubators to support enterprises in their early stages of activity. Indeed, the strongest expansion in the last 20 years is recorded between the "third industrial revolution" and the aftermath of the financial crisis (Rifkin 2016).[1] The number of European accelerators and incubators has increased dramatically in the aftermath of the financial crisis, reflecting an impressive counter-cyclical aptitude of startups and small and medium-sized enterprises (SMEs), and incubators have played a crucial supportive role. Between 2007 and 2013, the number of incubators rose by nearly 400 percent, boosted by the launch of several specific national incubation programs to reignite growth and absorb enterprise shutdowns and unemployment (Mignogna 2014).

The incubation process in its most traditional form is structured in different interrelated phases: (1) selection of ideas for new product or service and/or recognition of opportunities; (2) decision to proceed and selection; (3) gathering required resources (e.g., information, financials, human resources); (4) actual launch of the new venture, (5) building and development of the successful business; and (6) final collection of the rewards (Baron and Shane 2007). The output of the incubation process depends on several factors such as: (1) individuals (e.g., skills, motivation, individual characteristics); (2) collective (ideas, inputs of externals, interaction within the incubator and with investors, customers and potential employees); and (3) institutional issues (e.g., government policies, economic conditions, technologies). Once the idea is thoroughly validated, incubators play a crucial role in bringing together its different elements and forces to develop the business in a friction-less environment.

As the market evolved, incubation features changed, resulting in new forms of development, incubation and models (Lewis et al. 2011). Besides the rather standardized early stage business development, diverse target-focused incubators have emerged. Technology, culture, philanthropy and agribusiness are some recent developments, expanding the range of opportunities to support virtually any emerging business. As incubators expanded across the globe, changes to their organizational models were introduced, leading to greater flexibility of their business models and to a more complex articulation of activities/services performed. Nowadays, a major proportion of incubators also provide *pre-incubation* services, as a way to consolidate previous business plans for future endeavors (Masutha et al. 2014), as well as *post-incubation* activities. It has been observed that, on average, businesses that went through a phase of pre-incubation performed better either during or after incubation than those that directly entered the incubation phase (Rodrigues et al. 2013). The *post-incubation* phase is, in turn, a rather uncommon activity among incubators, despite surveys of incubator managers highlighting interest in tighter relationships with more grown-up firms as regards both *service* and *agent* goals. As a *service*, startups often demand follow-up activities. Post-incubations feedback and follow-ups can be used to enhance the incubation process. As *agent*, developed startup team members can serve as consultants or mentors for further incubation activities of new projects. The literature on the subject indicates that support after the incubation is also favored by startups, with the objectives as: (1) a realistic rating of the market situation; (2) a realistic market forecast; (3) designing and developing an organizational culture; and (4) design and implementation of continuous management and consulting activities (Flanschger 2012).

As incubators accumulate skills and the market consolidates, new opportunities also emerge outside the traditional incubation boundaries of startups, approaching local or regional production networks, SMEs and established firms. *External incubation* is one of the tools used by incubators to gather higher expertise and increase their capacity to meet greater demand, reaching a larger number of firms through consulting services, training, coaching and other activities (Kipper et al. 2014). The experience of incubator managers and their continuous advancements in services and performances allows incubators to intervene in the strategic planning of new business projects, giving guidance and promoting enhanced policies for smaller and traditional businesses and those with basic technology. External incubation entails the involvement of incubators in local or regional development projects. The integration of the incubator into regional innovation systems fulfills the crucial purpose of interfacing knowledge transfer and goods and services production, bringing innovation into existing businesses for further enhancement, and thereby generating larger technology firms and increasing the competitiveness of the firms involved (Lahorgue 2004).[2]

The institutional recognition of incubators as crucial pivots of local innovation systems leads the way to greater public commitment and financing of the incubators. In Italy, 15 incubators are of mixed ownership, while 25 are entirely publicly funded.[3] Moreover, of these 25 incubators, nine belong to universities, seven are entirely public and two have mixed ownership. Despite the strong participation of public financing in the domain and the growing need for transparency in public budget expenditures, to date there is no general mechanism to assess the efficiency of business incubators (Dossena et al. 2012). While a rather small number of private incubators focus solely on providing returns on shareholder investments, the vast majority are oriented toward enabling technology and knowledge transfer to the market, relying on public sources and offering little attention either to profits or to effectiveness to develop sustainable models for their operations. Despite the fact that the very first examples of incubators were non-profit, the current trend is to establish for-profit incubators by taking an equity stake in the startups in terms of scope (Barbéro 2014). This circumstance additionally highlights the need to set standard indicators to reflect aggregated results of incubation, for the purpose of both comparison and improvements.

Traditionally, scholars have considered that the commercialization of technology developed in incubators is measured precisely with the aggregation of two factors: the technology transfer occurring by means of spin-off firms that leverage university research; and the management of intellectual property obtained by means of the royalties accrued through licensing agreements (Becker and Gassman 2006). A well-established body of literature (extensively reviewed by Rothaermel et al. 2007) has examined the impact of the process of knowledge valorization, in particular, technology transfer and commercialization, but with ambivalent results (Miglietta and Peirone 2012). In Europe this debate is particularly intense, because several European universities, which are the birthplace of outstanding technology and research, still do not perform well enough in terms of technology transfer efficiency (Saublens 2011; European Commission, State of Innovation Union 2011). Moreover, only a few of them have developed solid and fruitful relationships with venture investors (resulting in the so-called "European Paradox"; see Conti and Gaule 2011); and even fewer rely exclusively on private resources (CSES 2012). A better understanding of the underlying processes of incubation and the assessment and monitoring of their performances over time is crucial to enhance the effectiveness of incubators and the allocation of resources.

7.3   INCUBATORS AS DRIVERS OF ENTREPRENEURIAL ECOSYSTEMS

Business incubators are organizations geared toward speeding up the growth and success of startups and early stage firms, attracting equity injection from angel investors, state governments, economic-development coalitions and other financial investors. The essence of their multilevel activity reflects the complexity of the collective and systemic nature of entrepreneurship, articulated in direct connection to each of the six domains that comprise an entrepreneurial ecosystem contained in Isenberg's theory (2014). Their arbitrator role conveys bilateral relationships where every element of the incubator is considered a part of a structure that guarantees the effective and positive interaction of the incubatees with the external context. This entrepreneurial ecosystem framework enables a thorough analysis of this incubation process:

1. *Cultural domain*: incubators actively integrated in society and conscious of macro-tendencies contribute to regulate the influence of factors affecting startups' internal dynamics such as tolerance of risks and mistakes, the vision of the social status of the entrepreneurs, their personal ambitions and hunger for success, valuing the creation of wealth and values such as equality and reciprocal respect. Incubators may promote themes such as culture, innovation and solidarity that can constitute the principal elements of their activity (Mercier-Laurent 2011).
2. *Policy*: incubators may integrate the enforcement of public policies by supporting the definition of business strategies and the adoption of right actions to deal with urgencies and mitigate risk impacts on the

business. They also contribute to the development and/or optimization of public strategies, constantly monitoring the legislative framework, the presence of incentives, institutions or information sources, such as research institutes.

3. *Finance*: part of the incubator's activity is to assess the availability of dedicated finance and attract it, aiding the incubatees to navigate among different equity solutions, for example, business angels and angel investors, microloans, venture capital funds, private equity, and so on.

4. *Human capital*: incubators may propose particular programs of entrepreneurial training and skills acquisition, oriented to market requests. Their connection to educational institutions stimulates knowledge exchange and guarantees the correct structure and approach (Corbett et al. 2014), since scientific theories shall be targeting market validation and the elements of the entrepreneurial ecosystem (Schwarzkopf 2016). The mission of incubators may also include attracting talents and ideas, thereby giving them the chance to grow rapidly.

5. *Markets*: incubators may assess venture-friendly markets for products, potential customers and distribution channels. They may also contribute to creating synergies and networks, whereby post-incubation support represents a further way to favor the inclusion of startups in the wider entrepreneurial ecosystem.

6. *Support*: in most cases, incubators occur where effective infrastructural support is in place and help startups analyse its relevance to the realization of their ideas (e.g., telecommunication and transportation infrastructures, entrepreneurship-promoting associations and energy). They integrate or replace different kinds of centralized support such as institutional, legal, investment and technical advice.

Being able to operate and transform ideas into value, incubators need to investigate the entrepreneurial ecosystem of their specific territory to correctly assess its conditions. In other words, this means actively operating in the center of the flow of updated and verified information about the politics, economics and social situations in the area, markets and law, technological advances and innovations, top performers, evolution of knowledge processing, tendencies and trends. The correct analysis of these external inputs (Boutillier et al. 2016) allows incubators to address means and extents to leverage favorable conditions for the launching of startups.

According to the "Four Circle Entrepreneurial Ecosystem" theory, proposed by Schwarzkopf (2016), to succeed in the go-to-market phase, new enterprises need to pass the test of four levels of environmental factors, where each level has its own peculiarities and difficulties. The role of incubators is to accelerate this process and set enhancement tools to reach functionality and cooperation among all levels.

7.4 SELECTING THE PERIMETER: OUTLINING THE INCUBATOR IN THE EUROPEAN AND ITALIAN CONTEXTS

Despite a large literature on the matter, a comprehensive benchmark to standardize and define incubators can be complex to establish, and the above-mentioned characteristics of incubators in today's businesses make up such complexity. In fact, with the growth of the number of incubators and enlargement of the range of their activities, it is not always easy to measure whether a given incubator is categorically an incubator (Essig 2014). Prior to their performance assessment and aggregation, it is necessary to define the perimeter of the incubator in terms of scope, outlining the common factors that categorize incubators to differentiate them from other business assistance programs. To this extent, the European Union (EU) has established a procedure to obtain the *status* of Certified Incubators, compliance with which entails that the incubator be officially recognized as such.[4] The EC-BIC incubator is a program that certifies incubators upon membership to the European Business and Innovation Centre Network. Membership certification is based upon an administrative request to be submitted and approved with regard to the following criteria: (1) Mission; (2) Organization; (3) Services to Innovative Individual Entrepreneurs/Startup Enterprises and SMEs; (4) Activity Measurement and Evaluation; and (5) Quality.

At the national level, a number of governments have further ratified this membership by establishing national registries. In this case, national chambers of commerce or other ad hoc institutions are responsible for their registration. Both these registers do not set standards to identify incubators, but rather offer simple *ex post* certification. The Italian government has nationally transposed this provision by instituting the Registry of Certified incubators, membership in which requires any business assistance program to fulfill the following requirements:

1. *Rationale*: the certified incubator for innovative startup is a corporation that shall guarantee perfect patrimonial autonomy.
2. *Management*: it needs to be administered or managed by individuals of recognized competence in the field of enterprise and innovation and shall have a minimum equity capital of euro 10,000.00, and a minimum number of members (three to nine).

3. *Administrative*: it must be registered in a special section of the Registrar of Companies.

Across European countries, a number of best practices define the main requirements that a business support facility should have to be categorized as a business incubator. This approach links to the principles and guidelines defined by the Centre for Strategy & Evaluation Services (CSES) in 2012, and concerns:

1. *Efficiency*: there is a positive ratio between the financial resources spent in the incubation and in proved/heterogeneous skills of its management (more resources allocated/better the management).
2. *Effectiveness*: the demonstration of the relationship amongst services and activities provided and the achievement of specific entrepreneurial objectives.
3. *Relevance*: the extent to which the results obtained though the incubation process serve solely the same facility or broader political objectives.
4. *Utility*: the ability of incubators to provide business development through services and agents focused on startups and from the viewpoint of customers.
5. *Sustainability*: the robustness and length of time to maintain results achieved and to plan/monitor the allocation of resources – internal or external.

Combining both approaches described above, we are able to outline the incubator perimeter in terms of scope in the Italian framework. The assessment results in a perimeter of 73 incubators that need to be benchmarked against the 30 facilities registered as *certified incubators*.

7.5   ASSESSING INCUBATORS' QUALITY AND RESULTS

Incubators require a flow of strong investments from public institutions and private investors that often imply long-term returns. Despite a number of different funding models for incubators, evidence resulting from CSES (2012) analysis shows that public support for the establishment of incubators in Europe is still a critical issue weighing on national budgets, and the previously highlighted macroeconomic role is responsible for this situation. In 2012, public funding accounted for about 37 percent of operating revenues of EU recognized incubators: a high proportion of the setup costs of most incubators (CSES 2012). Incubator operating costs average around €500,000 per year, with the highest proportion of cost relating to staff (41 percent), followed by client services (24 percent), and maintenance of buildings and equipment (22 percent). Other costs, such as for utilities, account for 13 percent. While many incubators are able to recover significant proportions of these costs from tenants (averaging around 40 percent), public subsidy remains pretty high in most cases.

In 2012 almost three-quarters (77 percent) of European incubators operated on a not-for-profit basis (CSES 2012). In 2014 this rate was higher, topping 90 percent (Matejun 2014). This feature highlights the growth in allocation of public budgets, thereby underscoring their crucial role in macroeconomic goals to countervail the consequences of the economic crisis. However, this data refers only to incubators certified in conformity to the analysis performed in Section 7.4, and inspires the rationale of this chapter: a homogeneous perimeter in terms of scope is a prerequisite condition for evenly measuring the evolution, outcomes and impact of all incubators – whether they request a certification or not. The perimeter shall be assessed solely upon the effective performance of incubation activities. Its lack undermines the efficacy of any subsequent aggregation, thereby hindering any assessment of incubators' performances and monitoring of their advancements.

Some business incubators have attempted to establish individual internal systems for assessing their performances over time, but this condition may be limited to quantitative data or qualitative data that does not allow aggregation. As such, these systems fail to demonstrate the tangible added value of business incubation and their comparative advantages. Moreover, as evidence shows (Flanschger et al. n.d.), the performance of business incubators should be judged primarily in terms of results achieved (i.e., the impact they have on the creation of new businesses, the wider economic development and other priorities). A key message of this research is therefore that we need to judge incubator performance in terms of long-term impact achieved rather than short-term measures, in alignment with indicators proposed in the literature, such as occupancy rates or failure rates (CSES 2012).

In Italy, most incubators use different indicators to evaluate their performances, depending on drivers, such as:

1. number of incubated firms
2. net results of the resident firms
3. number of employees
4. net funding received.

In consideration of this condition, since 2009 the Italian government has tried to assess overall results of incubators' support using various methodologies. Comprehensive and thorough research was performed in 2012 using interviews and questionnaires with the office workforce and incubator managers, along with periodic surveys to quantify the exact size of the industry (i.e., firms, employment, turnover, institutional linkage between other data, and knowledge transfer). The Bank of Italy issued the most recent data in 2012 (Auricchio 2013). This approach has produced a comprehensive report displaying an overall consolidated industry, with good growth prospects that are critically dependent, however, on external funding. The methodology has provided a first complete picture of the incubators' situation in Italy, although it might be expensive to implement on a regular basis.

A different approach in the aforementioned administrative membership in the "certified incubator" system. This certification envisions regular evaluation activities with reference to performance, at both national and EU levels (European Commission 2014). The majority of these methodologies do not manage to define a global perimeter of analysis, are mostly done *on the spot*, and are typically centered on specific requests from institutions. Moreover, and at least in the Italian framework, this certification in March 2015 was limited to 30 facilities, thereby highlighting that the majority of national facilities that call themselves "incubators" have not requested such accreditation and are, hence, excluded from the analysis.

Although the two methodologies reported above have different objectives and outputs (the former aims to identify how incubator resources are used and the importance of each sector for more funding, while the latter wants to establish a registry of all facilities), outcomes of both show overall incubator industry consolidation and progressive growth in terms of number and value of Italian incubators, with minor attention given to their effectiveness as tangible drivers of economic development.

The literature has highlighted several indicators to measure incubators' performance based on, for example, *occupancy, jobs created, firms graduated* (Allen and McCluskey 1990), or *tenant revenues, number of patent applications per firm, number of discontinued businesses* (Philips 2002) and others such as *internal processes, organization, impacts and outcomes* (Mian 1996; Colombo and Delmastro 2002; Chan and Lau 2005). International best practices tend to confirm the existence of a relationship between these indicators and the positive performance of incubators over time.

Some are purely *quantitative indicators*, hence easier to measure, and concern the following aspects:

1. *Size of the incubator/number of firms hatched.* According to these standards, the minimum space recommended is 2,000 square meters, which is needed to accommodate between 20 and 30 firms, in order to achieve economies of scale (Lalkaka 2006).
2. *Length of stay.* A three-year time span is recommended. This period is applicable to an average incubator with unskilled capacities (Aernoudt 2004).
3. *Number of administrative staff* – indexed to space/incubated firms. At least two managers should be appointed to support between 20 and 30 resident startups. This number allows sufficient flexibility to cover potential inadequacies, and ensure access, support and administrative advice at all times. Ideally, the ratio of managers to incubated firms should not exceed 1:20.
4. *Contribution of the incubator to business performance.* This represents the added value the incubator gives to incubated firms concerning financial support.

Others are *qualitative* indicators, and therefore their assessment concerns the following aspects:

1. *Success rate of the incubated firms.* The main objective of the incubator is to accelerate the process of business launching and minimize the chances of failure. To be considered effective, the incubator shall achieve a survival rate of 85 percent of its incubated firms over time (Radojevich-Kelley and Hoffman 2012).
2. *Destination of graduate firms.* Global Best Practices (Rothaermel and Thursby 2005) suggest performing follow-up monitoring of the graduated firm's final location in order to establish the magnitude of long-run, local economic benefits. Follow-ups are generally not regulated by policies and hence are casual and not continuous (Guceri-Ucar and Koch 2013).
3. *Employment generation.* The employment generated is often used to measure the economic and social impact of a developed firm. The indicator is given by the number of people working in the incubated firms, assuming a minimum of two full-time employees at the early stage (Fritsch and Noseleit 2013).
4. *Creation of wealth.* The incubated firm success in generating an increase in capital. This is harder to measure, but rates of growth in sales or taxes of incubated firms may reflect this outcome (Bhatli et al. 2015).

On the demand side, the reasons driving entrepreneurs to decide to establish their startup in a business incubator entail performance indicators such as the location, the favorable image of the incubator, the quality, the price and flexibility of the structure, and finally the spaces and services it provides, rather than the certification. With specific reference to the latter, startups may be encouraged by the endorsements the incubator can release for administrative tasks rather than by its efficacy in providing incubation services.

We use the above-mentioned benchmarks to identify four areas of analysis, described in the following section.

7.6   METHODOLOGY

Although various approaches have been developed for the analysis of business incubators, starting with the first systematic overview of incubator performance in the 1990s (Allen and McCluskey 1990), for the purpose of this analysis we have chosen to identify from existing approaches a set of indicators to thoroughly evaluate and represent incubators' capabilities This comprises factors such as: *Validity* (the ability to measure the factor in terms of scope); *Reliability* (consistency in using the same result applied in similar situations); *Measurability* (by means of available data and need for data certification); and *Relevance* (with regard to other indicators). We use these settings to assign weights and scores.

The main goal of the analysis is to obtain harmonized outcomes of incubators' performance on the basis of the analysis of the above-mentioned literature. Since business incubators are complex organizations, the results of the analysis may be correctly evaluated only by use of a standard set of indicators. To collect the data, we perform individual surveys among different actors referring to the same hub: stakeholders, representatives and government agencies with reference to each incubator. Subjects of the interviews shall provide data that are reliable and comparable (as quantitative as possible) in order to allow a consistent analysis pursuing the identification of common traits and correlations (Van Vught and Ziegele 2012). We then calculate each incubator's average score.

A *"360 degree"* perspective is necessary to assess the impact of business incubation over time (*added value*) and inter-sector (*comparative advantages*). In order to harmonize results, we therefore established a weighed system to account for different business incubators' situations based on a scoreboard of *type*, *age*, *location* and *financials*. The incubators' ecosystem is quite broad, and each incubator has goals and objectives proportionate to its audience. The scoreboard aims to harmonize these differences. For example, while technology-based incubators pursue the creation of strong, competitive firms in the global market, traditional incubators offer support to firms whose markets are local or national, and whose growth is rarely accelerated. The indicators also need to reflect the different conceptions of success of each incubator type, as well as *lifetime* and *location*. In other words, an older incubator may have more cumulative expertise and more success stories than a younger one. Likewise, being located alongside efficient infrastructures increases the opportunities for incubated firms to reach technologically advanced products, whereas a location where knowledge production is not as strong tends to develop firms relying on simpler technologies (Lahorgue 2004). Finally, we add the scrutiny of the incubator *financials* as part of the scoreboard, as the income source may vary in each incubator and its valuation shall be indexed to other factors. Its definition therefore helps to define the source of the incubator's funding and its market position. The scoreboard is based upon the following drivers: *Years of Activity; Dimension; Prevailing areas of activity; Localization; Branches; Proximity to technological hubs; Proximity to research centers; Proximity to entrepreneurial districts; Incomes from rent & services; Incomes from contracts and grants: Incomes from cash operating subsidies; Incomes from investment: Incomes from other sources.* Each question comprises a score ranging from 1 to 10 manually selected using given benchmarks. The benchmarks account for inner differences among incubators. Young ones may face difficulties that are not shared with older ones; the number of startups incubated may vary from incubators as well the value of each startup incubated, and so on.

For the incubator's efficiency assessment, we establish the analysis based on the aforementioned literature, according to which we identify four categories of analysis:

1. *Analytics.* Aimed at the evaluation of the management and to identify consolidation and quality of the incubator equipment. The section is directed at evaluating the target startups, the target startups' financials, the existence of a parent organization, the existence of a sponsoring institution, and, lastly, the existence and relevance of the incubator network.
2. *Internal processes.* Aimed at the evaluation of the effectiveness of the management of the incubator and of its degree of institutional openness. The section comprises the evaluation of the selection process of the incubator, the average time of incubation, the existence and relevance of potential follow-up activities, the evaluation of the incubator's organizational processes, internal policies and control systems.
3. *Customers.* Aimed at the evaluation of the degree of autonomy and diversification of sources of financing operations. A crucial matter for all incubators is their long-term sustainability. The section focuses on

the evaluation of incubator development, the outcomes of its activity on the startups, and the impact on the outside network. Lastly, we consider the percentage of revenue from royalties and from other sources.

4. *Firms*. Aimed at the evaluation and monitoring of the volume and quality of services provided to the incubator's residents, and is hence based on the startups in terms of scope. The section is aimed at evaluating the percentage of funds raised spent on training for startups and entrepreneurs, the percentage of startups incubated that participated in fairs, events and merchandizing, the number of jobs created, the criteria for selecting the management and resources of the startups.

Each question allows the selection of a score – reflecting, respectively, a weight ranked from 1 to 12 based upon a matrix of relevance/reliability from 1 to 10. Surveys are submitted to all incubators identified in the perimeter – with a minimum of three representatives of the incubator and ideally one executive, one graduated startup. The same survey shall be submitted on a yearly basis, in order to gather updates and develop a monitoring cycle of the advancements.

The results provide three categories according to the range of each incubator total score as indexed in the scoreboard. The range allows the establishment of several outcomes, such as semiotic squares, indicating each incubator's positioning vis-à-vis the dimensions under consideration; charts with individual advantages and advancements; overall efficacy either on specific areas or wide ranging – on a broader area.

7.7   LIMITS OF THE METHODOLOGY

This methodology is aimed at defining the perimeter and performance indicators of incubators on the basis of the best practices currently in force. As such, it shall need to be repeated regularly in order to gather updated and comprehensive results and requires effort from incubator stakeholders to provide initial results and continuous follow-ups.

The degree of accuracy depends on several variables, each of which may affect the aggregated results. The main challenges concern the lack of "control groups" in the incubator ecosystems. In other words, the complexity in identifying a proper financial model to evaluate the financial and social returns using an accepted and commonly used methodology (Hackett and Dilts 2004).

Moreover, this methodology may not succeed in assessing the long-term impact of various links and variables connecting the incubator and its surrounding environment, as it focuses on the incubator and its peers rather than its environment. The complexity of the concept of *business incubation* (sum of tangible and intangible assets) and the gaps identified above suggest the need to further refine the issue by advancing a more refined methodology combining longitudinal (i.e., the study of the same group of people at more than one point in time: incubator managers, tenants and non-tenants/control groups) and cross-sectional studies (i.e., the study of a set of people at a single point in time: stakeholders forming the surrounding environment of the incubator). In addition, reviews of the local economic context (statistics, secondary quantitative data) should also be undertaken. Lastly, the definition of a single methodology that encompasses different types of business incubation environments is not practical: we partially address this limitation by establishing drivers and definition of the incubators, and a subsequent mapping of its whole perimeter. However, there is the risk of falling short in providing the complete picture.

For a more detailed analysis, the assessment should include qualitative approaches through face-to face-questionnaires, as well as group discussions (on-site visits) and case studies. Nevertheless, important progress in the consolidation of this analysis as a way to track and monitor incubator performance and evolution over time would be to perform follow-ups on a continuous basis. This would provide a better understanding of the incubators, and by the development of a taxonomy that may help define adequate strategies for each kind of business incubator.

7.8 CONCLUSIONS

The research concerns the participation of incubators in entrepreneurial ecosystems and the way it can be assessed. Incubators' mission is not limited to collecting, processing and sharing knowledge to foster new waves of entrepreneurship, but involves the emergence of several success factors (i.e., character, experience, knowledge, connections) in new firms (Schwarzkopf 2016). If we consider university incubators, for example, focused on the analysis and dissemination of theoretical frameworks, they often outperform the mere knowledge transfer by combining academic competencies, on-the-job experience, talents and ideas. By providing entrepreneurs with soft skills recognized as crucial entrepreneurial traits (Schwarzkopf 2016), they are more likely to leverage on successful incubated companies to identify and spread broader and wide-ranging entrepreneurial best practices.

In terms of incubators' participation in the entrepreneurial ecosystem, the Italian experience reveals strengths as well as difficulties. On the one hand, there are problems inherent in an industry that is not homogeneous, and hence highly connected to variability in regulations, economic outlooks and overall entrepreneurial environment. On the other hand, the scenario is not well defined as it encompasses several differences in terms of age, location, dimensions and models. However, following the mapping and assessment activity (i.e., partially covered by the certified incubator accreditation), additional assessment of incubators' efficacy and performance is essential for planning governmental actions regarding incubators. Such metrics indentification is in fact crucial in many respects: for the startup industry, as it represents a tool to help establish that incubators may be tangible drivers of economic development and knowledge transfer; for investors, as it represents an empirical dataset to support and drive the identification of relevant, efficient and growth driven sectors and where to address investments.

This chapter is a preliminary introduction to further analysis that will start in the first quarter of 2017, and is still ongoing, and aims to fulfill the gaps highlighted in research on Italian business incubators by answering several inquiries concerning performance over time. The success of the research depends on the participation of incubator representatives and incubated startups. An assessment of the state of the art of incubators that recognizes best practices for scaling incubation methodologies is key for enhancing the incubation process, and the results and their continuous update may benefit the incubator industry as a whole, especially in establishing a regulated system in this emerging new area of practice.

NOTES

1. The author refers to the third industrial revolution as a shift toward energy converging with the internet and creating new businesses and employment based on five pillars: renewable energy; buildings as micro-power plants; energy storage; internet and grids; and energy conveying grids. These areas are particularly interesting as specific areas of activities for incubators.
2. Some authors have highlighted the possibility for incubators to become financially self-sufficient (Johnsrud 2004) by increasing the value of the startups through private equity investments or taking profits from the sale of an innovative product. However, other authors argue that this option is odd given that the period required before the investment reaches breakeven is generally pretty long and risky (Cheng and Schaeffer 2011).
3. Mixed ownership entails funds supplemented by private participation in the capital. These results arise from assessments performed from our research group with regard to the Italian perimeter and based upon indicators analysed in Section 7.4.
4. The certified incubator for innovative startup is a corporation that shall guarantee perfect patrimonial autonomy. It must be administered or managed by persons of recognized competence in the field of enterprise and innovation and shall have at least euro 10,000 as minimum working capital and a minimum number of members (three to nine). It must be registered in a special section of the Registrar of Companies. To obtain registration it

is necessary to indicate the requirements to qualify the company as a certified incubator. In order to retain such registration, it is mandatory to quantify the activities, number of resident startups, number of employees and staff hosted, the growth rate and the number of patents registered.

REFERENCES

Aernoudt, R. (2004), Incubators: tool for entrepreneurship? *Small Business Economics* **23**(2), 127–35.

Allen, D.N. and McCluskey, R. (1990), Structure, policy, services, and performance in the business incubator industry, *Entrepreneurship Theory and Practice* **15**(2), 61–77.

Auricchio, M., Cantamessa, M., Colombelli, A. et al. (2013), Gli incubatori d'impresa in Italia, Working paper, Banca d'Italia, Roma.

Barbéro, J.L., Casillas, J.C., Wright, M., and Ramos Garcia, A. (2014), Do different types of incubators produce different types of innovations? *Journal of Technology Transfer* **39**(2), 151–68.

Baron, R. and Shane, S. (2007), *Entrepreneurship: A Process Perspective*. New York: Nelson Education.

Becker, B. and Gassmann, O. (2006), Corporate incubators: industrial R&D and what universities can learn from them, *Journal of Technology Transfer* **31**(4), 469–83.

Bhatli, D., Borella, P., Jelassi, T., and Saillant, N. (2015), Startup accelerators: entrepreneurial match makers. In *Ideas in Marketing: Finding the New and Polishing the Old*, New York: Springer Verlag, pp. 259–69.

Boutillier, S., Carré, D. and Levratto, N. (2016), *Entrepreneurial Ecosystems: 2 (Innovation, Entrepreneurship, Management: Smart Innovation Set)*, New York: Wiley-ISTE.

Chan, K.F. and Lau, T. (2005), Technology incubator programs in the science park: the good, the bad and the ugly, *Technovation* **25**(10), 1215–28.

Chandra, A. (2007), Approaches to business incubation: a comparative study of the United States, China and Brazil, Networks Financial Institute Working Paper, 2007-WP: 29, 2007.

Chandra, A., He, W. and Fealey, T. (2007), Business incubators in China: a financial services perspective, *Asia Pacific Business Review* **13**(1), 79–94.

Cheng, S. and Schaeffer, P. (2011), *Evaluation without Bias: A Methodological Perspective on Performance Measures for Business Incubators*, Région et Développement no. 33-2011 LEAD, Universite du Sud – Toulon.

Chengappa, L. and Geibel, R. (2014), What European incubators can learn from their American counterparts: an analysis of the critical success factors for a startup incubator, *Journal of Tourism and Hospitality Management* **2**(10), 40–47.

Colombo, M.G. and Delmastro, M. (2002), How effective are technology business incubators: evidence from Italy, *Research Policy* **31**, 1103–22.

Conti, A. and Gaulé, P. (2010), Is the US Outperforming Europe in University Technology Licensing? A New Perspective on the European Paradox, DRUID Working Papers 10-04, DRUID, Copenhagen Business School, Department of Industrial Economics and Strategy/Aalborg University, Department of Business Studies.

Corbett, A.C., Katz, J.A. and Siegal, D.S. (2014), *Academic Entrepreneurship: Creating an Entrepreneurial Ecosystem (Advances in Entrepreneurship, Firm Emergence and Growth)*, Emerald Group Publishing.

CSES (Centre for Strategy & Evaluation Services) (2012), Valuation of the Indicators of the Entrepreneurship and Innovation Programme Operational Guidance on Indicators, February, PO Box 159, Sevenoaks, Kent TN14 5WT, UK.

Dossena, G., Bassani, S., Bettinelli, C., and Sanz, L. (2012), Parchi Scientifici Tecnologici e loro contributo ai sistemi locali per l'innovazione: evidenze empiriche, *Sinergie Italian Journal of Management* **84**, 157–77.

Essig, L. (2014), Ownership, failure, and experience: goals and evaluation metrics of university-based arts venture incubators, *Entrepreneurship Research Journal* **4**(1), 117–35.

European Commission – Enterprise DG (2014), *Benchmarking of Business Incubators*, Brussels, Ares(2014)77245, 15 January. Available at: https://ec.europa.eu/growth/tools-databases/eip-raw-materials/en/content/european-commission-dg-enterprise-and-industry-homepage.

European Commission, State of Innovation Union (2011).

Flanschger, A. (2012), Controlling in technologiebasierten Jungunternehmen unter spezieller Berücksichtigung der Rolle des Inkubators. Verlag der Techn. University of Graz.

Flanschger, A. et al. (n.d.), Do start-ups need an incubator after incubation? Evidences from Austria, Graz University of Technology, Department of Business Economics, Kopernikusgasse 24/II.

Fritsch, M. and Noseleit, F. (2013), Start-ups, long- and short-term survivors, and their contribution to employment growth, *Journal of Evolutionary Economics* **23**(4), 719–33.

Guceri-Ucar, G. and Koch, S. (2013), Business incubation practices and software start-up success in Turkey. Lecture Notes in *Business Information Processing (LNBIP)*, Volume 150, pp. 178–82.

Hackett, S.M. and Dilts, D.M. (2004), A systematic review of business incubation research, *Journal of Technology Transfer* **29**(1), 55–82.

Isenberg, D. (2011), *Introducing the Entrepreneurship Ecosystem: Four Defining Characteristics*, Forbes-Leadership, http://www.forbes.com, 25 May, accessed 2016.

Isenberg, D. (2014), What an entrepreneurship ecosystem actually is, *Harvard Business Review* 12 May.

Johnsrud, C. (2004), Business Incubation: Profitability v.s Economic Development.

Kipper, L.M., Rodrigues, E., and Ferrari, A.G. (2014), Universities and incubators: key factors driving entrepreneurship and socioeconomic development, *Independent Journal of Management & Production* **5**(4), 25–70.

Lahorgue, M.A. (2004), Pólos, Parques e Incubadoras: instrumentos de desenvolvimento do século XXI. Brasília, DF: Anprotec.

Lalkaka, R. (2006), Technology business incubators: critical determinants of success, *Annals of the New York Academy of Sciences* **7**(8), 270–90.

Lewis, D.A., Harper-Anderson, E. and Molnar, L.A. (2011), *Incubating Success. Incubation Best Practices that Lead to Successful New Ventures*, University of Michigan Institute for Research on Labor, Employment, and the Economy, University of Michigan, Ann Arbor, MI.

Marks, K.H., Robbins, L.E., Fernandez, G., Funkhouser, J.P. and Williams, D.L.

(2009), *The Handbook of Financing Growth: Strategies, Capital Structure, and M&A Transactions*, Hoboken, NJ: John Wiley and Sons.

Masutha, M. and Rogerson, C.M. (2014), Business incubation for small enterprise development: South African pathways, *Urban Forum* **26**(2), 141–55.

Matejun, M. (2014), *Small and Medium-sized Enterprises in the European Union: Development Challenges in 2014–2020 perspective*, Lodz University of Technology, Lodz.

Mercier-Laurent, E. (2011), *Innovation Ecosystems*, Hoboken, NJ: Wiley-ISTE.

Mian, S.A. (1997), Assessing and managing the university technology business incubator: an integrative framework, *Journal of Business Venturing* **12**, 251–85.

Mignogna, A. (2014), *Analisi dei portafogli e comparazione delle performance di alcuni incubatori di impresa in Italia*, Research Paper, Politecnico di Milano, Rome.

Phillips, R.G. (2002), Technology business incubators: how effective as technology transfer mechanisms?, *Technology in Society*, **24**(3), 299–316.

Radojevich-Kelley, N. and Hoffman, D.L. (2012), Analysis of accelerator companies: an exploratory case study of their programs, processes, and early results, *Small Business Institute® Journal* **8**(2), 54–70.

Rampado, N. (2013), *Dinamiche imprenditoriali e innovazione: il rapporto tra incubatore e start-up*, Università Ca' Foscari Venezia.

Rashid, S. and Rashid, U. (2012), Work motivation differences between public and private sector, Federal Urdu University of Arts, Science and Technology Islamabad, Pakistan, CECOS University of IT and Emerging Sciences, Peshawar, Pakistan, *American International Journal of Social Science* **1**(2), 24–46.

Rifkin, J. (2016), How the Third Industrial Revolution will create a green economy. *NPQ* **33**(1), 6–10.

Rodrigues, E., Pedó, R. and Kipper L.M. (2013), *Entrepreneurship as Basis for Economic Diversification: A Case Study at UNISC's Technological Incubator*, Valladolid, Spain: ICIEOM – CIO.

Rothaermel, F.T. and Thursby, M. (2005), Incubator firm failure or graduation? The role of university linkages, *Research Policy* **34**(7), 1076–90.

Rothaermel, F.T., Agung, S., and Jiang, L. (2007), University entrepreneurship: a taxonomy of the literature, *Industrial and Corporate Change* **16**, 691–791.

Saublens, Ch. (2011), *EU-Drivers: Universities' Involvement in Regional Smart Specialisation Strategy*, EURADA, 36 pp.

Schwarzkopf, C. (2016), *Fostering Innovation and Entrepreneurship: Entrepreneurial Ecosystem and Entrepreneurial Fundamentals in the USA and Germany*, Gabler: Springer.

Tavoletti, E. (2013), Business incubators: effective infrastructures or waste of public money? Looking for a theoretical framework, guidelines and criteria, *Journal of the Knowledge Economy* **4**(4), 423–43, December.

van Vught, F.A. and Ziegele, F. (2012), *Multidimensional Ranking: The Design and Development of U-Multirank*, Rotterdam: Springer Science & Business Media, pp. 84–96, 21 February.

APPENDIX

Table A7.1   *Italy overview in terms of incubator numbers and main features*

Indicator	Geography	No.	No. startups incubated
Region	Calabria	1	NA
	Campania	3	10>50
	Emilia Romagna	6	>50
	Friuli Venezia Giulia	4	10>50
	Lazio	2	NA
	Lombardia	31	<50
	Marche	3	10>50
	Piemonte	6	<50
	Puglia	1	NA
	Sardegna	2	NA
	Sicilia	2	<50
	Toscana	5	<50
	Trentino Alto Adige	2	10>50
	Veneto	4	<50
Certification	YES		32
	NO		40
Source of finance/ operations	Businesses		10
	Banking		1
	Enterprises		1
	Institutions		16
	Mixed		15
	Private sources		19
	University based		9
	Not specified		1
Governance	Non-profit		2
	Consortium of companies		3
	Social cooperative		1
	SPA		8
	SRL		13
	SNC		21
	Cooperative		1
	SRLS		4
	Not specified		19
Services	Development and spaces		36
	Development, spaces and financing		11
	Development, spaces, financing, strategy		4
	Not specified		21

Table A7.2 Dimensions of analysis

Dimensions	Indicators' Incubation Process	Description	Degree of Reliability (0–10)	Assessment and Description	Score
ANALYTICS	Target companies	Incubated startups' growth potential	8	HIGH: Startups have the potential to grow into high growth companies (typically technology product based or technology enabled service based)	6
				MEDIUM: Startups are chasing opportunities to grow into profitable regional or local companies.	4
				LOW: Startups chase opportunities to pursue small-scale industry opportunities, agency-like (niche markets and sectors: food processing, handicraft exports and tourism).	2
	Target companies' financials	The startups' financial position at the moment of exit from the incubation program	9	HIGH: Equity investible companies with globally competitive perspectives (10 x ROI).	3
				MEDIUM: Small percentages of equity are investible; potential to be acquired or merged with larger entities. Mostly financed through debt investment or self-funding (5 x ROI).	2
				SMALL: Largely financed via debt investment or self-funding (2 x ROI).	1
	Parent organization	The incubator in force/existing partnerships with private/public institutions	7	HIGH: Partner organization is either: leading financial institution; research center; leading non-governmental or corporate groups; top angel & VC groups.	9
				MEDIUM: Partner organization is: medium financial institution, research center, local non-governmental or company, SMEs.	6
				SMALL: None or minor partner organization.	3
	Sponsoring	The incubator official sponsoring from any private/ public	5	HIGH: Net sponsoring covers >50% incubator operational expenses.	9
				MEDIUM: Net sponsoring covers 15>50% incubator operational expenses.	6

Table A7.2 (continued)

Dimensions	Indicators' Incubation Process	Description	Degree of Reliability (0–10)	Assessment and Description	Score
		institution		LOW: Net sponsoring covers < 15% incubator operational expenses.	3
	Network	Incubator network (access to experts, mentors, tutors, accommodation and/or other business support designed to nurture new businesses)	5	HIGH: Support network is constant and business support is institutionalized and regulated by internal processes and agreements.	3
				MEDIUM: Partial support network and constant business support is institutionalized and regulated by internal processes and agreements, but covers only specific needs.	2
				LOW: None or minor network of experts and accommodation services and constant business support, not institutionalized nor regulated by internal processes and agreements.	1
INTERNAL PROCESSES	Startups' selection	Incubator selection processes, defined tools and extents used for choosing a startup over another	7	HIGH: The incubator selection process is institutionalized, updated regularly, regulated by internal processes and policies and involves external peers for further evaluation.	3
		Criteria of selection define perimeter of activity and expectations		MEDIUM: The incubator selection process is partially institutionalized, and regulated by internal processes and policies, may involve external peers and ask is based upon partially documental proof.	2
				LOW: The incubator selection process is not institutionalized nor regulated by internal processes and policies; it does not involve external peers and does not required documental proof.	1
	Average time of incubation	Incubator timespan of incubation per startup	4	HIGH: The incubation process requires more than 2 years and comprises tailored milestones and procedures.	3
				MEDIUM: The incubation process requires between 1 and 2 years and comprises partial tailored milestones and procedures.	2

Criterion	Description	Score	Scoring levels	
Follow-up on incubation	Incubator's follow-up activities are institutionalized, to what extent these are regulated by internal processes and policies; bear in mind that effective follow-up involves > 50% of startups	7	LOW: The incubation process requires less than 1 to 2 years and comprises minor tailored milestones and procedures.	1
			HIGH: Follow-ups are regulated by internal processes and policies and occur regularly to provide continuous feedback flow (at least 1 each quarter).	6
			MEDIUM: Follow-ups are regulated by internal processes and policies and occur yearly in order to provide partial flow of information (at least 1 each quarter).	4
			NONE: Follow-ups are not regulated by internal processes and policies and may not occur yearly.	2
Organizational processes, policies and systems	Incubator's abilities to develop capabilities that will support startups at scale and in a sustainable manner through policies and and control systems	5	HIGH: Organizational processes, policies and systems are updated at least 2 times yearly and are also assessed/measured by external peers/outsourced. Internal controls are in place and revised yearly.	12
			MEDIUM: Organizational processes, policies and systems are updated at least yearly and are assessed/measured also by internal peers and not outsourced. Internal controls are in place but not revised.	8
			LOW: Organizational processes, policies and systems are updated at event and less than 1 time per year, and are assessed/ measured by internal peers and not outsourced. Internal controls are not in place.	4

Table A7.2 (continued)

Dimensions	Indicators' Incubation Process	Description	Degree of Reliability (0–10)	Assessment and Description	Score
CUSTOMERS	Development	Incubator's capabilities in transferring to the private sector and commercializing the results and products of scientific research and development conducted by graduated companies	5	HIGH: Patents or external royalties from graduated companies involve > 40% of companies.	9
				MEDIUM: Patents or external royalties from graduated companies involve > 20% to < 40% of companies.	6
				LOW: Patents or external royalties from graduated companies involve < 20% of companies.	3
	Outcomes	Incubator's net value of successful exits of incubated startups	7	HIGH: Value of exits per startup per year arising from the incubated startups is below 5% of total revenues.	9
				MEDIUM: Value of exits per startup per year arising from the incubated startups is between 5% and 10% of total revenues.	6
				LOW: Value of exits per startup per year arising from the incubated startups is below 20% of total revenues.	3
	Impact	Incubator's overall effect on local or national industry and impacts	3	HIGH: The effect on local or national industry and the impact of companies incubated in the long term is strong and certified by rewards, certificates and public awards.	2
				MEDIUM: The effect on local or national industry and the impact of companies incubated in the long term is moderate	1

Category	#	Metric	Description		Score
			of companies incubated; its long-term impact on the economy and local community		
			and not certified by rewards, certificates and public awards. LOW: The effect on local or national industry and the impact of companies incubated in the long term are validated by rewards, certificates and public awards.		0
	7	Percentage of revenue from royalties and others	Incubator's net value concerning royalties and technology transfer	HIGH: > 10%	9
				MEDIUM: 5 > 10%	6
				LOW: < 5%	3
COMPANIES	8	Percentage of funds raised spent in training for startups and entrepreneurs	Incubator's capabilities to encourage startups to institute training programs, teaching leadership, encouraging learning and self-improvement, and optimizing team efforts toward quality and safety	HIGH: > 10%	3
				MEDIUM: 5 > 10%	2
				LOW: < 5%	1

Table A7.2 (continued)

Dimensions	Indicators' Incubation Process	Description	Degree of Reliability (0–10)	Assessment and Description	Score
	Percentage of startups incubated that participated in fairs, events and merchandizing	Incubator's capabilities to lead startups in participating in fairs, lobbying activities and merchandizing constitute an important driver for the startups and leverage an important asset for the incubator capable of promoting its operations	6	HIGH: > 50% MEDIUM: 20 % > 50% LOW: < 20%	6 4 2
	Jobs created	Net amount of jobs created by each startup on a yearly basis divided by the number of startups to any extent (including external	5	HIGH: range > 10 MEDIUM: range 6–10 LOW: range 0–6	12 8 4

consultants, projects and outsourced activities). This concerns only startups undergoing incubation processes

Management & resources of the startup | To what extent management and resources of the startup are selected amongst experienced professionals with specific background related to the field of activity and perform training regularly | 5

HIGH: The management of the startup is selected amongst experienced professionals with specific background related to the field of activity (minimum 5 years activity) and resources and perform training regularly (yearly). | 3

MEDIUM: The management is selected amongst experienced professionals with partially related background related to the field of activity and also with less than 5 years experience and do not perform training regularly (at least yearly). | 2

LOW: The management and resources are selected amongst professionals with no specific background related to the field of activity and resources and do not perform training. | 1

Table A7.3 *Weights of analysis (to mitigate quantitative assessment)*

Dimensions	Indicators' Incubation Process	Description	Mitigating Factors (0–10)	Score Selection
AGE	Years of activity	Years since incorporation	*New or young incubators may face difficulties in their early stages*	1 – young firms 10 – old firms
TYPE	Dimension	Average number of startups per year/at average fair value/at cost of each startup	*The number of average startups per year shall be indexed to the average capitalization of each startup – considering different industries/geographies*	1 – low value 10 – high value
	Prevailing specialization	Choose one or more if "mixed"	*Depending on the specialization as it can be a competitive, hygiene or constraining factor (i.e. high specialization limits number of potential candidates)*	1 – highly specialized 10 – not specialized
LOCATION	Local area	In km, 00	*City of main location is a factor affecting potential growth and efficacy of the incubator*	1 – distant from hub/district 10 – close to hub/district
	Branches	In km, 00	*City of potential branches/foreign countries' branches of the incubators that contribute to knowledge transfers, spillovers and multinational footprint*	1 – distant from hub/district 10 – close to hub/district
	Proximity to technological hubs	In km, 00	*Proximity to technological hub brings value to incubators if a relation with it is strong and continuous and well defined in goals for mutual projects*	1 – distant from hub/district 10 – close to hub/district

Category	Attribute	Unit	Description	Scale
	Proximity to research centers	In km, 00	*Proximity to research centers brings value to incubators if a relation with it is strong and continuous and transfer occurs*	1 – distant from hub/district 10 – close to hub/district
	Proximity to entrepreneurial districts	In km, 00	*Proximity to entrepreneurial district brings value to incubators if a relation with it is strong and continuous and if the specialization levers on the district's core focus*	1 – distant from hub/district 10 – close to hub/district
FINANCIALS	Rent & services	In euros, 00	*Incubator's annual income from rents – coworking (not incubation driven)*	1 – low income 10 – high income
	Contracts and grants	In euros, 00	*Incubator's annual income from contracts and public grants (part of public promotion)*	1 – low income 10 – high income
	Investments	In euros, 00	*Incubator's annual income from equity investments performed (at costs – not at fair value)*	1 – low income 10 – high income
	Other sources	In euros, 00	*Incubator's annual income from other sources (private sponsors, consulting services provided from the incubators: indicate the sources)*	1 – low income 10 – high income:

8. Towards "skarse" entrepreneurial ecosystems: using agent-based simulation of entrepreneurship to reveal what makes regions tick

Elias G. Carayannis and Mike Provance

8.1 INTRODUCTION

The formation of new ventures draws considerable attention in the strategy, organizational theory, and entrepreneurship literatures. One of the central perspectives that scholars in these fields adopt is that of knowledge and the development of capabilities. New ventures pursue knowledge in order to establish capabilities and increase their competitiveness by acting on opportunities. How ventures gain this knowledge remains a hotly contested question among small business scholars. One camp believes that entrepreneurial activity is primarily a product of localized knowledge spillovers that lead to agglomeration of economic activity (Krugman 1991). Other scholars suggest that entrepreneurs actively form broad-reaching knowledge networks to overcome the limitations imposed by resource and geographic constraints (Almeida and Kogut 1999; Rosenkopf and Almeida 2003). From both vantage points, the outcomes of entrepreneurial activity are measured in terms of regional impact – the growth of economies as a result of regional innovation system dynamics.

Entrepreneurial ventures alter competitive dynamics in a region by introducing alternative products and services into the market, which in turn improve the economic conditions of the market (Freeman and Engel 2007). Carayannis (2009, p. 236) has defined sustainability of this entrepreneurial activity in regions as ongoing "creation of viable, profitable and scalable firms that engender the formation of self-replicating and mutually enhancing innovation networks and knowledge clusters," which suggests that a cornerstone of sustainable new venture formation in regions is external knowledge acquisition.

These mechanisms are influenced by the composition of the regions too. Institutions co-located with a new venture in a region significantly influence the new knowledge the venture acquires. Much of the existing literature considers the relationship between the new venture, the entrepreneur's social capital, and firm performance. However, relatively less research has been devoted to examining the influence of these on the new venture's knowledge acquisition activities and the resulting sustainability of regional entrepreneurial activity. This chapter focuses on the formation of alliances by new ventures, one particular form of knowledge acquisition process that has been established as critical to new venture success in the high technology sector.

This process and the environment within which it occurs lead to the central question of this study: How does the institutional context of a region influence new ventures' knowledge acquisition actions during their growth, and in turn the level of sustained entrepreneurial activity within the region? Entrepreneurial knowledge is knowledge used to shape the new venture during the formative stages of a venture's growth. The acquisition of new knowledge plays a crucial role in the formation and growth of each new venture (Wiklund and Shepherd 2003). When the level of new venture formation is compared across regions, however, the conditions under which this growth occurs also become relevant.

This chapter uses simulation methodology to examine regional effects of institutions and knowledge acquisition on new venture formation (Provance 2010). The foundation for using simulation to study organizational dynamics is quite strong despite some opposition. Some scholars have argued that simulation may be used to elucidate complex linkages in organizational settings that are difficult to observe in the field or through other empirical methods, while research critical of the method has suggested that simulation creates models that are distantly removed from the phenomena they seek to explain (Zott 2003). In response, Davis and colleagues clarified the most relevant uses of simulation for organizational research: "Simulation is particularly suited to the development of simple theory because of its strengths in enhancing theoretical precision and related internal validity and in enabling theoretical elaboration and exploration through computational experimentation" (Davis et al. 2007, p. 482).

A growing body of empirical work exists regarding the formation and structure of alliances by entrepreneurs. However, this work draws from disparate strands of organizational theory, often with conflicting or disconnected conclusions. What is evident from all of this research is that the processes associated with the acquisition of knowledge by entrepreneurs from external sources have complicated interdependencies and contingencies. For this reason, simulation provides a methodology that enables this study to address the question of how a region's institutional context influences the structure of entrepreneurs' alliances and the rate of regional new venture formation. What follows is a discussion of the relationship between institutional influence, entrepreneurial alliance structure and new venture formation. Then, a computational design for the simulation is described, results from running the simulation are analysed, and conclusions regarding the contributions of this study are offered.

8.2   EXTERNAL KNOWLEDGE ACQUISITION AND INSTITUTIONS

Entrepreneurs possess scarce resources that they must allocate in order to maximize their appropriation of entrepreneurial rents. Early in the life of the venture, the allocation of these resources, particularly knowledge resources, involves the creation of new capabilities. The allocation also emphasizes gaining access to additional resources (Alvarez and Barney 2005). A primary source of access comes from alliance networks developed by new ventures to expedite growth and gain competitive advantage. An entrepreneurial venture's network is a complex organizational structure that at different points in the firm's growth may act as a constraint or cost to formation or as a catalyst of continued growth (Ariño et al. 2008; Eisenhardt and Schoonhoven 1996).

Like social networks, alliance networks are constructed from a core containing strong, redundant ties and peripheral connections that are considered weak and populated with structural holes, or positions of disconnection between network participants (Burt 1992; Granovetter 1973, 1985). Entrepreneurs gain competitive advantage from their asymmetric access to heterogeneous external knowledge, which is more likely to contain untapped and unique resources. At the same time, entrepreneurs struggle to access diverse sources of knowledge because they are more likely to lie on the periphery of regional knowledge networks and be unevenly distributed throughout regions. They initially lack the capabilities to build far-reaching networks, and thus are at a disadvantage in reaching these sources of valuable knowledge. Also, entrepreneurs will exhibit intrinsic heterogeneity in their abilities to create the networks. New ventures achieve more sustainable levels of growth when they develop capabilities from combinations of knowledge resources that enable them to build more robust peripheral network structures (Almeida and Kogut 1999; Eisenhardt and Schoonhoven 1996).

The interactions between institutions and entrepreneurs are governed by economic systems comprised of parallel activity systems. Carayannis and Campbell (2009, p. 202) describe the model as "a multi-layered, multimodal and multi-lateral system, encompassing mutually complementary and reinforcing innovation networks and knowledge clusters consisting of human and intellectual capital, shaped by social capital and underpinned by financial capital." In other words, entrepreneurship occurs as an endeavor within a complex system of systems throughout which knowledge is the primary content. This system never rests or reaches equilibrium. It has previously been described as a Triple Helix of Innovation linking the knowledge-based activities of academia, industry, and government over time (Etzkowitz and Leydesdorff 2000), to which Carayannis and Campbell (2009) added a fourth helix of society – the interactions of media and culture. Variety in the flows of knowledge between layers of the innovation system and use of knowledge by system participants produces heterogeneity in the quality and rate of entrepreneurial activity within and between regional innovation systems (i.e., communities, geographies, or countries). The sustainability of this activity produces greater economic performance for a region (Carayannis et al. 2008).

Broader institutional forces structure interactions that create and sustain markets, influence the allocation of resources across markets, and guide the behaviors of actors within those markets (North 1991; Scott and Meyer 1994). Markets serve as institutions that naturally and directly shape the rate, quality, and location of entrepreneurial activity (Fligstein 2001). Competitive forces likewise play influential roles in shaping the nature of entrepreneurial action. These dynamics are viewed generally as the actions and responses of members in a market (competitors, partners, and so on) seeking to gain competitive advantage (Smith et al. 1991). In markets characterized as dynamic, or changing, the innovation system represents a central engine of growth in the presence of these forces. The model framing the research presented here connects institutional forces with the innovation system, and innovation- and competition-related behaviors of organizations in that system with the knowledge acquisition actions of new ventures seeking access to it.

The choice by an entrepreneur of which knowledge acquiring activities to pursue carries significant risks, so the decisions of how and when to acquire new knowledge from outside the new venture weighs heavily on its growth and success. Prior literature has identified two central means of knowledge acquisition by entrepreneurs: networks of social capital or knowledge, and the localized spillover effects of industry agglomeration in a region (Agarwal et al. 2007). These two perspectives overlap because formal knowledge networks may include nodes that are also part of the agglomerated local spillover (Tallman and Phene 2007). However, the perspectives vary significantly in their implications for new venture formation and growth. A fundamental assumption of this study is that agglomeration theory underestimates the value of heterogeneity of knowledge resources present within regions and of cross-region knowledge acquisition for inducing entrepreneurial behaviors that produce longer-lasting new ventures within a region (Carayannis 2009; Klepper and Sleeper 2005; Krugman 1991). Alliance formation provides an important source of this variation (Nelson 2004; Spilling 2007).

8.2.1   Knowledge-mediating Institutions

Regions benefit from the introduction of institutions into their innovation systems. Institutions can catalyse the emergence of new ventures by providing mechanisms that make the formation of network connections to sources of specialized knowledge and capabilities easier (Saxenian 1994). Other institutions introduce efficiency into the innovation system by reducing variation in the knowledge available to organizations in the region. These institutions favor older incumbent firms, which are likely to be more focused on exploitation of existing knowledge than exploration for new knowledge (March 1991). These institutions influence the strategic actions of new ventures and incumbent firms in the region, including the search for new knowledge and development of new capabilities. Search for new knowledge is generally accepted as occurring progressively, beginning with local search and expanding outward when improvements in the firm's knowledge fail to materialize, although alliances have been recognized as mechanisms to move quickly beyond (or skip) localized search into more distant domains (Rosenkopf and Almeida 2003; Stuart and Podolny 1996). Institutions that increase the availability of diverse knowledge reduce the search requirements on new ventures that must allocate scarce resources to capability development. Conversely, institutions that reduce variability in the value of novel knowledge cause new ventures to increase their investments in search of new knowledge.

The institutional context employed here is the socio-political institutional infrastructure present within a region. Specifically, the simulation models three types of institutions present in economic markets: Knowledge standardizing institutions, knowledge production-stimulating institutions, and knowledge variation-inducing institutions. Examples of these are provided in Table 8.1.

Knowledge standardizing institutions are defined here as those social and regulatory structures that limit the potential for novel knowledge production within a particular domain (i.e., scientific, economic) by reducing the degree of variation in the nature of knowledge or making that knowledge public, thereby removing its novelty, but also increasing its replication efficiency. Technology standards organizations and patent offices serve as

Table 8.1   Knowledge-mediating institutions

Knowledge Standardizing Institutions	Technology standards organizations
	International trade treaties
	Patent offices
Knowledge Production-Stimulating	Economic development funding
Institutions	Department of Defense agencies
	Trade and industry associations
	Confidentiality agreements
Knowledge Variation-Inducing	Universities
Institutions	Scientific institutes
	Federal scientific research funding

examples of this type of institution as their primary missions include the proliferation of a consistent, replicable public knowledge base. *Knowledge production-stimulating institutions* are mechanisms designed to facilitate the creation and movement of more knowledge without regard to its novelty. These institutions play important roles in the dissemination of knowledge through social network structures and as gatekeepers or clearinghouses of new knowledge that has value in its public spillover, such as specialized knowledge generated and distributed through the involvement of economic development organizations or trade associations. *Knowledge variation-inducing institutions* possess different missions from the first two types. These institutions focus on exploration by encouraging (through access to financial, human, and other capital resources) the pursuit and accumulation of novel knowledge by organizations, often by new ventures.

The importance of all three types of institutions has been noted previously (Carayannis and Alexander 1999; DiGregorio and Shane 2003; Ozsomer and Cavusgil 2000). The work by Carayannis and Alexander (1999) emphasizes the importance of well-developed collaboration between public and private entities on industry performance at a regional or national level, but focuses on the performance of publicly traded or larger investor-backed firms. These firms benefit from standardization because of the production efficiencies it produces. Similarly, Ozsomer and Cavusgil (2000) see similar effects of increased competition and technology exploitation benefiting larger, central players in their ecological examination of the global personal computer industry. DiGregorio and Shane (2003) found that institutional factors play central roles in the spin-off of new ventures from universities, particularly with respect to knowledge and innovation captured as intellectual property.

8.3   SIMULATION DESIGN AND METHODOLOGY

The simulation methodology employed in this study builds on the relevancy of simulation to simple theory. Simple theory may be described as the logical explanation of a phenomenon that has few constructs and related propositions, uses propositions that – while likely correct – are weakly situated in empirical research, or explains the less understood interactions between better known basic processes (Davis et al. 2007). Knowledge acquisition through alliances by fledgling ventures falls into the category of simple theory. This simulation uses a previously published computational model (Provance 2010) that represents regional entrepreneurial activity as a dynamic Poisson system in which institutions, entrepreneurs, incumbent firms, buyers, and knowledge sources interact.

8.3.1   Simulation Model

The simulation uses a landscape model in which the agents participate in a complex innovation system within local, interconnected neighborhoods (Epstein and Axtell 1996). These neighborhoods are computationally defined as lattice points on a torus-shaped lattice structure. A torus refers here to a two-dimensional square space in which the most distant points are located on the centers of two symmetrical shapes created when the entire landscape is bisected either horizontally or vertically. This geometry ensures that the simulation is not analytically biased towards points in the center, while agents on peripheral lattice points get "trapped." Agents may pass off one edge and enter at the same lateral point on the opposite edge (Epstein and Axtell 1996). Conceptually, the lattice points depict regional innovation systems (e.g., national innovation systems). Thus, the entire lattice structure models a global innovation system across which institutional practices, organizational resources, and market structures vary (Carayannis and Campbell 2009).

   Complex systems are distinguished by stocks of resources possessed by agents and interactions between them that generate flows of these resources in the system. In this simulation, the resources are clusters of specialized knowledge that firms and incumbents use to produce innovations for buyers. The knowledge resources and innovation requirements are codified as 28-bit binary strings. The simulation design consists of seven processes that represent interactions of the agents and knowledge resources (Figure 8.1): new venture creation, new venture capability generation, firm transition, product innovation, product adoption, buyer requirement evolution, and institutional knowledge mediation.

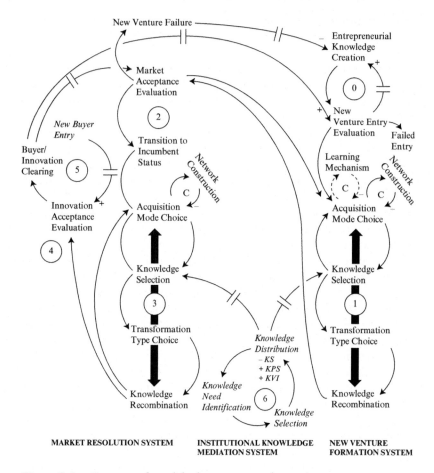

Figure 8.1   Conceptual model of new venture formation

Collectively, these seven processes comprise the three subsystems of the model: New Venture Formation, Market Resolution, and Institutional Knowledge Mediation. *New venture creation* (0) is the process through which nascent entrepreneurs decide to start new ventures. Nascent entrepreneurs enter the simulation probabilistically at a rate established during the initialization of a simulation run, and are granted a small amount of knowledge on a randomized basis. *New venture capability generation* (1) is an innovation process the drives new venture growth during the simulation. The primary objectives of new ventures in the simulation are acquisition of new knowledge to create capabilities and transition to incumbent status. New ventures acquire new knowledge through formal network connections (e.g., alliances) or by absorbing localized spillovers of knowledge. Once acquired, the knowledge is transformed into innovation capabilities.

A firm's external knowledge accumulation process is defined in the literature as the combination of acquisition and assimilation activities, although it uses different models across papers. Todorova and Durisin (2007) summarize these differences (i.e., Cohen and Levinthal 1990; Zahra and George 2002) in their reconceptualization of absorptive capacity. This study examines two significant components of this process for new ventures: acquisition of knowledge from external sources, and transformation of acquired knowledge into useful internalized knowledge. In this simulation, the new venture is assumed to possess relatively little extant knowledge, so it must focus on acquisition from its inception. For this reason, other mechanisms of the knowledge appropriation process are held constant across agents, assuming each agent uses the knowledge acquired with perfect efficiency given the constraints it has, such as imperfect market information and innovation capability (specified as the difference between its extant knowledge and the market need it attempts to address).

Firm transition (2) occurs when a new venture's capability generation efforts have created a sustainable organizational form. After each period of capability generation, the knowledge string of the new venture is compared with the requirement strings of all of the buyers in the region. If the new venture fails to find a match over the first ten (10) periods of its existence, then the simulation removes it from the model and logs the event as a new venture failure. *Product innovation* (3) creates a mechanism for incumbent firms to engage in innovation. A subsystem of knowledge acquisition and transformation similar to the one for new venture capability generation is used in this process, but with different configuration parameters. *Product adoption* (4) represents the way in which buyers accept innovations produced by firms. This process is the culmination of the innovation process, and results in market needs being removed from the landscape. If the match occurs and the product is adopted, the incumbent firm's sales score is increased and the buyer that adopted the product is removed from the lattice point.

Buyer resolution (5) controls the rate and nature of entry for new customer requirements on the lattice structure. New customers are generated at a rate established during configuration of the simulation. This rate is then affected by the density of existing buyers in the market, and the numbers of incumbent firms and new ventures in the lattice point. As new customers are generated in the system, these customers are assigned sets of preferences, defined as knowledge requirements for innovations to be adopted. *Institutional knowledge mediation* (6) influences the degree of variation in available knowledge within a region. It will affect the knowledge acquisition results of both incumbent firms and new ventures, and the value of loose knowledge clusters and requirements of buyers, by reducing or increasing the variation in knowledge transferred to the agents.

The three types of institutions described above are modeled in the simulation as institution agents that manipulate knowledge flows within a lattice point according to different behavioral rules established for each type of institution. These behaviors are defined in Table 8.2.

8.3.2 Variables and Configurations

The variables measured to analyse the simulation come from the parameters of the particular configuration used in the simulation and the measures of system performance generated during a simulation run. The

Table 8.2   Types of institutional knowledge-mediating agents

Institutional Agent	Actions
Knowledge Standardizing	• Institution copies knowledge from whichever incumbent firm has highest innovation sales level in lattice point ("winning design") • Institution selects 3-bit piece of knowledge within winning design string that is common to most buyer agents in lattice point • The selected 3-bit string is distributed to all incumbent firms and new venture agents in focal and adjacent lattice points based on a loss function
Knowledge Production-Stimulating	• Institution identifies knowledge string of any length that is common to most buyers • Institution selects 3-bit piece of knowledge from initially selected string (or less if the initially selected string is 1–2 bits in length) • The selected 3-bit piece is distributed to incumbent firm, new venture, and loose knowledge cluster agents in the lattice point and other lattice points based on a loss function
Knowledge Variation-Inducing	• Institution identifies knowledge missing in region (up to 3 bits not present in any buyer string) • Institution selects string and distributes to buyer and new venture agent(s) on some uniformly distributed probability

simulation uses configurations that reflect the institutional context and innovation system characteristics of economic regions that vary in initial conditions. These regions could emulate national and global contexts, such as contrasting the innovation environment of Boston and Silicon Valley, or Norway and India.

Variables. The outcome measures of interest in this simulation study are the regional rate and level of new venture formation. These measures are computed by lattice point as a probability of new venture formation (defined as survival to a stable growth state – or transition to incumbent status) and aggregate number of new ventures that form, respectively. New venture formation occurs when the match between a new venture's knowledge and a buyer's requirements exceeds the system's threshold for transition to an incumbent firm state in that lattice point, which is set during initialization. The level of regional new venture formation is calibrated to empirically tested levels of survival for new firms (Watson and Everett 1996).

Analysis of the simulation is based on four types of variables: system-wide parameters, manipulated variables, process variables, and outcome measures. Since the simulation is a dynamic Poisson model, parameters may be altered by changes in states in the system through feedback and feed-forward loops. In particular, system parameters include a *Configuration Identifier* and dummy variables for the presence of each of the three types of institution in a lattice point – *Knowledge Standardizing Institution, Knowledge Production-Generating Institution,* and *Knowledge Variation-Inducing Institution.* The manipulated variable is *Probability of Formal Knowledge Acquisition,* and process variables include the *Average Numbers of Formal* and *Informal Actions* that agents produce, *Network Size* and *Node Closeness Centrality* and their squared terms, and *Average Age of the New Ventures* at the end of the simulation run.

Network Size and Node Closeness Centrality are social network analysis metrics that define the structure of an incumbent's or new venture's network. Network size is defined as the number of partners a particular agent (incumbent or new venture) is connected to. These connections are bidirectional by convention in this simulation, meaning either partner may avail itself of knowledge from the other partner. Node Closeness Centrality is one of several measures of centrality used to define the importance of a node, or agent, in the network based on the nature of network characteristics. Node Closeness Centrality is used here because it is based on geographic proximity, which is the manner in which networks are constructed in the simulation (Wasserman and Faust 1994). The primary output measures used to evaluate performance are the *Probability of New Venture Formation* and *Average Number of New Ventures Formed.*

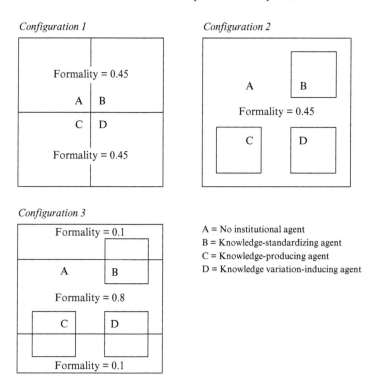

Configuration 1

Formality = 0.45

A | B

C | D

Formality = 0.45

Configuration 2

A   B

Formality = 0.45

C   D

Configuration 3

Formality = 0.1

A   B

Formality = 0.8

C   D

Formality = 0.1

A = No institutional agent
B = Knowledge-standardizing agent
C = Knowledge-producing agent
D = Knowledge variation-inducing agent

Figure 8.2   Simulation configurations for regional analysis of new venture formation

Configurations. The primary mechanism for inducing variation in the simulation is the manner in which system variables are configured across the landscape. Running different configurations allows the researcher to examine changes in performance that are linked to parameters on the landscape and variables influencing new venture behavior. For this study, three configurations are employed. These are depicted in Figure 8.2.

These configurations are designed to emulate realistic environments in which institutional contexts vary. While they are not models of actual environments, they possess characteristics consistent with elements of entrepreneurial centers of activity, such as Silicon Valley, Cambridge, England, or Israel (Saxenian 1994; Senor and Singer 2009). The empirical significance of predecessor models from this simulation provides evidence to support the use of these configurations here (Carayannis et al. 2011; Provance 2010).

Configuration 1 is a landscape consisting of four adjacent regions, each one except for A (see Figure 8.3) containing a different one of the three types of institutions. The radius of impact for institutions in this configuration is set to 3, which means that one type of institution's knowledge mediating activities can reach up to three regions away in any direction. The parameter for determining the formal or informal acquisition of knowledge by new ventures is set to 0.45 for formal acquisition, 0.45 for informal acquisition, and 0.1 for neither. The "neither" condition is introduced into the model to allow for internal exploitation activities and to avoid an assumption that firms are only knowledge acquirers.

Configuration 2 introduces "non-institutionalized" space between the institutionalized regions (B, C, and D) that prevents one type of institution from influencing the knowledge acquiring activities of an agent in another institutionalized region directly. The agent may still be affected through the partners it may choose for formal knowledge acquisition. The parameters for knowledge acquisition formality are consistent with those in Configuration 1. Configuration 3 is identical to Configuration 2, except that it divides the parameters for formality into two sections of the landscape, one where formal knowledge acquisition probability is set to 0.8, informal is 0.1, and neither is 0.1. These conditions are reversed in the other section, so that formal is 0.1, informal is 0.8, and neither is 0.1.

8.4   RESULTS AND ANALYSIS

The simulation is run three times on each of the three configurations, generating a dataset approaching 180,000 agent observations, which reduces to 3,600 lattice point observations on average. Each configuration generates on average 60,000 agents over three runs, which aggregates to approximately 180,000. When these observations are aggregated to measures of regional performance (e.g., probability of new venture formation) for this study, the resulting dataset includes 3,600 observations over three configurations (20 x 20 matrix = 400 lattice points x 3 runs / matrix = 1,200 lattice point observations per configuration x 3 configurations = 3,600 observations). Running repeated trials of the same configuration reduces bias issues and provides a statistically significant sample for analysis.

Analysis consists of three stages: model validity, graphical analysis, and pattern analysis. The simulation model was tested to evaluate the robustness and stability of the design, which proved sufficiently valid for further analysis. Once the model architecture and programming was eliminated as a likely source of variation in the results, the lattice point data for the three configurations were graphically analysed. The results presented here are captured at the end of the simulation run. A duration of 65 periods was determined for the simulation runs in the studies because it represented

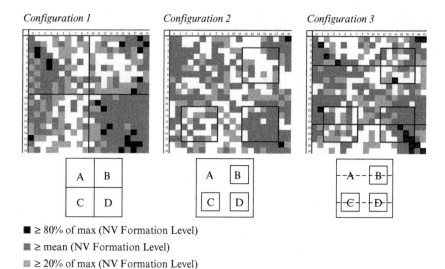

■ ≥ 80% of max (NV Formation Level)

▨ ≥ mean (NV Formation Level)

▨ ≥ 20% of max (NV Formation Level)

Figure 8.3   New venture formation levels across configurations and regions

a span during which the simulation reached a state of stable function for several periods. For the sake of convention, 65 periods may be thought of in terms of years, more or less. Since agents make choices about actions probabilistically on a continuous basis, any agent may experience zero to several events (or actions) within the course of one period.

Two simulation variables provide insights into the effects of regional variation in institutional conditions: Average Number of New Ventures Formed, and Probability of New Venture Formation. Average Number of New Ventures Formed provides data on historic performance, while the Probability of New Venture Formation offers predictions regarding future system behaviors. To make visual analysis of these outputs easier, the levels of new venture formation and probabilities of new venture formation in Figures 8.3 and 8.4, respectively, have been tiered using a modified Pareto distribution. The darkest regions represent lattice points where results are 80 percent or more of the maximum value of the measure on the lattice. The next darkest regions show lattice points where the values are greater than the mean of the measure across lattice points, and the lighter gray indicates lattice points at the 20 percent (of maximum value) mark. White lattice points represent the lowest performance (< 20 percent).

Average Number of New Ventures Formed captures aggregate, absolute levels of new venture activity and growth by identifying the number of new ventures that survive to incumbent firm status in a lattice point. Figure 8.3

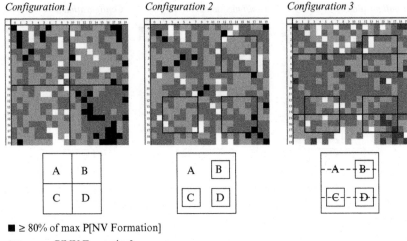

*Figure 8.4   Survival rates for new ventures, expressed as probability of
              formation occurring across configurations and regions*

depicts an example of one run from each configuration (1, 2, and 3), showing levels of new venture formation by lattice point, or "neighborhood."
Other runs exhibited similar results. As Figure 8.3 indicates, the distinct
institutional contexts are demarcated with letters A through D. From
this graphical analysis, two factors seem to predominate the new venture
formation events on the landscape. First, the knowledge standardizing and
knowledge production-stimulating institutions seem to reduce the absolute
levels of new venture formation below levels produced in regions with no
formal institutions operating in them. These observations seem to be more
or less consistent across all three configurations.

In Configuration 1 (and supported by evidence in Configurations 2
and 3), the knowledge acquisition activity in A leading to higher levels of
new venture formation appear to spill into the knowledge standardizing
region (B). This spillover does not appear to be due to the characteristics
of B because it also occurs on the fringe outside B in Configurations 2 and
3. Some of the spillover seems to flow into region D, too. However, this
region exhibits its own high levels of new venture formation across all three
configurations. Consistently higher levels of new venture formation are
present across most of the lattice points within Region D. These observations gain additional support from a graphic analysis of the probabilities
of new venture formation across the lattice structure.

Figure 8.4 depicts the probability of new venture formation by lattice point. The results are consistent with those presented for "New Venture Formation Level," but also demonstrate the effects of formal knowledge acquisition reaching beyond local neighborhoods, or lattice points. In Figure 8.3, significant white space (low levels of formation) appears in between contiguous areas of heightened new venture activity. In Figure 8.4, moderate levels of the probability of new venture formation – an indicator of future system behavior – replace these low levels. So, the historical time of the simulation exhibits agglomeration effects to some degree. If new ventures in lattice points were to use informal knowledge acquisition predominantly, then the results shown in Figure 8.4 would mimic more closely the results from Figure 8.3.

Statistical analysis of the simulation output corroborates these findings. In order to develop statistical evidence that was valid given the non-linear, dynamic nature of the simulation, this study employed a two-staged analytical approach that focused on identifying variation in patterns across the regions based on the simulation parameters. The analyses use New Venture Formation Level and Probability of New Venture Formation, along with assignments of an observation to a Configuration Identifier and region on the lattice structure (Group).

The first analyses use analysis of variance methods to isolate the regions exhibiting significant differences in performance from the rest of the simulation landscape. Comparing the three configurations with ANOVA (results not reported here) for variation between them produced mixed results (for 1–2 and 1–3: $p < 0.001$; for 2–3: not significant). However, the results were sufficient to proceed to analysis of each of the configurations. Tables 8.3 and 8.4 present analysis of variance results when testing both the aggregate New Venture Formation Level and Probability of New Venture Formation across regions within each configuration.

In the analysis of New Venture Formation Level (Table 8.3), all three configurations exhibited differences in the means of New Venture Formation Levels, while Configurations 1 and 2 also exhibited differences in the variance across groups ($p < 0.05$ and $p < 0.005$, respectively). Post hoc Bonferroni tests revealed that the mean differences were primarily linked to significantly higher means for the knowledge variation-inducing regions than for the other three regions ($p < 0.001$) across all three configurations. Testing the Probability of New Venture Formation yielded similar results, although only Configuration 1 showed significance in the variance between group populations (Table 8.4).

These statistical results confirmed the graphical analysis, which showed the greater level of impact knowledge variation-inducing institutions had on the development of sustainable regional entrepreneurship and the

Table 8.3   *Analysis of variance for absolute levels of new venture formation across regions*

Configuration 1

Source	SS	df	MS	F	Prob > F
Between groups	47,848.92	3	15,949.64	81.49	0.000
Within groups	234,074.04	1,196	195.71		
Total	281,922.96	1,199	235.13		

Barlett's test for equal variances: $X^2(3) = 9.98$ Prob $>X^2 = 0.019$

Configuration 2

Source	SS	df	MS	F	Prob > F
Between groups	20,203.84	3	6,734.61	44.57	0.000
Within groups	180,737.56	1,196	151.12		
Total	200,941.40	1,199	167.59		

Barlett's test for equal variances: $X^2(3) = 25.98$ Prob $>X^2 = 0.000$

Configuration 3

Source	SS	df	MS	F	Prob >F
Between groups	16,879.34	3	5,626.45	31.91	0.000
Within groups	210,901.65	1,196	176.34		
Total	227,780.99	1,199	189.98		

Barlett's test for equal variances: $X^2(3) = 5.16$ Prob $>X^2 = 0.161$

Table 8.4   *Analysis of variance for probability of new venture formation across regions*

Configuration 1

Source	SS	df	MS	F	Prob > F
Between groups	3.42	3	1.14	32.57	0.000
Within groups	41.81	1194	0.04		
Total	45.23	1197	0.04		

Barlett's test for equal variances: $X^2(3) = 17.19$ Prob $>X^2 = 0.001$

Configuration 2

Source	SS	df	MS	F	Prob > F
Between groups	0.93	3	0.31	8.31	0.000
Within groups	44.28	1192	0.04		
Total	45.20	1195	0.04		

Barlett's test for equal variances: $X^2(3) = 2.815$ Prob $>X^2 = 0.421$

Configuration 3

Source	SS	Df	MS	F	Prob > F
Between groups	0.99	3	0.33	7.52	0.000
Within groups	52.49	1195	0.04		
Total	53.48	1198	0.05		

Barlett's test for equal variances: $X^2(3) = 5.16$ Prob $>X^2 = 0.161$

relative negative effect that the other institutions had on entrepreneurial activity.

The results from this simulation were analysed further using Tobit regression on the Probability of New Venture Formation. Regression may be used for its value at identifying patterns within populations of data on a more complex level than analysis of variance allows. In this case, the method is being used inductively (without a priori hypotheses) to investigate agent behaviors at a regional, or lattice point, level of analysis. The use of regression on the data resulting from agent-based modeling reveals systematic patterns that emerge from the interdependent actions of individual agents, which has been justified previously in simulation research (Cederman 2003; Earnest 2009). Tobit regression is appropriate to this study because the variable of interest is a bounded, continuous one with an upper limit of 1.0 and a lower limit of 0.0, and Tobit regression relaxes assumptions of normality in linear regression. The regression models used here focus on the manipulated variables as sources of "independent" influence, while certain system parameters are used as controls. The correlation table for these variables is provided in Table 8.5.

Three models were analysed using Tobit regression: (1) a simple model of formal and informal actions, and institutional context; (2) introduction of structural agent network measures to the first model; and (3) tests of curvilinear characteristics in the relationship between network structure and probability of new venture formation. In all three, the average age of new ventures in the lattice point and the configuration identifier were used as controls. The average age of new ventures, which was significant and positive ($p < 0.005$), would be expected to influence formation levels because of issues regarding crowding within the lattice point. Increasing populations of new ventures initially increase and then decrease the likelihood of entry of nascent entrepreneurs after a certain point as a function within the simulation. Also, path dependence in the innovation process may result from more agents (incumbent firms and new ventures) locating in a particular region, since the likelihood of these agents sharing information will increase. This latter explanation is consistent with the arguments of agglomeration raised by Klepper, Krugman, and others (Klepper and Sleeper 2005; Krugman 1991). The regression results of the three models are shown in Table 8.6.

In Model 1, formal and informal actions (a and b) exhibit negative and significant relationships with probability of formation ($p < 0.005$). One possibility is that the levels of these actions are endogenous to the outcome; the longer it takes for a new venture to reach the transition to incumbent firm (definition of formation), the more actions are likely to be undertaken. Two factors may reduce the endogeneity explanation,

Table 8.5 Correlation matrix for lattice point aggregated simulation data

	(1)	(2)	(3)	(4)	(5)	(6)	(7)	(8)	(9)	(10)	(11)	(12)
1 Prob[New Ven. Surv]	1.00											
2 Prob[Formal Acquis.]	0.08	1.00										
3 Prob[Informal Acquis.]	0.31	(0.59)	1.00									
4 Network Size	0.04	(0.41)	0.87	1.00								
5 Network Size^2	0.01	(0.30)	0.81	0.97	1.00							
6 Node Closeness Centrality	0.36	(0.43)	0.70	0.63	0.54	1.00						
7 Node Closeness Centrality^2	0.35	(0.44)	0.70	0.63	0.55	0.99	1.00					
8 Know Standardizing Inst	(0.06)	0.01	0.00	0.05	0.04	0.07	0.05	1.00				
9 Know Production-Gen Inst	(0.05)	0.07	(0.02)	0.02	0.02	0.00	(0.01)	(0.18)	1.00			
10 Know Variation-Induce Inst	0.17	0.03	(0.05)	(0.13)	(0.13)	0.05	0.04	(0.18)	0.01	1.00		
11 Age of New Venture	0.73	0.19	0.37	0.17	0.13	0.30	0.29	(0.02)	(0.01)	0.09	1.00	
12 Configuration Type	(0.07)	(0.05)	0.02	(0.07)	0.03	(0.17)	(0.09)	(0.19)	(0.14)	(0.14)	(0.08)	1.00

Table 8.6   *Results of Tobit regression analysis on probability of new venture formation*

		Model 1		Model 2		Model 3	
(a)	Prob[Formal Acquis.]	−0.02***	(0.002)	0.01***	(0.002)	0.01***	(0.002)
(b)	Prob[Informal Acquis.]	−0.01***	(0.002)	0.03***	(0.004)	0.04***	(0.004)
(c)	Network Size			−0.13***	(0.008)	−0.13***	(0.015)
(d)	Network Size^2					−0.001	(0.002)
(e)	Node Closeness Centrality			0.42***	(0.032)	0.92***	(0.135)
(f)	Node Closeness Centrality^2					−0.60***	(0.151)
(g)	Know Standardizing Inst	−0.01	(0.009)	−0.02*	(0.008)	−0.02*	(0.008)
(h)	Know Production-Gen Inst	−0.04***	(0.009)	−0.04***	(0.008)	−0.04***	(0.008)
(i)	Know Variation-Induce Inst	0.04***	(0.009)	0.02*	(0.008)	0.02**	(0.008)
(j)	Age of New Venture	0.03***	(0.001)	0.02***	(0.001)	0.01***	(0.001)
(k)	Configuration Type	−0.001	(0.004)	−0.01**	(0.004)	−0.002	(0.004)
	Constant	0.14***	(0.025)	0.20***	(0.029)	0.05	(0.051)
	Sigma	0.14***	(0.002)	0.13***	(0.002)	0.13***	(0.002)
	N	1998		1998		1998	
	X^2	1660.55		2022.98		2040.22	
	Log Likelihood	1066.57		1247.79		1256.40	

Notes: * $p < 0.1$ ** $p < 0.05$ *** $p < 0.005$.

however. The simulation includes a fixed duration (10 periods) for new ventures to achieve the transition before they are treated as failures, so the relationship between these variables should appear weaker. Also, a reasonable explanation for the relationship is to view the choice to act as a cost to the new venture. Every action adds to the overall cost of survival for the new venture, which taxes the capital resources of the venture and increases its risk of failure.

Model 1 also shows significance in the effects of two types of institutions (knowledge production-stimulating, and knowledge variation-inducing) on the probability of formation. The presence of Knowledge Production-Stimulating Institution agents had a negative and significant ($p < 0.005$) relationship with the Probability of New Venture Formation, while the effects of Knowledge Variation-Inducing Institution agents were positive and significant ($p < 0.005$). These results are consistent with the visual analysis of the lattice point data, confirming that, within this simulation environment, Knowledge Production-Stimulating Institution agents reduce sustainability in a region while Knowledge Variation-Inducing ones contribute to a greater likelihood of high levels of new venture formation.

Models 2 and 3 introduce structure network metrics as explanatory variables for system behavior. The introduction of these variables has a significant effect on the relationships between formal and informal actions and the Probability of New Venture Formation by reversing the direction ($p < 0.005$). The correlations between these variables differ in direction, however. This suggests that the effects of network structure on the relationship between levels of actions are not statistical artifacts, but rather an explanation of system behavior. As new ventures create networks the value of actions to their successful formation increases. These results suggest that smaller networks improve sustainability of entrepreneurship in a region. Further analysis of the network structural variables demonstrates a significant, concave (inverted U-shape) relationship ($p < 0.005$) between Node Closeness Centrality and Probability of New Venture Formation consistent with the premise that entrepreneurs go outside their local regions through their networks to acquire novel knowledge (Almeida and Kogut 1999).

8.5   DISCUSSION

The importance of gaining insights into entrepreneurship has increased dramatically over the last two decades, as regions grow increasingly dependent on entrepreneurial activity and innovation to recover or maintain their prosperity. The use of a complex systems lens and simulation methodology to study this phenomenon has also gained prominence (McKelvey 2004). Studying complex systems does not involve identifying sources of linear causality. Rather, it reveals the array of systems at work, discrete patterns of behaviors by participants in the system, and differences in ends that result from the system starting under different initial conditions (Bar-Yam 1997; Carayannis and Campbell 2009).

This chapter uses a complex systems lens to explore the external knowledge acquisition actions of new ventures and the impact of these actions on regional sustainability of entrepreneurship. Rather than focusing on characteristics of entrepreneurs or industry conditions that lead to the formation of new ventures, this simulation study examines the effects of interactions between entrepreneurs and institutions in the process of new venture formation from a knowledge perspective. Knowledge is a fundamental building block of entrepreneurial ventures. Understanding how variation in the acquisition of knowledge impacts the sustainability of these ventures provides scholarly perspective on the process of entrepreneurship and guidance to entrepreneurs in their decisions on how to acquire new knowledge. It also reveals to policymakers how their efforts to catalyse entrepreneurial activity create intended and unintended institutional and competitive forces on the very same entrepreneurs. The results of this simulation reinforce elements of regional theory on entrepreneurial activity, but also contribute to advances in the field by revealing complexities associated with the development of institutions to spur economic development through entrepreneurship (Florida 2005; Florida and Kenney 1988).

Use of the simulation method is not without its limitations. The success of simulation-based research comes from an ability to simplify the interactions on the landscape and manipulate only one or two variables in order to examine the changes that occur from initial conditions (Davis et al. 2007). This simplification reduces noise that would be present otherwise in real systems. This study attempts to mitigate these issues by developing simulation conditions that vary, which creates a "noise" of its own while maintaining the validity of the model. For example, three distinct types of institutions are introduced on parts of the landscape so their interaction and overlap may be controlled; yet, their impacts on new ventures may – because of overlapping acquisition actions – have ripple effects throughout the landscape and make accurate pattern identification more difficult. The approach used to analyse simulation results attempts to overcome this issue by triangulating on the conclusions drawn here regarding regional sustainability of entrepreneurship through different analytical methods.

Simulation may be subject to criticism that it reveals what the researcher intended to find. This study employed methods accepted in the field to ensure the robustness and validity of the simulation model. It also used a range of initial conditions to ensure that conclusions drawn from the results of the simulation runs could be generalized across a similarly wide set of conditions in real economic systems to develop new streams of research. The results of this study suggest that institutions vary in their influence on regional levels of sustainable entrepreneurship. Institutions that contribute to the variety of specialized knowledge present in a market, such as universities or R&D funding directed towards expanding scientific knowledge, are more likely to make positive impacts on a region's ability to foster and sustain an entrepreneurial climate. By contrast, institutions that constrain the flows of knowledge in a region drive entrepreneurial ventures to pursue knowledge acquisition activities more distantly and in turn create instability in the entrepreneurial climate of the region.

These revelations provide opportunity for further research, which include development and testing of more refined and realistic scenarios in the simulation, and qualitative and quantitative research that builds on the insights. In particular, testing these results with data that spans a spectrum of political economies may uncover how generalizable these insights may be. The simulation has great potential for continued expansion and development. For example, additional analytic methods (e.g., qualitative interviews and case studies) may enable deeper exploration of the nature of interactions between entrepreneurs and institutions that occur during the simulation. In turn, these findings may be reduced to more sophisticated and realistic behaviors of agents in the simulation.

8.6   CONCLUSION

This chapter examined the embeddedness of new ventures within social and institutional structures in order to inform our understanding of their formation processes. New ventures, facing scarce knowledge resources with which to develop capabilities and other resources for competitive advantage, engage in appropriation of new knowledge from external sources. These appropriation activities occur through absorptive capacity mechanisms, largely ones that emphasize acquisition and transformation of novel knowledge. Through simulation, this study supported arguments regarding localized spillover of knowledge and agglomeration of new ventures within innovation-intensive regions, but only after new ventures acted independently to create formal networks that acquired knowledge from more distant regions. The knowledge appropriation actions of early new ventures in the formation of a region's entrepreneurial capacity created a critical mass of knowledge flows into the region.

Further analysis demonstrated the substantial influence that institutions have on the formation of new ventures. Institutions that increase the diversity of knowledge flows make positive impacts on the survival of new ventures and sustainability of entrepreneurship in a region, while heterogeneity-reducing institutions (such as ones that replicate existing knowledge or produce standardized knowledge) impede the progress of new venture formation at firm and regional levels. These findings are quite relevant to practitioners in the field of entrepreneurship, since they directly influence the choices of policymakers and economic development professionals who seek to improve the economic viability of their regions. Institutions that produce diversity of knowledge include funding organizations such as the National Science Foundation, National Institutes of Health, and private foundations. These types of organizations catalyse the pursuit of new and different knowledge as parts of their charters. By contrast, knowledge-limiting institutions such as patent offices and technology standard setting bodies improve the production of information, but reduce variability in the range of knowledge produced.

The simulation study presented here opens up new channels of research for entrepreneurship and innovation scholars. The methodology demonstrated a wide range of behaviors in new ventures based on different initial conditions, and developed conclusions regarding the nature of new venture network structure and interaction with institutions that reinforce existing propositions and provide starting points for future theoretical and empirical research. New ventures undoubtedly affect the vitality of regional economies. This research extends this understanding by demonstrating how competitive and institutional dynamics interact in co-evolutionary ways with new ventures as they grow.

REFERENCES

Agarwal, R., Audretsch, D., and Sarkar, M.B. (2007). The process of creative construction: knowledge spillovers, entrepreneurship, and economic growth. *Strategic Entrepreneurship Journal*, **1**(3–4), 263–86.

Almeida, P. and Kogut, B. (1999). Localization of knowledge and the mobility of engineers in regional networks. *Management Science*, **45**(7), 905–17.

Alvarez, S.A. and Barney, J.B. (2005). How do entrepreneurs organize firms under conditions of uncertainty? *Journal of Management*, **31**(5), 776–93.

Ariño, A., Ragozzino, R., and Reuer, J. (2008). Alliance dynamics for entrepreneurial firms. *Journal of Management Studies*, **45**(1), 147–68.

Bar-Yam, Y. (1997). *Dynamics of Complex Systems*. Reading, MA: Perseus Books.

Burt, R. (1992). *Structural Holes: The Social Structure of Competition*. Cambridge, MA: Harvard University Press.

Carayannis, E.G. (2009). Firm evolution dynamics: towards sustainable entrepreneurship and robust competitiveness in the knowledge economy and society. *International Journal of Innovation and Regional Development*, **1**.

Carayannis, E.G. and Alexander, J. (1999). Winning by co-opeting in strategic government-university-industry R&D partnerships: the power of complex, dynamic knowledge networks. *Journal of Technology Transfer*, **24**(2–3), 197–210.

Carayannis, E.G. and Campbell, D. (2009). "Mode 3" and "Quadruple Helix": toward a 21st century fractal innovation ecosystem. *International Journal of Technology Management*, **46**, 201.

Carayannis, E.G., Kaloudis, A., and Mariussen, A. (eds) (2008). *Diversity and Heterogeneity in the Knowledge Economy and Society*, Cheltenham, UK and Northampton, MA, USA: Edward Elgar Publishing.

Carayannis, E.G., Provance, M., and Givens, N. (2011). Knowledge arbitrage, serendipity, and knowledge formality: their effects on sustainable entrepreneurial activity in regions. *IEEE Transactions on Engineering Management*, **58**(3), 564–77.

Cederman, L.E. (2003). Modeling the size of wars: from billiard balls to sandpiles. *American Political Science Review*, **97**, 135–50.

Cohen, W.M. and Levinthal, D.A. (1990). Absorptive capacity: a new perspective on learning and innovation. *Administrative Science Quarterly*, **35**.

Davis, J.P., Eisenhardt, K.M., and Bingham, C.B. (2007). Developing theory through simulation methods. *Academy of Management Review*, **32**.

DiGregorio, D. and Shane, S. (2003). Why do some universities generate more start-ups than others? *Research Policy*, **32**.

Earnest, D. (2009). Simulating the K Factor: an agent-based model of distributive conflict in international negotiations. Paper presented at the 2009 International Studies Association annual meeting, 15–19 February, International Studies Association, New York.

Eisenhardt, K.M. and Schoonhoven, C.B. (1996). Resource-based view of strategic alliance formation: strategic and social effects in entrepreneurial firms. *Organization Science*, **7**.

Epstein, J.M. and Axtell, R.L. (1996). *Growing Artificial Societies: Social Science from the Bottom Up*. Cambridge, MA: MIT Press.

Etzkowitz, H. and Leydesdorff, L. (2000). The dynamics of innovation: from national systems and "Mode 2" to a triple helix of university-industry-government relations. *Research Policy*, **29**, 109.

Fligstein, N. (2001). *The Architecture of Markets*. Princeton, NJ: Princeton University Press.

Florida, R. (2005). *The Flight of the Creative Class. The New Global Competition for Talent*. New York: Harper Business, Harper Collins.

Florida, R. and Kenney, M. (1988). Venture capital and high technology entrepreneurship. *Journal of Business Venturing*, **3**, 301–19.

Freeman, J. and Engel, J.S. (2007). Models of innovation: startups and mature corporations. *California Management Review*, **50**, 94.

Granovetter, M. (1973). The strength of weak ties. *American Journal of Sociology*, **78**.

Granovetter, M. (1985). Economic action and social structure: the problem of embeddedness. *American Journal of Sociology*, **91**.

Klepper, S. and Sleeper, S. (2005). Entry by spinoffs. *Management Science*, **51**.

Krugman, P. (1991). Increasing returns and economic geography. *Journal of Political Economy*, **99**.

March, J. (1991). Exploration and exploitation in organizational learning. *Organization Science*, **2**.

McKelvey, B. (2004). Toward a complexity science of entrepreneurship. *Journal of Business Venturing*, **19**, 313.

Nelson, R.R. (2004). The market economy, and the scientific commons. *Research Policy*, **33**.

North, D.C. (1991). Institutions. *Journal of Economic Perspectives (1986–1998)*, **5**.

Ozsomer, A. and Cavusgil, S.T. (2000). The effects of technology standards on the structure of the global PC industry. *European Journal of Marketing*, **34**.

Provance, M. (2010). Tying it together: three essays on the roles of knowledge, entrepreneurial action, and institutions in the formation of new ventures. Doctoral dissertation, George Washington University.

Rosenkopf, L. and Almeida, P. (2003). Overcoming local search through alliance mobility. *Management Science*, **49**.

Saxenian, A. (1994). *Regional Advantage: Culture and Competition in Silicon Valley and Route 128*. Boston, MA: Harvard University Press.

Scott, R. and Meyer, J. (1994). *Institutional Environments and Organizations*. Thousand Oaks, CA: Sage.

Senor, D. and Singer, S. (2009). *Start-up Nation: The Story of Israel's Economic Miracle*. New York: Twelve.

Smith, K.G., Grimm, C.M., Gannon, M.J., and Chen, M.J. (1991). Organizational information processing, competitive responses, and performance in the U.S. domestic airline industry. *Academy of Management Journal*, **34**.

Spilling, O.R. (2007). Entrepreneurship and heterogeneity. In Carayannis, E.G., Kaloudis, A., and Mariuseen, A. (eds), *Diversity in the Knowledge Economy and Society*, pp. 140–64. Cheltenham, UK and Northampton, MA, USA: Edward Elgar Publishing.

Stuart, T.E. and Podolny, J.M. (1996). Local search and the evolution of technological capabilities. *Strategic Management Journal*, **17**.

Tallman, S. and Phene, A. (2007). Leveraging knowledge across geographic boundaries. *Organization Science*, **18**.

Todorova, G. and Durisin, B. (2007). Absorptive capacity: valuing a reconceptualization. *Academy of Management Review*, **32**.

Wasserman, S. and Faust, K. (1994). *Social Network Analysis: Methods and Applications*. Cambridge: Cambridge University Press.

Watson, J. and Everett, J.E. (1996). Do small businesses have high failure rates? *Journal of Small Business Management*, **34**.

Wiklund, J. and Shepherd, S. (2003). Knowledge-based resources, entrepreneurial orientation, and the performance of small and medium-sized businesses. *Strategic Management Journal*, **24**.

Zahra, S. and George, G. (2002). Absorptive capacity: a review, reconceptualization, and extension. *Academy of Management Review*, **27**.

Zott, C. (2003). Dynamic capabilities and the emergence of intraindustry differential firm performance: insights from a simulation study. *Strategic Management Journal*, **24**.

9. Looking beyond the current status of the conversation on entrepreneurial ecosystems and the diffusion of startups: where do we go from here?

Giovanni Battista Dagnino and Elias G. Carayannis

9.1 ENTREPRENEURIAL ECOSYSTEM: FROM DEFINITION TO CONFIGURATION

It is pretty popular to say that entrepreneurship is the fundamental engine for economic growth and social development. Actually, the value of entrepreneurship rises above economic growth to perform vast and enduring social impact. This condition impinges on the sense of viral positivity and contagious optimism that can be felt in all the effective cradles of new entrepreneurship, such as startup incubators, accelerator programs and co-working spaces, business angel network gatherings, venture capitalist meetings and pitches, and city and regional agencies for entrepreneurial development. This is actually the way to support and nurture the so-called entrepreneurial ecosystem's "can-do" attitude: an attitude that has long been one of the most (if not *the* most) significant features of the California-based mother of all entrepreneurial ecosystems: Silicon Valley (Hamel, 1999).

Though Silicon Valley has a path that is now much more extended in time (Saxenian, 1996), the story of entrepreneurial ecosystems studies and topical discussion is very recent and moves clearly in the direction from definitional approaches to static and configurational postures to eventually a few initial dynamic views of entrepreneurial ecosystems. In July 2010 *Harvard Business Review* published an article by Daniel Isenberg, a professor of practice at Babson College, entitled "How to start an entrepreneurial revolution." In this article, Isenberg illustrates the environment in which entrepreneurship tends to prosper. Drawing from many examples throughout the globe, Isenberg argues that entrepreneurs tend to be more successful when, on the one hand, they have easy access to the human, financial and professional skills and resources they need. And, on the other hand, when they operate in "entrepreneurial friendly" settings in which government and local policies actively encourage and safeguard entrepreneurs. This fertile actor network is termed the "entrepreneurship ecosystem."

After this pioneering definitional contribution, researchers begun to look into entrepreneurial ecosystems. Adopting a configurational approach, Spigel (2017) has recently suggested that entrepreneurial ecosystems are characterized by a triad of important attributes: (a) *cultural* attributes (a culture of entrepreneurship and histories of successful entrepreneurship); (b) *social* attributes that are accessed through social ties (workers' talent, fresh capital to invest, social networks and entrepreneurial mentors); and (c) *material* attributes grounded in specific places, such as central government and local policies, universities, support services, physical infrastructure and open local markets). Spigel complements his approach by using two case studies extracted from Canadian uprising environments in Calgary and Waterloo that were respectively termed "market-driven" and "dense and innovative" (Spigel, 2017). In the second part of the paper, opening up to a more dynamic understanding of entrepreneurial ecosystems, he argues that it is important to look at the *interdependencies* between these kinds of elements that generate and reproduce the overall ecosystem (Motoyama and Watkins, 2014), because research on entrepreneurial ecosystems focuses exclusively on individual cultural, economic and policy elements, thereby overlooking key ecosystem relationship interaction.

Conversely, examining the Dutch entrepreneurial ecosystem, Stam (2014) makes a distinction between *framework* conditions of ecosystems, given by formal institutions, culture, physical infrastructure and market demand, and *systematic* conditions, given by networks, leadership, finance, talent, knowledge and support services. This is, again at least in the initial part, another clear configurational approach that looks at attributes and pillars or components for making up entrepreneurial ecosystems.

On the ground of a longitudinal qualitative study of the whole life cycle from birth to termination of a Canadian ICT ecosystem, Minà et al. (2016) depict how entrepreneurial ecosystem evolution relies on high cooperation as concerns the value creation process and on high competition in respect to the value capture process. In such a way, they realize how the ecosystem's members interpret and balance cooperation and competition in the process of value creation and value capture. By grasping how value creation and value capture are coupled in the entrepreneurial ecosystem's evolution,

Minà et al. (2016) propose to tackle the issue of "ecosystem evolutionary life cycle".

Finally, Cohen (2006) examines the applicability of the emergent entrepreneurial ecosystem literature to the development of a "sustainable valley," where communities turn into the center of entrepreneurial innovations. Cohen explores how components of the formal and informal network, physical infrastructure and culture within a community may have a say in building up a sustainable entrepreneurial ecosystem. A specific community, that of British Columbia city in Victoria, was utilized to lay out the framework for the infrastructure necessary to create such an ecosystem.

9.2   TOWARDS A DYNAMIC ENTREPRENEURIAL ECOSYSTEM APPROACH

As we have seen in this book, an entrepreneurial ecosystem encompasses a group of firms, including startups, and one (or sometimes more) orchestration entities that share goals and choose to tap into economies of scale and scope, network effects pooled with flexibility and robust entrepreneurial drive. Economies of scale and scope can be used in various functions and processes, such as business development and financing, market analysis and communication, managing human capital, while startups participating in the ecosystem focus their attention on research and development, and new product development and distribution.

Some key conditions typically epitomize a *healthy* ecosystem. The ecosystem is customized around its own unique environment: it should not try to be something it is not such as the "next Silicon Valley" (Shavinina, 2004). However, it supports open and constant dialogue among the entrepreneurship stakeholders and works out an environment in which government policies support entrepreneurs and new entrepreneurship, accepts failure of new ventures, and actively encourages potential and actual investors to participate in new ventures. The existence of this basket of conditions is important since it can become the solid bedrock for activating a "virtuous loop," where all the cultural biases against failure and operating a business are removed and entrepreneurial success is passionately promoted. These conditions favorable to business in turn attract entrepreneurs, new ventures and new financiers, thereby enhancing the conditions for entrepreneurial ecosystems to actually exist and thrive.

In this perspective, entrepreneurial ecosystems can be observed as *complex adaptive systems* (Gell-Man, 1994; Holland, 1999), where each element cannot be considered in isolation from the others. As occurs in biological ecosystems, it is the constant interaction of the components and the networks that are created that define the ecosystem (Moore, 1993). Complex adaptive systems are *complex* since they are dynamic networks of interactions; their relationships are not aggregations of the individual static entities, that is, the behavior of the whole is not predicted by the behavior of the components. It is in fact the set of positive-sum relationships and synergies between actors working together that define the system. They are *adaptive* since individual and collective behavior self-organize in line with the change-initiating micro-event or collection of events (Miller and Page, 2007). As such, interdependent and interacting factors, such as family and social networks, education system and research centers, innovation hubs, financial institutions, local infrastructure, government policies and cultural and social norms may play a fundamental role in facilitating entrepreneurial ecosystems. It is therefore not the single element, but the interaction among all the elements comprising the entrepreneurial ecosystem that eventually contributes to its success or failure over time.

On the basis of the complex adaptive system interpretation of entrepreneurial ecosystems evolution, we need a dynamic approach to entrepreneurial ecosystems that entails understanding how they emerge, remain vital and eventually decline over time. A more dynamic view of entrepreneurial ecosystems evolution might leverage and benefit from the complex, adaptive systems perspectives as well as draw upon recent advancements on firm clusters literature to adopt an entrepreneurial ecosystem life cycle standpoint. As such, it involves a "sequential process with an evolutionary logic: a triggering event coupled with entrepreneurial spark set in a process of coevolution in which technology, institutions and business models arise and reinforce increasing returns that improve the competitive advantage of the region in attracting talent, finance and firms" (Stam, 2014, p. 6; Braunerhjelm and Feldman, 2006). The "happy incidents" story of Carayannis and Provance to interpret regional stickiness (in this volume) heads exactly towards this dynamic direction.

This intriguing circumstance may be the fertile basis to eventually design and formulate a cumulative knowledge and value-based theory of entrepreneurial ecosystems, which may provide the fundamental groundwork to allow an appreciation of entrepreneurial ecosystems' evolutionary paths, developing life cyles and evolving governance systems. While the chapters in this volume have collectively marked the path towards this direction, in the years to come we look forward to seeing additional inquiries and case studies that might forge a more compelling and advanced dynamic understanding of the entrepreneurial ecosystem.

REFERENCES

Braunerhjelm, P. and Feldman, M.P. (eds) (2006). *Cluster Genesis: Technology-based Industrial Development*. Oxford: Oxford University Press.
Cohen, B. (2006). Sustainable valley entrepreneurial ecosystems. *Business Strategy and the Environment*, **15**(1), 1–14.
Gell-Mann, M. (1994). *The Quark and the Jaguar: Adventures in the Simple and the Complex*. San Francisco, CA: Freeman.
Hamel, G. (1999). Bringing Silicon Valley inside. *Harvard Business Review*, **77**(5), 70–84.
Holland, J.H. (1999). *Emergence: From Chaos to Order*. Reading, MA: Perseus Books.
Isenberg, D. (2010). How to start an entrepreneurial revolution. *Harvard Business Review*, **88**(6), 41–50.
Miller, J.H. and Page, S.E. (2007). *Complex Adaptive Systems: An Introduction to Computational Models of Social Life*. Princeton, NJ: Princeton University Press.
Minà, A., Dagnino, G.B., and Ben-Letaifa, S. (2016). Competition and cooperation in entrepreneurial ecosystems: a life-cycle analysis of a Canadian ICT ecosystem. In F. Belussi and L. Orsi (eds), *Innovation, Alliances and Networks in High-tech Environments*, pp. 65–81. Abingdon, UK: Routledge.
Moore, J.F. (1993). Predators and prey: the new ecology of competition. *Harvard Business Review*, **71**(3), 75–83.
Motoyama, Y. and Watkins, K.K. (2014). *Examining the Connections within the Startup Ecosystem: A Case Study of St. Louis*. Kauffman Foundation Research Series on City, Metro, and Regional Entrepreneurship. Available at: http://www.kauffman.org/~/media/kauffman_org/research%20reports%20and%20covers/2014/09/examining_the_connections_within_the_startup_ecosystem.pdf. Accessed 4 May 2017.
Saxenian, A. (1996). *Regional Advantage: Culture and Competition in Silicon Valley and Route 128*. Boston, MA: Harvard University Press.
Shavinina, L. (ed.) (2004). *Silicon Valley North: A High-tech Cluster of Innovation and Entrepreneurship*. Bingley, UK: Emerald Group.
Spigel, B. (2017). The relational organization of entrepreneurial ecosystems. *Entrepreneurship Theory and Practice*, **41**(1), 49–72.
Stam, E. (2014). *The Dutch Entrepreneurial Ecosystem*. Available at SSRN: https://ssrn.com/abstract=2473475.

Index